A World Safe for Capitalism

Columbia Studies in Contemporary American History
Alan Brinkley, General Editor

Columbia Studies in Contemporary American History
Alan Brinkley, General Editor

See p. 249 for a complete list of titles in this series

A World Safe for Capitalism

*Dollar Diplomacy and America's Rise
to Global Power*

Cyrus Veeser

COLUMBIA   UNIVERSITY   PRESS   NEW   YORK

Columbia University Press
Publishers Since 1893
New York, Chichester, West Sussex
Copyright © 2002 Columbia University Press
All rights Reserved
Library of Congress Cataloging-in-Publication Data
Veeser, Cyrus.
A world safe for capitalism: Dollar diplomacy and
America's rise to global power / Cyrus Veeser.
        p. cm.
    Includes bibliographical references and index.
    ISBN 0-231-12586-0 (cl) — ISBN 0-231-12587-9 (pa)
    1. United States — Foreign economic relations —
Dominican Republic. 2. Dominican Republic —
Foreign economic relations — United States. 3. San
Domingo Improvement Company (New York, N.Y.)
4. Debts, Public — Dominican Republic — History.
5. Loans, American — Dominican Republic — History.
6. United States — Foreign relations — Dominican
Republic. 7. Dominican Republic — Foreign
relations — United States. I. Title.

HF1502.Z4 U57 2002
337.7307292'09'034 — dc21

                              2002019283

Dedicated to the memory of my parents, Harry Veeser and Elise Karagozian Veeser and to my favorite Dominicanists, Lilian, Gaby and Minerva.

Contents

List of Illustrations

Acknowledgments

The personal debts I incurred in researching and writing this book spread across several continents, recapitulating the credit network that linked the United States, the Dominican Republic, and Europe at the end of the nineteenth century.

The idea for this study came to me fully formed in an Irish bar on Eighth Avenue near 46th Street, where Emelio Betances and I had stopped to discuss his dissertation on the formation of the Dominican state, since published as *State and Society in the Dominican Republic*. My adviser, Eric Foner, later looked over a list of possible dissertation topics and counseled, "Do the Dominican Republic." In the early stages of the project, Emelio Betances, Herbert Klein, Frank Moya Pons, Lisa McGirr, Ariel Salzmann, Gerald Sider, and David Nasaw offered advice that guided my research. I also owe thanks to Elizabeth Blackmar, Robert McCaughey, Eric McKitrick and James Shenton of the Columbia history department for their support and intellectual guidance. In the Dominican Republic, three accomplished historians generously shared their knowledge, contacts, and resources — Roberto Cassá, Jaime Domínguez, and Raymundo González. Jaime arranged for me to read microfilm of French foreign ministry records at the Maison Francaise in Santo Domingo, going so far as to lend me his microfilm viewer. The staff at the Archivo General de la Nación extended themselves far beyond their official duty, often spending hours helping me decipher the cryptic longhand of Ulises Heureaux. I thank Eddy Jaquez, Rosmery Fanfán, and Adalgiza Cabrera especially. All three shifts of waiters at El Dumbo adjusted to my puzzling presence in what for me was an air-conditioned, 24-hour research facility.

In New York, participants in the Mellon working seminar at Columbia University read and commented on several chapters of this work. Sven Beckert, Emelio Betances, Alan Brinkley, Roberto Cassá, Jaime Domínguez, Norman Finkelstein, Charles Tilly, Richard Turitz, and Hobart Spalding also commented on portions of the manuscript. Martha Biondi and Adele Oltman, in particular, took pains to work through early versions of several chapters. Betsy Blackmar found the time to both read and encourage. Anders Stephanson provided a regular antidote to my empirical tendencies, while Eric Foner made astute editorial suggestions about material far removed from his own areas of interest. Martin Sklar offered incisive objections to the representation of Gilded Age capitalism and corruption in chapter 1. Anonymous reviewers for *Diplomatic History* offered useful comments on an article version of chapter nine. Gaynor Ellis brought a merciless but salutary intolerance for academic jargon to her reading of these chapters.

In England, Andrew and Ruth Seager made possible a stint of compressed research at the Public Record Office and the Guildhall Library. I benefited from the advice of librarians at those institutions as well as the U.S. National Archives, Library of Congress Manuscript Division, Columbia University Rare Book and Manuscript Library, Columbia University School of Law Special Collections, Moorland-Springarn Collection at Howard University, and Benjamin J. Feinberg Library at SUNY/Plattsburgh. A grant from Ful-bright/I.I.E. allowed me to spend over a year doing research in Santo Domingo, and I owe a special thanks to Mary Fedorko for her interest in this project. Barbara Burke provided food, lodging, and critical readings on my many trips to Washington, D.C.

A summer research grant from Bentley College allowed me to revise the manuscript for publication. At Columbia University Press, Peter Dimock, Anne Routon, and Leslie Bialler provided level-headed encouragement and hard-nosed editorial advice.

Harold Veeser managed to read the entire manuscript critically even as he urged me to carry the project to its always provisional conclusion. Elise Veeser provided material and emotional support all along the way, but sadly is not here to see the final product. Lilian Bobea offered her own vision of Dominican history and also proved that Dominican-American relations, if founded on equality and mutual respect, can be wonderful indeed.

Abbreviations

AF	Area File of the Naval Records Collection, Area 8, United States National Archives
AGN	Archivo General de la Nación, Santo Domingo
CE	Correspondencia Epistolar de Ulises Heureaux, Archivo General de la Nación, Santo Domingo
CFB	Council of the Corporation of Foreign Bondholders, Guildhall Library, London
CM	Presidencia de la República, Copiadores de Carlos Morales Languasco, Archivo General de la Nación, Santo Domingo
DI	Diplomatic Instructions of the Department of State, Haiti and Santo Domingo, United States National Archives
DL	Notes from the Dominican Legation to the State Department, United States National Archives
FO 23	General Correspondence before 1906, Dominican Republic, Foreign Office, Public Record Office, Kew, England
FO 140	Embassy and Consular Archives, Dominican Republic, Foreign Office, Public Record Office, Kew, England
FRUS	Foreign Relations of the United States
FWH	Frederick William Holls papers, Rare Book and Manuscript Library, Columbia University
GO	Gaceta Oficial, Archivo General de la Nación, Santo Domingo
JBM	John Bassett Moore papers, Columbia University School of Law Special Collections

JHH	Jacob Hollander papers, United States National Archives
MHC	Ministerio de Hacienda y Comercio, Archivo General de la Nación, Santo Domingo
MIP	Ministerio de lo Interior y Policía, Archivo General de la Nación, Santo Domingo
MRE	Ministerio de Relaciones Exteriores, Archivo General de la Nación, Santo Domingo
NYT	*New York Times*
NYTr	*New York Tribune*
UH	Presidencia de la República, Copiadores de Ulises Heureaux, Archivo General de la Nación, Santo Domingo
USM	Despatches from United States Ministers to the Dominican Republic, United States National Archives

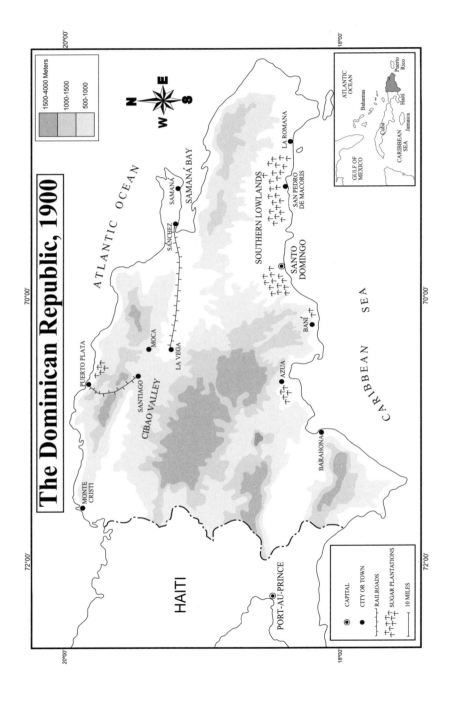

The Dominican Republic, 1900

HAITI

ATLANTIC OCEAN

CARIBBEAN SEA

SAMANÁ BAY

SAMANÁ

SÁNCHEZ

SOUTHERN LOWLANDS

LA ROMANA

SAN PEDRO DE MACORIS

SANTO DOMINGO

BANÍ

AZUA

PUERTO PLATA

MOCA

LA VEGA

SANTIAGO

CIBAO VALLEY

MONTE CRISTI

BARAHONA

PORT-AU-PRINCE

1500-4000 Meters
1000-1500
500-1000

ATLANTIC OCEAN

GULF OF MEXICO

Bahamas

Cuba

Jamaica

CARIBBEAN SEA

Haiti

Puerto Rico

20°00'

18°00'

72°00'

70°00'

CAPITAL
CITY OR TOWN
RAILROADS
SUGAR PLANTATIONS
10 MILES

A World Safe for Capitalism

Introduction

Economic Power and American Expansion, 1892 to 1907

On January 22, 1905, Americans opened their Sunday newspapers to discover that Theodore Roosevelt, their irrepressible president, had taken charge of another Caribbean country. Wire reports from Santo Domingo, the capital of the Dominican Republic, announced that the United States had signed an agreement giving it "virtual control" over that Caribbean nation. "This Country to Adjust Claims, Preserve Order, and Increase Efficiency of Administration," reported the *New York Times*.[1] The United States was not annexing the Caribbean republic — in fact, Washington "guarantees the complete integrity of Dominican Territory," the *Times* clarified. But the United States would control Dominican finances and see to it that all the creditors of the heavily indebted nation were repaid.

Americans might have been surprised that January morning, but they had no reason to be shocked. The Dominican intervention of 1905 came at the end of a dozen years in which the United States had, by any measure, emerged as a great power. Between the early 1890s and 1905, the country surpassed Great Britain to become the world's leading industrial producer, developed the world's richest multinational corporations, among them U.S. Steel (1900) and International Harvester (1902), and built a deep-water navy that ranked second only to the British Navy in major battleships by 1906.[2] As early as 1902, the British editor of the *Review of Reviews* declared that "the advent of the United States of America as the greatest of world-Powers is the greatest political, social, and commercial phenomenon of our times."[3]

Although it had joined the exclusive club of great powers, the United States still played a smaller role in world affairs than did Britain, France, Germany, or Russia. Indeed, the first region to feel the impact of American power was the greater Caribbean, which consisted of small, weak, poor republics and the few remaining European colonies in the New World. American influence in the area dated back well into the nineteenth century, when U.S. capitalists invested in railroads, plantations, and public utilities while merchants built a brisk trade in both manufactured goods and foodstuffs.[4] The U.S. political presence began in earnest in 1898, when the country went to war with Spain, won a quick victory, and took possession of Puerto Rico. Spain's other Caribbean colony, Cuba, became formally independent, but the Platt Amendment to its 1902 constitution made the new nation a U.S. protectorate.[5] Then, in 1903, President Theodore Roosevelt sent the U.S.S. *Nashville* to keep Colombia's navy from crushing a rebellion in that nation's northernmost province, Panama. The renegade province proclaimed its independence and quickly signed a treaty granting the United States the right to build an isthmian canal in an American-controlled canal zone. In less than a decade Puerto Rico, Cuba, and Panama had passed under some form of U.S. control.

Now, in January 1905, Americans learned that U.S. officials would take over Dominican custom houses, the source of nearly all government revenue in that nation. The officials would turn over 45 percent of the revenue to the Dominican government for its expenses. The other 55 percent would be set aside to pay the country's many creditors, primarily Americans and Europeans. Fair treatment of European as well as American creditors would prove to the great powers that the United States was worthy to join their ranks.

Even in the age of San Juan Hill and the Panama rebellion, Roosevelt's Dominican intervention was unprecedented. The takeover of Dominican finances was "one of the momentous steps in the history of American international relations," *Collier's* magazine declared. "It is obvious that this is the beginning of a new and profoundly important policy which can not logically stop with Santo Domingo." *Harper's* noted that the Dominican Republic "will occupy toward the United States substantially the same position which is now occupied by Egypt with relation to Great Britain."[6] Present-day historians agree with these contemporary assessments. The Dominican intervention, according to Emily Rosenberg, "represented an attempt by policymakers to find an alternative to colonialism that would still institute the supervision they deemed necessary for fiscal and social reform."[7]

As they digested the news from Santo Domingo, few Americans suspected that the new customs receivership was the culmination of a process that had begun years before, during the Gilded Age. In his lengthy message to the Senate calling for approval of the receivership, Roosevelt mentioned, but did not dwell on, the interests of the San Domingo Improvement Company (SDIC), a New York-based company that had taken over the foreign debt of the Dominican Republic in 1893. Only insiders at the highest level of government, and officials of the SDIC itself, could recognize that the little-known New York corporation had played a key role in triggering the American takeover of Dominican finances.

Neither contemporaries nor historians since have paid much attention to the Improvement Company. From its creation, however, the SDIC aligned itself with Washington's strategic goals in the Caribbean. The SDIC's president, Smith M. Weed, was a prominent New York Democrat and close friend of Grover Cleveland. When he formed the company in 1892, Weed sought personal assurances from President Benjamin Harrison and Secretary of State James G. Blaine that Washington supported his plan to take the control of Dominican finances away from a European firm. "American capital is of the stay at home kind," a letter to the *New York Times* pointed out apropos of the SDIC, "and when it does journey across the seas it is in search of some great prize or is assured that it will be protected if need be by the power of the United States."[8]

From 1893 through 1899, Weed and the Improvement Company controlled Dominican finances and worked closely with Dominican president Ulises Heureaux.[9] The company tried, and failed, to move the country's peasant farmers toward cash-crop, export agriculture. The SDIC had greater success in financial markets, borrowing some $30 million by selling Dominican bonds in Europe. But those loans and the printing of paper money pushed the republic toward financial ruin, turning Dominicans against Heureaux and his ally, the Improvement Company. When a group of assassins at last ended Heureaux's life in July 1899, the SDIC became a full-fledged pariah, universally reviled by the Dominican people.

The company was not, however, reviled by Washington. After a new Dominican government expelled the SDIC from the island in 1901, Washington became a forceful champion of the company's rights. From 1901 to 1904, both the State Department and the U.S. Navy became active in supporting the company's claims against the Dominican government. Washington's good offices escalated from the occasional dispatching of warships for their "moral effect" on the Dominicans, to the withholding of recognition from a new president who refused to acknowledge the SDIC debt, to the continuous deployment of the U.S. Navy's Caribbean Squadron in Dominican waters to quell political turmoil that kept the government from paying the company. The fusion of the SDIC's private interests and Washington's Caribbean policy became complete in 1904, when President Roosevelt appointed American officials to collect Dominican customs revenue exclusively on behalf of the Improvement Company. To dispel any doubts about Washington's support of the SDIC, the American collectors arrived in the republic aboard a U.S. warship.

For years, American policymakers had assumed that the SDIC's grip on Dominican finances served U.S. geopolitical interests in the Caribbean. Yet, by 1904, it was becoming clear to U.S. officials in the Dominican Republic that the company had created as many problems as it solved. The country was bankrupt and in a state of nearly constant revolution. As a result, several European foreign ministries hinted that they might intervene in order to force the Dominican government to pay money owed to their citizens. By the last weeks of 1904, Roosevelt and Secretary of State John Hay decided that to restore political and financial stability in the Dominican Republic and quiet the clamor of the Europeans, the U.S. government would have to do more than simply try to collect the SDIC's debts.

Few Americans in 1905 understood, of course, that the disastrous results of the Improvement Company's private control over Dominican finances had pushed Roosevelt toward a new and higher order of interventionist logic. That logic took the shape of a new policy applicable to all of Latin America, the Roosevelt Corollary to the Monroe Doctrine. The corollary arrogated to the United States the right, in fact the obligation, to intervene anywhere in Latin America that "wrongdoing or impotence" threatened "civilized society," in Roosevelt's words.[10] Americans naturally assumed that "wrongdoing" referred to the Dominicans and their failure to honor their international obligations — that is, to pay their debts. But the customs receivership tacitly elbowed aside another "wrongdoer," the Improvement Company itself. By substituting U.S. government supervision of Dominican customs for the SDIC's private control, the receivership was also a step toward extending federal power over corporations, a hallmark of domestic policy during the Progressive Era.

Naturally, U.S. foreign policy never freed itself entirely from the cronyism typical of the SDIC's relationship with Washington officials in the dozen years before 1905. Nevertheless, American foreign policy did evolve from the "uncertainty" and "improvisation" of the early 1890s toward the self-conscious, executive-driven, interventionist strategies of the early twentieth century.[11] The creation of the Dominican customs receivership was a turning point in that development. In place of the narrow, venal goals of the Improvement Company Roosevelt substituted a grand vision of rehabilitation for the Dominican Republic based on the proposition that "it is supremely to our interest that all the communities immediately south of us should be or become prosperous and stable."[12] In the coming years, the United States would pressure a number of Latin American nations to accept U.S. supervision of their finances in exchange for fresh loans from U.S. banks — the essence of the new Dollar Diplomacy.[13]

The SDIC's fifteen-year relationship with Washington policymakers thus provides a unique window on the ways that private business interests influenced American foreign policy just as the United States became a world power. At first, the Improvement Company venture might appear to be a "smoking gun" proving that Washington policymakers were servants of American capitalists. At the very least the Dominican case seems to tip the scales against such historians as Richard Collin, a leading expert on U.S.-Caribbean relations, who deny the influence of business interests on policymakers. "The United States may have had its share of international capitalists," writes Collin, "but the Roosevelt Administration — President Theodore Roosevelt, Secretary of State John Hay, and most of the working under-secretaries — were upper-class American aristocrats who found any business demeaning and the marginal enterprise of Latin American adventurers especially sleazy."[14]

In fact, American investors in the Dominican Republic did have close ties with Washington policymakers. Smith M. Weed, founder of the SDIC, was a lifelong ally of Grover Cleveland. John T. Abbott, the SDIC's man in Santo Domingo after 1899, was former U.S. Minister to Colombia, with his own contacts at the State Department. The SDIC's primary agent of influence in Washington after 1901, John Bassett Moore, was a renowned jurist and scholar of international law, former assistant secretary of state, and frequent adviser to presidents and the State Department from the 1890s on. Moore had regular, friendly contact with both John Hay and Theodore Roosevelt. In fact, throughout its history, the SDIC depended on cooperation between "aristocrats" of the executive branch and the "sleazy" entrepreneurs who controlled Dominican finances. At times sleazy investor and high-minded policymaker were one and the same person.

Far from showing the indifference of American policymakers to the concerns of U.S. investors in the Caribbean, then, the story of the SDIC seems to embody the investment-driven imperialism that English economist John A. Hobson described in his classic work, *Imperialism*, first published in 1902. Hobson saw the same economic forces pushing U.S. expansion as had spurred Britain's scramble for new colonies in the late 1800s. Indeed, Hobson believed that business interests in the United States were even more powerful than those in Britain. "The stronger and more direct control over politics exercised in America by business men enables them to drive more quickly and more straightly along the line of their economic interests than in Great Britain. American Imperialism is the natural product of the economic pressure of the sudden advance of capitalism which can not find occupation at home and needs foreign markets for goods and for investments."[15]

In the Dominican case, however, neither Hobson's model of business control over politics nor Collin's dismissal of sleazy entrepreneurs explains the evolution of U.S. policy from 1893 to 1907. For many years the Improvement Company *did* enjoy exaggerated influence over the State Department. That is why Theodore Roosevelt had to redefine the relationship between the executive branch and the company when the Dominican Republic became an international flashpoint in late 1904. Evidence examined for the first time in this book shows that the Roosevelt Corollary itself was the outcome of this conflict between private interest and public policy. While the Improvement Company, through John Bassett Moore, urged Roosevelt to do no more than defend the company's narrow interests, as it had done in the past, the president instead launched a sweeping new policy that injured the SDIC even as it moved Dollar Diplomacy to a higher plane.

In exploring what might be called the prehistory of Dollar Diplomacy, this study goes beyond the scope of traditional diplomatic history. Bringing developments in New York, Washington, Santo Domingo, Brussels and London into the same field of vision integrates processes that are usually examined separately. The narrative introduces a multinational cast of public and private actors — State Department officials, Caribbean rulers, Democratic Party leaders, bankers, economists, international lawyers, sugar planters, naval officers, and European bondholders, among others. A single narrative that traces the interplay of government action and private initiative presents a more complete picture of the genesis of Dollar Diplomacy than we have had in the past.

The Dominican case does not merely illustrate changing American strategies for modernizing the Dominican Republic. It also traces the steps that moved the executive branch to assume significant new tasks in Latin America, comparable in a way to the vast extension of U.S. commitment abroad after World War II. By proposing an economic remedy to a political problem, Roosevelt's customs receivership looked forward to American policies of the mid-twentieth century that linked security and peace to integration in the world capitalist system — policies embodied in the Marshall Plan, the International Monetary Fund and the World Bank, and the General Agreement on Tariffs and Trade. Post-World War II American leaders consciously interwove economic and political strategies to "foster a world environment in which the American system" could "survive and flourish," according to NSC-68, a key planning document from 1950.[16] By seeking to create a world safe for capitalism, they were following in Roosevelt's footsteps in solving the Dominican crisis of 1904–5.

The book is divided into nine chapters. Chapter 1, "The Gilded Age Goes Abroad," describes the origins of the San Domingo Improvement Company in the distinctive political economy of the late nineteenth century. The company's organizers were not outwardly oriented "cosmopolitans" with deep pockets.[17] The president of the SDIC was a political entrepreneur whose wealth derived from his access to government largesse. Neither in resources, structure, nor personnel did the SDIC compare with the major investment banks or large corporations that spearheaded economic expansion elsewhere in Latin America.[18] The SDIC took control of Dominican finances without commanding the reserves of capital or coercive power needed to enforce its own contracts, much less remake Dominican society.

Chapter 2, "Remapping the Caribbean," looks at Washington's increasingly active Caribbean policy in the early 1890s. A reciprocal trade treaty with the Dominican Republic that opened the U.S. market to sugar was an incentive to the launching of the SDIC. Equally encouraging to the company were negotiations between Dominican President Ulises Heureaux and Washington for the lease of a naval station at Samaná Bay on the republic's northeast coast. The SDIC's intrusion in the Caribbean was thus encouraged as a private complement to official steps to draw the Dominican Republic into the political and economic orbit of the United States.

Chapter 3, "Peasants in the World Economy," surveys the social, economic, and political conditions of the nation that the Improvement Company presumed to control from its offices at 36 Wall Street. The Dominican

Republic was undergoing a slow transition from near-subsistence peasant farming toward cash-crop agriculture. Even so, many Dominican peasants still had scant contact with the international market; instead they grew food crops and raised cattle, pigs, and chickens to feed their families. These peasants would prove hostile to modernizing schemes that threatened their independent lifestyle.

Chapter 4, "Dictating Development," considers attempts by Heureaux and the Improvement Company to move Dominican peasants away from subsistence farming and herding toward an export-oriented agriculture. In 1894, the Improvement Company took J. Lawrence Laughlin, a University of Chicago economist, to Santo Domingo to help implement the gold standard. The following year, the Dominican congress revised agricultural laws to keep peasants from raising livestock unless they owned land. Both policies were failures that undermined the company's hoped-for commercial revolution in the Dominican Republic. Chapter 5, "The Cash Nexus," details the ways that Heureaux and the Improvement Company went on to multiply the Dominican foreign debt, flood the country with paper money, and destabilize the local economy. The resulting economic chaos emboldened a group of conspirators to assassinate the dictator in 1899.

Chapter 6, "Old Wine in New Skins," analyzes the increasingly close relationship between the Improvement Company and Washington after the company's expulsion from the island in 1901. In chapter 7, "A Reign of Law Among Nations," the Improvement Company's lawyer, John Bassett Moore, defends the SDIC against the Dominicans before an international arbitration tribunal. Moore's brief calling for a radical restructuring of the Dominican state pointed the way toward a more decisive official intervention and, paradoxically, toward the waning of the SDIC's influence in Washington. American naval officers confirmed the need of the U.S. government to move beyond a policy of knee-jerk support of the Improvement Company, as shown in chapter 8, "A World Safe for Capitalism." That chapter traces the formulation of Roosevelt's famous corollary as a reaction to the SDIC's failure to create political and financial stability in the Dominican Republic.

The final chapter, "From the Gilded Age to Dollar Diplomacy," examines the replacement of the proto-Dollar Diplomacy of the Improvement Company by a rationalized, capitalized, and nationalized version imposed by Roosevelt. The SDIC's narrow interests ultimately lost out to the broad new goals of the U.S. government as the Gilded Age gave way to the Progressive Era.

A final note on sources. My intention throughout has been to take Dominican perspectives seriously by balancing U.S. sources with Dominican
documents. My hypothesis was that when American capitalists and U.S.
gunboats arrived in Santo Domingo, Dominicans actively steered the course
of events despite their manifest political, financial, economic, and military
weakness. The Dominican sources for this study proved to be plentiful and
articulate. The Archivo General de la Nación in Santo Domingo holds some
forty large copybooks containing the outgoing correspondence of Ulises
Heureaux for the entire period of the SDIC's tenure in the republic. In more
than 100 long, substantive, detailed letters to the Improvement Company,
Heureaux reveals the complex power relations and financial operations of
the period. The letters also reveal a strangely intimate relationship between
the metropolitan financiers and their creole client.[19] The files of the Dominican ministries of finance, commerce, and foreign relations were also
useful, although Heureaux's personalist rule meant that he himself made all
important and most minor decisions in those areas.

In the United States, the SDIC's archive was not preserved, and the personal correspondence of the company's president, Smith M. Weed, has survived only through 1892, the year the Improvement Company was formed.
This significant gap was filled, in part, by other private papers. In the base-
ment of the Columbia University Law School I had a quintessential moment
of discovery when a dusty but neatly wrapped packet of documents labeled
"San Domingo Improvement Company" emerged from a box of John Bassett
Moore's correspondence. The papers of Moore, one of the nation's leading
theorists of interstate relations as well as counsel to the SDIC, and the correspondence of another prominent SDIC attorney, Frederick William Holls,
exposed hitherto unknown links between the SDIC and high government
officials, including Grover Cleveland, Theodore Roosevelt, and several secretaries of state.

To understand both the financial and geopolitical context of Dominican-
American relations, I consulted State Department documents, the archive
of the council of the Corporation of Foreign Bondholders in London, British
Foreign Office documents, and diplomatic and commercial records from
the French foreign ministry. The European sources provided a different and
illuminating perspective on the growth of American influence in the Dominican Republic. Unless otherwise noted, all translations from Spanish and
French are my own.

1   The Gilded Age Goes Abroad

The San Domingo Improvement Company and the Political Economy of the 1890s

One of Santo Domingo's greatest needs is an influx of industrious and progressive people. With such an increase of productive power and improved means of interior communication, which railroads will afford, Santo Domingo will be able to demonstrate to the world the correctness of the estimate formed by the United States commissioners, who visited the country in 1871, when they said in their report that, taken as a whole, Santo Domingo is one of the richest and most fertile regions on the face of the earth.
— Handbook of Santo Domingo[1]

I have had to entrust my fate to different people, because no man, alone and isolated, can do anything. . . . Only God created out of the void. As a mere man, I have to start with something, I need some particle from which I can build something more.
— Ulises Heureaux[2]

On the last day of the year 1892, an American steamship chartered in Florida sailed into Puerto Plata, the largest seaport on the north coast of the Dominican Republic. On board was a group of American investors who, a few months earlier, had bought the entire foreign debt of the Caribbean republic. Charles W. Wells, the vice president of the San Domingo Improvement Company (SDIC), Frederick William Holls, a New York lawyer who had helped secure U.S. government support for the company's entry into Caribbean finance, as well as George Weed, son of SDIC president Smith M. Weed, intimate friend of Grover Cleveland. The *New York Times* noted that the three businessmen "took a pleasure party of ladies and gentlemen with them, and everybody had a good time."[3] Dominican newspapers, under the thumb of president Ulises Heureaux, did not mention the arrival of the "pleasure party" of Americans.

Wells, Holls, and Weed did not stay in Puerto Plata, but continued by steamer to Samaná Bay, the extraordinary harbor carved into the country's northeast coast, which American naval strategists had coveted for decades.[4] There they took advantage of a railroad line built by British capitalists to penetrate some 62 miles into the island's agricultural heartland. After touring the interior, they sailed on, passing the sugar-growing lowlands along the southern coast to reach the capital, Santo Domingo. "San Domingo seems to be enjoying great prosperity," Holls noted with enthusiasm. "The sugar and coffee plantations have largely increased and their owners seem to be making money." Statistics backed the impression: sugar production was growing rapidly, spurred by North American capital.[5]

The American investors had come to Santo Domingo on a ticklish mission. Their corporation, the San Domingo Improvement Company, had bought control of the Dominican foreign debt from a Dutch firm, Westendorp, six months earlier. The New Yorkers had gone to Santo Domingo to see how their imperial venture would play out in practice. They faced the delicate task of coming to terms with Ulises Heureaux, a dictator who ruled the Dominican Republic with an iron fist. Heureaux, who became president for the first time in 1882, used force, bribery, and fraud to stay in power longer than any other Dominican leader until the Trujillo dictatorship, which would begin in 1930.[6]

The first contacts between the New Yorkers and the Dominicans had not been cordial. When the SDIC notified the Dominican government that they had bought the country's foreign debt, Minister of Finance Juan F. Sánchez replied "with all our habitual courtesy . . . that the Dominican government considers the transfer null and void."[7] Westendorp, Sánchez alleged, had violated its contracts by transferring the company's rights without the government's consent. Another overture went sour later in August, when an agent of the SDIC failed to attend a meeting scheduled to take place in Santo Domingo. The company's apology must have seemed improbable to officials in Santo Domingo. "It may not be unknown to Your Excellencies," explained the SDIC, "that the summer heat has been extreme in New York this season, and that it has prostrated very many people, and has driven a large portion of our business population to the mountains and the seaside. This extreme heat has affected physically the gentleman who was to go for us to San Domingo."[8]

It was to overcome the Dominican government's resistance to the Westendorp buyout that the New Yorkers finally did arrive in Santo Domingo early in 1893.[9] The men arrived in the Caribbean brimming with confidence. True, Westendorp had sold the Dominican debt because of chronic problems with the Heureaux regime. But those problems were easy to explain, and avoid. "Messrs. Westendorp are understood not to have received the support of their own Government in the enterprise, and hence they were dependent on their own powers to enforce payments as they fell due," the *New York Times* noted in its first report on the Improvement Company. The SDIC, on the other hand, had been promised the firm support of Washington, support the men believed would go far beyond the "good offices" that the Department of State routinely provided to American businessmen abroad.[10] "It is intimated," the *Times* observed, "that officials of the National Government are interested also, and that eventually the work of the syndicate will be merged into an American protectorate over the island."[11]

The organizers of the SDIC no doubt shared the prejudices about race, religion, culture, and class that other elite Americans harbored toward tropical peoples. In this light their first encounter with the Dominican president was all the more remarkable. The company's lawyer, Frederick William Holls, stayed in touch with Andrew Dickson White, who years earlier had dabbled in another Dominican adventure. White, later president of Cornell University and ambassador to Russia, had studied the feasibility of annexing the Dominican Republic at the request of President Ulysses S. Grant some twenty-three years earlier. Holls consulted with this elder statesman of Dominican annexation and, in one long letter, gave a detailed portrait of the Dominican leader. "The present President, General Ulysses Heureaux," Holls wrote,

> a coal black negro, is one of the most remarkable men I have ever met. He . . . made himself President by a series of atrocious massacres and revolutions but for six years he has governed the country not only with an iron hand but also with a very enlightened purpose, and with great wisdom. He has never seen European civilization except as it exists in Jamaica and Nassau but he is well educated, and speaks English very well.

After several weeks of negotiating to obtain what, on paper, they already possessed, Holls admitted that not even a "first-class New York lawyer" could have "stated his position more clearly and forcibly, or seen through our own schemes & given us more trouble, than did this remarkable man."[12] Simply to encounter a black man in a position of both real and symbolic authority must have disoriented the Americans. In the years that followed, Heureaux would demonstrate that SDIC control, distant and abstract, could be frustrated by day-to-day resistance, through local knowledge and resources, and by means of other "weapons of the weak" that lay beyond the power of the New Yorkers to suppress.

Indeed, this first encounter between the new partners hinted at problems that would dog the SDIC throughout its tenure in the Dominican Republic. The U.S. government backed the SDIC in the belief that the private company's control of Dominican finances would make the republic a virtual protectorate of the United States. In fact, the company never gained full control of the country's finances, failed to achieve the modernizing goals that its name trumpeted, and in the end turned out to be as much a tool of Ulises Heureaux as it was of Washington or Wall Street. Far from creating a healthy business environment under benign American supervision, the Improvement Company and Heureaux sowed financial, economic, and political chaos. As a prototype of the later policy of Dollar Diplomacy, SDIC control of Dominican finances would prove to be such a resounding failure that it led to a rethinking of the proper role of American investment as an adjunct of U.S. foreign policy.

But these coming disasters could not be glimpsed by the American visitors to Santo Domingo in early 1893. At the time, the company's biggest worry was reaching an agreement with Heureaux. The SDIC needed to make concrete arrangements to raise money and convert the old loans by issuing new bonds. As a guarantee for the new bonds, the SDIC inherited the right to collect customs at the country's main ports of entry, the source of nearly all government income. After several weeks of meetings, the Dominican government gave up its objection to the transfer. "We finally succeeded," Holls reported, "in getting a series of contracts which we hope and think will prove very valuable."[13] Perhaps Heureaux gave his approval to the takeover because he found the New Yorkers more malleable than he had dared to hope. The Dominican congress, bullied by Heureaux, approved the contracts in March 1893, but it was less easy to convince ordinary Dominicans that the American takeover did not threaten the country's sovereignty. Heureaux immediately faced the desertion of one cabinet minister and a popular uprising.[14] The government suppressed the revolutionary outbreak, but the SDIC had been warned that the power of their new ally was not absolute.

With its contracts signed and popular opposition crushed, the SDIC could proceed with its declared mission of "improving" the Dominican Re-

public. In their six-year collaboration, the SDIC and Heureaux tried to reform Dominican society in basic ways, by building railroads, stabilizing the
currency, and moving the mostly peasant nation from subsistence farming to
cash-crop production. Theoretically, these changes would turn the Dominican Republic into a prosperous nation able to pay off old loans and the new
debt that grew rapidly as the SDIC brokered a series of loans from 1893 to
1897. "The island is rich and fertile, and under proper management should
be solvent, and more than that," a foreigner familiar with the country told the
New York Times in 1892. "That is why the better class of people would be
glad to see this American syndicate get in there and apply American business
methods to the place."[15]

While the SDIC and Heureaux worked to transform the country inter-
nally, they also repositioned it in the global financial system. This happened
because each time the SDIC sold Dominican bonds in Europe, it created
blocs of European bondholders ready to call on their governments to intervene should the Dominicans behave "irresponsibly" and default. Equally important, the SDIC situated the Dominican Republic within a changing geopolitical order. The sixteen years that the company operated (1892–1908)
coincided with the American "drive to hegemony" that has long been seen as
a turning point in U.S. foreign policy.[16] As the United States defined its
global interests in new ways, the SDIC's relationship with Washington
changed significantly. When the Improvement Company faced opposition
from the Dominican regimes that succeeded Heureaux, Washington backed
the company with the full force of its diplomatic and naval power. A turning
point came in 1904, however, when the State Department, the navy, and
Theodore Roosevelt himself became fed up with the company's exploitation
of the Dominican Republic for its own narrow ends. The rupture between
the SDIC and the American foreign policy establishment led to a new defi-
nition of Dollar Diplomacy expressed by the Roosevelt Corollary to the
Monroe Doctrine.

In the history of American expansion, the case of the San Domingo Improvement Company is unparalleled. By the 1890s Americans had far more
capital invested in Cuba and Mexico than in the Dominican Republic, while
corporations like W. R. Grace in Peru wielded considerable power over local
governments. Yet the partnership between the SDIC and Heureaux was
distinctive, both because an American company became an integral part of
a foreign state and because the company, from the start, served as a way for
Washington to exercise "control without responsibility" over a nearby and
strategically important neighbor. Surprisingly, the story of the company's

close ties to American policymakers and its influence on the formulation of
the Roosevelt Corollary have not previously been told.[17] Nor have the consequences of the company's control of Dominican finances and its promo-
tion of "modernization" in one of the least-developed nations of the Caribbean been seriously addressed.

The SDIC was a peculiar vehicle for direct investment in Latin America.
The company bore little resemblance to huge, well-financed multinationals
like the United Fruit Company which, in the early 1890s, were still the wave
of the future. The SDIC was firmly rooted in old ways of doing business,
above all in the cronyism and corruption typical of the 1870s and 1880s.
The organizers of the SDIC knew little about the Dominican Republic, but
they knew a great deal about using government contacts to gain private
wealth. In this sense, the Improvement Company represented the Gilded
Age going abroad rather than the cutting edge of a new, aggressive, world-
roving finance capitalism. To understand how such a company came to
control the finances of a Caribbean republic, it will be helpful to look at
the career of the SDIC's president, Smith M. Weed, in the political economy
of the Gilded Age.

In the years following the Civil War, state governments democratized the
economy by passing general incorporation and free banking laws, which
replaced earlier reliance on special charters and monopolies.[18] As a result,
competition invaded new sectors of the economy.[19] Rather than create equilibrium and efficiency, however, the new free-for-all economy led to "market
disorganization, 'wastes of competition,' business failures, recurrent depres-
sions, strikes and lockouts, social distemper, and political upheaval."[20] Facing
this new economic order, some entrepreneurs turned to government to cush-
ion against the harsh demands of bare-knuckled free enterprise.[21]

It was precisely from this milieu that Smith M. Weed, future president
of the San Domingo Improvement Company, emerged. A political insider
and master of patronage, Weed manipulated the state in order to accumulate
capital and evade competition in a dangerously democratized market.[22]
Weed's biography provides a resume of the forces that merged private investment and state initiatives into an anticompetitive strategy and illustrates
how the SDIC emerged as a foreign venture closely tied to the support of
Washington policymakers.

Smith M. Weed was born in 1833 in Belmont, a village in northernmost
New York State, the son of a manufacturer. After attending local public
schools in Plattsburgh, a town on the edge of Lake Champlain near the

Canadian border, he worked as a store clerk while reading law. In 1857 he graduated from Harvard law school and entered practice in Plattsburgh. His law firm grew into one of the largest in upstate New York, and Weed eventually opened an office in New York City.

Weed's political career began in 1865 with his election to the New York State assembly, an office he filled on and off until 1874. A Democrat regularly reelected from a strongly Republican district, Weed first won attention as an opponent of New York City's Tammany Hall machine. Weed championed the upstate reform Democrats, a group the *New York World* referred to as the "hay-loft and cheese-press Democracy."[23]

The 1870s saw Weed grow steadily more important in New York State Democratic circles. He became superintendent of the state insurance department and at different times served on the state legislature's committees on railroads and prisons, learning to exploit these positions to advance his private interests. Weed used his political influence to smooth the way for construction of a branch of the Delaware and Hudson Railroad connecting Montreal and New York through his hometown of Plattsburgh. He also wielded veto power over appointments in the state prison system, already an important source of patronage in upstate New York. Even a hagiographic portrait of Weed, published while he was still alive, could not avoid mentioning his reputation as a behind-the-scenes operator. "The Democratic Party of the State and Nation," observed the 1905 sketch, "owes much to Smith M. Weed, far more than appears on the surface. . . . Only the few who know their political history from the inside can justly estimate the meaning and value of [his] forty odd years of party service."[24]

Weed succeeded in projecting himself beyond his upstate district by forging strong personal bonds with national Democratic leaders. In the 1876 presidential campaign, Weed worked for Samuel J. Tilden, a fellow New Yorker and personal friend.[25] In the wake of that notoriously corrupt election, the degree of Weed's partisanship slowly emerged. New York newspapers revealed that Weed had traveled to South Carolina, one of three states that had disputed election returns. Traveling under a false name, Weed had sent coded telegrams to Democrat leaders in New York. "According to the translated dispatches," the *Times* reported, "Smith M. Weed was negotiating at one time for the purchase of members of the Returning Board for $80,000s."[26] Weed admitted the accuracy of the "cypher messages," but insisted that since South Carolina's popular vote had really gone for Tilden, he was simply trying to right a wrong. During a congressional investigation,

Weed maintained that Tilden knew nothing of the vote-buying scheme and denounced the plan when he learned of it later.[27]

Weed's loyalty evidently won him a place among the inner circle of New York Democrats, which included future President Grover Cleveland. The *Times,* which had once lauded Weed as a champion of reform, now dubbed him "the Mephistopheles" of the Tilden clique and commented that he was "well known to the people of New-York as a gentleman who always 'falls on the soft side of the fence.' "[28] While the vote-buying scheme became a public scandal, Weed's usual way of doing business stayed safely within the moral compass of Gilded Age politics, and he continued to thrive in the special niche he had carved for himself. Indeed, in the mid-1880s Weed gave up his law practice in order to devote himself full time to his various business endeavors. The largest of these was a vast mining operation centered in a remote area of the Adirondack Mountains in northern New York State. Weed was president and director of the Chateaugay Ore and Iron Company, which at times employed as many as 2,000 workers.

The success of Weed's iron company flowed directly from his political influence. The viability of the Chateaugay works depended on access to low-cost transportation for the heavy ore. A *New York Tribune* report on the origin of the company explained how Weed's political pull helped him exploit the otherwise inaccessible iron deposits. Allegedly, the company was set up after a hunting party in the Adirondacks noticed that their blazing campfire melted an outcropping of iron ore. "At the time of its discovery," the report continued,

> there was living in Plattsburgh a shrewd laywer, Smith M. Weed, who had no capital except his brains. The land at Lyon Mountain was owned by a resident of a distant city, but Mr. Weed leased it and then strove to interest capitalists in his scheme to develop the mine. . . . But the mine was almost inaccessible. Mr. Weed induced the State to build a railroad from Plattsburgh to Clinton Prison, at Dannemora, for the ostensible purpose of transporting provisions for the convicts, and then leased the railroad for the stupendous sum of $1 a year. . . . having thus secured a means for the transportation of his ore, he opened his mine.[29]

Despite Weed's manipulation of the state-owned railroad, the profitability of the mine was not yet assured. Like other mine owners, Weed depended on high tariffs to protect his iron from competition with more efficient British mines and mills. In the mid-1880s, as the Republican Party became more closely identified with protectionism, Weed's friend and mentor Grover Cleveland pushed the Democrats toward a limited free trade position. In 1887, Cleveland declared himself in favor of lower rates on raw materials, claiming the policy would make American industrialists more competitive internationally. A tariff bill sponsored by Congressman Roger Q. Mills proposed reducing duties on several raw materials, including bloom iron, the product turned out by Weed's Chateaugay works.[30]

Weed faced the unexpected prospect of suffering financial ruin at the hands of a President he considered a friend and benefactor. The *Tribune* noted the irony of Weed's position: "But what shall it profit a man to own an iron mine and be a prominent Democrat, if such a bill as the Mills bill, reducing the duty on bloom iron $2 a ton, is passed by the National Democratic Administration?"[31] Weed, together with Democrats from iron-producing regions of Alabama, lobbied vigorously and in the end defeated the reduced iron duties proposed by Mills.[32]

Twice between 1887 and 1890, Weed nearly emerged from backroom obscurity into national prominence. In 1887, Democrats in the New York State legislature nominated him unanimously for U.S. Senate, but he lost to the Republican candidate. In 1890, Weed believed he had the nod of Governor David B. Hill for the Senate, but instead Hill himself went to Washington in what the *New York Times* characterized as a "swindle."[33] These setbacks evidently convinced Weed that the limelight was not for him, and thereafter he contented himself with exploiting opportunities open only to a political insider. The *Tribune* identified Weed "as 'the power behind the throne'" during the second Cleveland administration (1893–1897).[34]

Long before Weed turned to overseas ventures, he had proven himself a minor master at using state power for private ends. Weed's correspondence with Grover Cleveland took up such prototypical patronage concerns as appointments to custom houses, the national mint, and foreign consulates. Weed used his political pull to avoid competing freely in an economy falling under the control of large corporations. As Altina Waller has pointed out, by relying on traditional structures of patronage and personalism, Weed represented the past, not the future. "What the *Times*, Weed's enemies, and historians have excoriated as 'corruption' was perceived by Weed and his allies as a legitimate appropriation of public funds in their struggle to remain competitive in a business environment increasingly dominated by corporate consolidation and monopoly," Waller perceptively notes.[35] Weaned on patronage, backroom politics, favoritism, and other "irrational," nonmarket practices, Weed moved easily through the close-knit world of politicians, attorneys, and businessmen who gave the Gilded Age its distinctive hue.[36]

When Smith M. Weed turned to overseas investment in the 1890s, he carried with him the assumptions about business-government collaboration that he had learned in New York State. Perhaps Weed looked abroad for grand opportunities which, as Waller suggests, New York State no longer offered to his brand of noncorporate promoters. Weed's first overseas venture concerned not the Dominican Republic, but Central America. His friendship with Grover Cleveland allowed him to play an active role in promoting one of the era's great unrequited projects — cutting an isthmian canal across Nicaragua.

For more than a decade after the failure of the de Lesseps canal project in Panama in 1889, supporters of two rival routes battled for U.S. government support. One was a sea-level route across Nicaragua, the other a shorter but more arduous route across Panama, which was still a province of Colombia. From the first, partisans of the Nicaragua canal argued that private capital could never carry out the tremendous undertaking. They pointed out that failure of the de Lesseps canal in 1889 had lost more than $250 million of private money, souring capital markets on the project. They sought help from the federal government, asking the United States to guarantee $100 million of bonds to be issued by the Maritime Canal Company, the firm that had undertaken the project. Naturally, a government guarantee would have made the bond issue attractive to investors.[37]

The question of federal canal aid was a lively political issue for most of the 1890s. Advocates warned that America's limited capital market for overseas ventures would force the canal organizers to seek money in Europe. Senator John Sherman painted a grim picture of the likely consequences:

The stocks and bonds [of the canal company] would have to be disposed of in the open market, and would be sold largely in Europe. Therefore, though the work would have been instituted and conducted by American citizens, the control and management of the corporation would necessarily drift into the hands of holders who have no regard to the important American interests involved in the enterprise.[38]

Despite the appeals of canal promoters and the support of President Harrison and Secretary of State Blaine, Congress gave no money to the project. It is not clear precisely when Smith M. Weed became a booster of the canal, although both the *New York Sun* and *Herald* reported at the time of Weed's death that "he organized the first company for the digging of the Nicaragua Canal."[39] In any event, by 1892 Weed was working actively to win federal support for the canal. In the heat of that year's presidential campaign, Weed wrote to his friend, Democratic candidate Grover Cleveland, urging him to take a public stand in favor of canal aid. "The people of the entire Pacific Coast are wild about it," Weed counseled the once and future President. "Inasmuch as you signed the bill that gave it life . . . it would be wise for you to refer to your own action . . . and to your belief in the great importance of the work to American commerce and defense."[40]

The subsidy failed to materialize, however, and in 1893 the Nicaragua Canal Construction Company, a subsidiary of the Maritime Canal Company, ran out of money. All work on the canal stopped, and the Construction Company was forced into receivership. This financial embarrassment did not halt Weed's efforts to win Cleveland, once again President, to the cause. Weed had, in the interim, become a vice president of the Construction Company and was working with a group of investors seeking to reorganize it on a more sound footing. "I desire to impress upon you," Weed wrote the President late in 1893, "that the parent company — the Maritime Canal Company . . . is solvent, and is in no way affected by the Construction Companies [sic] going into the hands of a receiver." Weed spoke eloquently of the benefits promised by the canal: "This canal is the greatest enterprise before the world at this time, and one fraught with more important consequences, to the people of the whole United States, than any other ever presented to it."[41] The fact that private capital could not make the venture profitable was, to Weed, no argument against it.

Weed did not limit his lobbying efforts to the President. In June 1894, Secretary of State Walter Q. Gresham sent off a testy reply to an entreaty from Weed. "You seem to think the Nicaragua canal matter should have precedence of the tariff and everything else," Gresham scolded. "It has been . . . the president's opinion, and I have concurred, with him, that the most important thing before congress is the tariff bill."[42] Weed's behind-the-scenes pressure on Cleveland and Gresham, like the public lobbying by Senator Sherman and others, did not prevail. The Nicaraguan canal promoters failed to tap sufficient private capital or public largesse to complete the project, and eventually the Nicaraguan route lost out to Panama. Weed's efforts to secure federal support for the canal show that he hoped to project abroad the same relationship to the state that had worked so well for him in New York. Weed had a visceral preference for concessions, monopolies, and subventions. When he died in 1920, one obituary credited him with having originated the policy of paying cash bounties to enlistees during the Civil War. It is unlikely that Weed deserved the laurels, but it is not surprising that the innovation was attributed to him, given his gift for extracting personal profit from public service.[43]

The canal episode is an important antecedent to Weed's launching of the San Domingo Improvement Company in 1892. Thoroughly embedded in the patronage networks and collusive practices of his age, Weed and his allies would carry these same ways of doing business to the Dominican venture. The attraction of Santo Domingo is easy enough to appreciate. As a patron, President Heureaux promised to be even more obliging than President Cleveland. Here was a state without checks and balances, its press muzzled, its territory small enough to be managed like a personal fiefdom. To a political capitalist of Weed's persuasion, the island republic truly was "a Garden of Eden," as he told the New York Times in 1894 — "the finest country I ever saw."[44]

The Dominican project took shape within a larger economic and political environment that, at first glance, hardly seemed propitious. However much Weed counted on political clout to shield him from the usual risks of foreign investment, 1892 was not a good year to go into Latin American securities. The late 1880s, when the Dutch firm of Westendorp started to issue bonds for the Dominican Republic, had been a boom period for Latin American lending. British portfolio investment in Latin America, for example, jumped from 123 million pounds in 1880 to 194 million pounds ten years later (that is, from roughly $625 million to nearly $1 billion). Direct investment in Latin American businesses leaped from 56 million to 231 million pounds ($250 million to $1.1 billion) in the same period. The boom ended suddenly in 1890, however, when Argentina announced it would suspend payments on its foreign debt. Baring Brothers, the British merchant banking house that had executed many of the loans, teetered at the brink of insolvency. To avoid a financial panic that would draw in other lenders on the London Exchange, the British government intervened.[45]

As a result of the Baring panic, Latin American loans found few sponsors or buyers in European capital markets in the early 1890s. The New York financial paper *Bradstreet's* noted in January 1892 that "the downfall of Argentine credit gave a decisive blow to the whole inflation of unsound government credits in the money markets of Europe. . . . financial instability has, it seems, been the rule with every South American state."[46] At the time, few if any foreign securities were traded in New York. London was the premier market for such bonds.[47] Loans were based on the sale of bonds, also called securities, notes, or paper, on the London stock exchange and stock markets in Paris, Brussels, Amsterdam, Geneva, and Berlin. The bankers or promoters who arranged the loan risked very little of their own funds. Because of lax regulation and strong demand for profitable investments, "the issue of external bonds was as easy as printing money."[48]

The collapse of the market for "questionable" loans had a paradoxical result. Throughout 1892, *Bradstreet's* and other financial journals reported a "plethora of money" in the capital markets of New York and Europe. "Advices from the European financial centers indicate a continuance of the easy conditions and low rates for money which recently made their appearance," the journal reported in April.[49] This accumulation of savings seeking profitable outlets convinced economists like Charles A. Conant and John Hobson that finance capitalism lay behind imperial expansion in the late 1800s.[50] By June, *Bradstreet's* wrote,

> The chief subject of complaint in financial circles throughout the civilized world is at this moment in regard to the steady accumulation of idle funds at every banking center and the dearth of employment therefor. . . . Interest rates have reached the minimum figures alike in American cities and in the financial center of British India. The marked feature of this unusual state of affairs is its failure thus far to stimulate activity in either general business or speculation.[51]

In fact, the conditions described by *Bradstreet's* had already stimulated Smith M. Weed to action. By early 1892, Weed and two partners, New York attorneys Charles W. Wells and Willard Brown, were negotiating to acquire the Dominican foreign debt from Westendorp. The demand for Latin American securities was at its lowest ebb in over a decade, yet the major capital markets were glutted and eager for secure, profitable investment. If a group of investors could establish the security of a bond issue — say, by letting it be known that the venture had the backing of the U.S. government — they stood to do well. Official support, as Martin Sklar has pointed out in a somewhat different context, "substituted sufficiently for the credit rating, as it were, that investors would normally require in placing their capital."[52]

Other developments also encouraged Weed. By 1892, Washington had demonstrated a heightened interest in the Dominican Republic by signing a reciprocity treaty with that nation and by attempting to lease Samaná Bay, events discussed in the next chapter. Intrigued by these developments, Westendorp approached the State Department to see if the U.S. government might itself assume the role of fiscal agent for Santo Domingo.[53] Not surprisingly, the United States declined to take the unprecedented step of assuming the foreign debt of another sovereign state. Although they declined Westendorp's offer, the American leaders did show interest in getting Santo Domingo's purse strings out of European hands. President Benjamin Harrison and Secretary of State Blaine met personally with the future organizers of the SDIC to encourage their venture. "The hope was expressed by those high officials," wrote one SDIC official, "that the important contracts between Westendorp & Co., and the Dominican Government, concerning the possession of the Custom Houses, would be brought into the control of Americans. They said they regarded the possession of the Custom Houses of San Domingo by Europeans . . . as dangerous to American interests and policy."[54]

The term Dollar Diplomacy would not be coined for more than a decade, but American policymakers were groping their way toward just such a policy. In the early 1890s, however, both the concept and the practice of Dollar Diplomacy remained embryonic. The executive branch had not yet developed a structure that could promote and supervise private initiatives intended to complement U.S. geopolitical interests. As will be seen, Washington encouraged the SDIC's promoters and would, in moments of crisis, give the company vigorous diplomatic support; but the policy was still a long way from Theodore Roosevelt's careful orchestration of private investment and government supervision in the Dominican customs receivership created in 1905. The SDIC belonged to an age that still believed in laissez-faire. Washington could grant virtual carte blanche to a private firm that seemed to serve national interests since, as David McLean notes, "it was almost unquestioned that loans to a foreign government carried with them political control, and that railway, road, mining, and other concessions ensured the regional dominance of the power whose financiers controlled them."[55]

It is not clear how much Weed and his associates invested to buy the Dominican debt from Westendorp. Years later, newspapers would report that the founders had paid only $1,500 to organize the company, but that scandalously low figure squared with New Jersey's laws of incorporation. The former American consul to Santo Domingo later alleged that the SDIC paid $3.5 million, but that sum seems far too large, given Weed's gift for risking as little of his own money as possible. After Heureaux's murder, the Dominican government claimed that the company had arrived in the country "without a dollar of capital, borrowed $65,000 from a wealthy Dominican . . . and began operations." That sum seems improbably small. It is more likely that the Americans simply offered to convert Westendorp's defaulted notes into reissued bonds, which with forceful support from Washington seemed far more likely to be repaid by the Dominicans.[56]

From the first, then, political backing by the U.S. government was an essential ingredient of the SDIC plan. Smith M. Weed, political entrepreneur par excellence, found that his political connections in the Democratic Party were not much use when Westendorp offered to sell its Dominican holdings, since a Republican president occupied the White House in 1892. That explains why Weed and his two associates turned to Frederick William Holls for help in forming the San Domingo Improvement Company. A German-American, Holls was an important Republican stump speaker in New York's German-speaking neighborhoods. Though a much younger man than Weed, Holls was a well-known international lawyer with important European connections. On occasion, he served as American legal counsel for the German government. A personal friend of Theodore Roosevelt, he regularly corresponded with such leading intellectuals as Andrew Dickson White, Hugo Munsterberg, and Edward Everett Hale. In 1899, the State Department would name him secretary to the first Hague Peace Conference.[57]

Like Weed, Holls belonged to an elite group of lawyers, businessmen, politicians, and government officials who easily merged private interest with the public good. Holls had strong ties to the Harrison administration and was especially close to Secretary of War Stephen B. Elkins, whom he called "secretary of politics." In one blunt letter to Elkins, Holls described the influential clique he represented. "I speak," Holls wrote, "for a *constituency* in this City, small but very powerful, which has the idea that you and [Secretary of State] Blaine are both my friends and that I can, if I try hard enough, induce you to take action or persuade to take action which is not opposed to public interest and which I have at heart."[58]

Holls soon had "at heart" a bold new project. A few months before the

SDIC was incorporated in New Jersey, Holls accepted a $500 retainer to help Weed and his associates with "the San Domingo matter."[59] In return, Holls gave the SDIC's promoters "cordial letters of introduction" to Secretary of War Elkins and assured the latter that he could "speak to them as freely as you could to me." Holls also asked Elkins to introduce Wells and Brown to Benjamin Tracy, Secretary of the Navy, and to "place them upon the same footing if possible [with him] which you so kindly provided for me." Tracy, a prominent New York attorney and judge before entering Harrison's cabinet, had pushed steadily and successfully for large appropriations to build a modern navy.[60]

Holls and the organizers of the SDIC knew that the U.S. government was seeking to lease Samaná Bay, and they actively associated their venture with the planned takeover. The private venture would reinforce, and be reinforced by, the official one. Holls visited State Department and other officials in early 1892 to gather assurances of support for Weed's project. In February 1892 he and Secretary of War Elkins discussed "the Samaná Bay matter," which had "taken more practical shape." Holls urged Elkins to arrange a meeting with the Secretary of the Navy. "This is a matter of supreme importance," he wrote, "and a chance which I am sure will not soon recur; it is a grand opportunity for patriotic work on the part of the Administration." His diaries make clear that Holls saw the lease of Samaná by the United States and the SDIC's buyout of the Dominican debt as two sides of the same coin. In September 1892, Holls reported that "the San Domingo scheme has assumed a new phase and a very favorable one as this Government is now committed to support the claims of our company energetically and promptly."[61]

As word of the pending negotiations with Heureaux leaked out, press reports regularly confused the government's overtures toward Samaná with Weed's private venture. Rumors of an American takeover of Santo Domingo had reached Europe as early as April 1892. The London *Times* published a Dominican denial that the U.S. government had annexed the republic. "The independence of the Dominican Republic," the *Times* advised, "has been for many years an accomplished fact of which its people are justly proud." The New York papers told a different story. The *Times* heralded the SDIC's creation in a December 1892 headline that blared: "SAN DOMINGO SYNDICATE: AMERICANS WHO PROPOSE TO ESTABLISH A PROTECTORATE."[62] To American editors, the fusion of strategic and private interests was plain enough.

At this early stage, it seems that SDIC officials expected the republic to pass under American control. After visiting Santo Domingo, Holls felt that annexation was the most desirable outcome. "I am more than ever con-vinced," he confided to Andrew Dickson White, "that you were right twenty years ago and that the policy recommended by you and endorsed by General Grant was conservative and wise." Yet, although Holls favored an American takeover of the republic, he was candid enough to admit that "the desire for annexation to the United States has passed away" among ordinary Domin-icans. He argued that the United States should at least control Samaná, either by leasing the bay or acquiring it through outright cession.[63] When, during a private meeting with SDIC officials, the Dominican president pro-posed ceding the bay as a quid pro quo for American support of a war against Haiti, Holls did not hide his enthusiasm. His hope that Washington would look favorably on the dictator's scheme was, however, disappointed.[64] Un-derwriting a war of conquest or absorbing the Dominican Republic outright were projects that only the most militant expansionists favored. American officials wanted control without commitment, the very thing that SDIC takeover of Dominican finances seemed to promise so happily. Taking pos-session of Samaná was one thing, absorbing the entire republic quite another.

Even without the project of annexation, the SDIC and the Department of State had a sense of shared mission at this stage. Washington had pledged itself to support the SDIC "energetically and promptly," and the company took its obligations to Washington seriously. Holls affirmed the SDIC's sen-sitivity to American strategic interests when he discussed a clause of the Dominican contract that required, in case of default, formation of an inter-national commission of control. The commission, which was to include representatives of Holland, Belgium, England, France, and the United States, would "take entire charge of the finances of the country about on the plan of the Egyptian Commission," a step that would obviously remove the republic's finances from American control. Holls added: "Of course we shall not under any circumstances call on England or France but these countries had to be named in order to pacify public opinion" — that is, among bondholders in Europe.[65]

In deference to the geopolitical concerns of the United States, Holls declared that the SDIC would never involve the two leading international powers, France and Britain, in supervising Dominican finances. Signifi-cantly, Germany was not even considered as a possible member of the com-mission. The company followed through on this informal pledge not to invite European intervention, in part for its own reasons. When the Dominican government eventually did default in 1897, the SDIC did not invoke its right to create the international commission foreseen in its contracts. Instead, the company doggedly pursued a bilateral solution through its champion, the U.S. government. That decision had major consequences. The failure to create a mechanism of international supervision contributed to the *sauve qui peut* frenzy of Dominican creditors between 1901 and 1904 and thus led to direct U.S. intervention early in 1905.[66]

Confusion of American strategic goals with the company's private interests would define Washington's policy toward the Dominican Republic for the next decade. The overlap of public and private spheres was perceptively described by a naval officer, evidently familiar with Santo Domingo, in a letter to the *New York Times* in early 1893. "It is to be presumed," the writer said,

> that the gentlemen who compose the syndicate know what they are undertaking and see in their scheme considerable profit, for it is a well-known fact that American capital is of the stay at home kind, and when it does journey across the seas it is in search of some great prize or is assured that it will be protected if need be by the power of the United States. Looked at in any way, this undertaking is a very significant one, and no man can tell to what it may lead. On the surface it is purely a business scheme, but it would take very little to give it a political character.[67]

As this prescient contemporary saw, the advent of the Improvement Company created a rare hybrid, ostensibly private but in fact highly charged with political import. The SDIC forged a direct link between the interstate and financial world systems, connecting the future of the Caribbean republic to the fate of an American company in Santo Domingo, and thereby to the geopolitical interests of Washington.[68]

Smith M. Weed and the SDIC stand in a curious relation to theories of imperialism, like those of Charles A. Conant, John A. Hobson, and Vladimir Lenin, that assume accumulations of surplus capital and falling rates of profit in metropolitan countries pushed investors to look overseas for better returns on investments. It is certainly true that the SDIC took advantage of surplus savings in Europe that sought higher rates of return. But Weed and his associates did not correspond to the powerful monopoly capitalists that both

Hobson and Lenin described. In fact, the organizers of the SDIC were lawyers and politicians, not bankers and financiers. They commanded political influence rather than vast cash reserves. They had only enough money to acquire the Dominican concession, not to make new loans. After the initial buyout, the company raised additional capital through bond issues in Europe. Dominican debentures were not even offered for sale in the United States.

The firm's buyout of the Dominican debt, then, might be better described as "political control over business" rather than "business control over politics." The gap between the sources of the company's capital — Europe — and its strategic support — Washington — planted a contradiction at the heart of the project. Another gap existed between the company's objective — making money — and Washington's goal — keeping Dominican finances out of European hands. As long as all ran smoothly in Santo Domingo, these latent contradictions could be ignored, no matter how disastrous the company's operations were for the Dominican people. When the crisis came, however, Washington would be forced to confront the consequences of delegating foreign policy functions to a private company. Indeed, that policy itself created conditions of financial and political disorder in the Dominican Republic that Washington policymakers would find intolerable.

Surprisingly, some of those distant events could be foreseen in 1893. The American naval officer whose letter was cited above offered a remarkably astute forecast of events in the Dominican Republic. He predicted that foreign control of Dominican finances would prompt the growth of a nationalist party "whose platform will be a promise, on gaining power, to overturn the Government which mortgaged their country to the alien." When the insurgent government canceled the American firm's contracts,

> the syndicate . . . will turn to Washington for support, and does anybody suppose for a moment that it will turn in vain!
> From the dispatch of a United States vessel-of-war to San Domingo 'for the protection of American interests' to active interference is a step too short to be measured. The next move will be some form of a protectorate that will give us the right to intervene, and from that condition to annexation is an easy and logical sequence.[69]

Less than a decade later, the "logical sequence" foreseen by the naval officer began to unfold. Although the United States did not annex the Dominican Republic, it did create a virtual protectorate by taking over the nation's custom houses. But the forecast erred in assuming that the government and the company would continue to work in perfect harmony. In fact, by 1904, the contradictions between the company's self-interest and a new, broader American policy had become manifest. By the time the Dominican government threw the SDIC out of the Caribbean, Theodore Roosevelt occupied the White House and American foreign policy was changing. Roosevelt had a grand vision of the American role in the world, and the narrow interests of the Improvement Company could no longer guide U.S. policy. When Roosevelt intervened in the Dominican Republic, it was not on behalf of the SDIC. Instead, he championed a rationalized, Progressive rehabilitation of the Caribbean nation consistent with the new status of the United States as a great naval and industrial power.

2 Remapping the Caribbean

U.S. Caribbean Interests and the Mission of the SDIC

The American people, and their government, want not so much
territories to rule, as markets open to their agricultural and
manufactured goods. . . . We admit that, for a long time, our
republic has bowed to this law of commercial domination. . . .
Yet, for better or worse, our commercial dependency on the
United States has been the inoculation that makes us immune to
more complete subjugation to American imperialism.
— *El Republicano*[1]

Big fishes may fight or be friends, but little fishes are always eaten.
— Dominican cabinet minister[2]

The San Domingo Improvement Company's takeover of the
Dominican foreign debt in 1892 was one event in a larger U.S. plan to
reorient the Caribbean economically and politically in the early 1890s. The
term "plan" may seem to attribute too much intentionality to a foreign policy
establishment that was still "mostly informal, extemporaneous, and unsys-
tematic."[3] But in fact, under President Benjamin Harrison and Secretary of
State James G. Blaine, Washington pursued commercial and strategic goals
in the Western Hemisphere coherently and with unflagging attention.[4] The
American offensive in the Caribbean included reciprocal trade treaties
signed with the Dominican Republic and with Spain (for Cuba and Puerto
Rico) as well as ongoing efforts to lease Samaná Bay as a naval base and
coaling station. Combined with the SDIC's takeover of Dominican finances
in 1892, a precocious attempt at Dollar Diplomacy, this combination of
economic and strategic initiatives reflected an aggressive, if premature, policy of Caribbean expansion.[5]

In geopolitical terms, projecting American power in the Caribbean was
a low-risk policy. By the 1890s, the European nations most committed to

imperialism — Britain, France, and Germany — had arrived at de facto acceptance of American predominance in the Caribbean, even if they did not
formally recognize the Monroe Doctrine. This deference to American interests was granted grudgingly, even by Britain, which by the early 1900s
would rely on the United States to protect its interests in the Western Hemisphere.[6] Nevertheless, as intra-European rivalries heated up in Africa and
elsewhere, none of the great powers wanted to risk a direct challenge to the
United States on its own turf. Washington had already begun the ambitious
naval construction program that would make the U.S. Navy, by 1906, second
only to Britain's in ships of the line.[7] While no European power was happy
to see the Caribbean slide into the American orbit, none saw the region as
important enough politically or economically to justify actions that might
alienate the United States.[8]

Even so, the United States remained suspicious of European designs
toward the Caribbean, above all those of Germany.[9] Moreover, European
deference in the political arena did not imply a retreat from commercial
and financial competition. Trade rivalries actually sharpened in the Caribbean, as Germany in particular sought New World markets.[10] When the
United States took steps to capture Caribbean commerce, European foreign
ministries reacted vigorously, protesting American reciprocal trade treaties
as violations of the most-favored-nation principle. Ultimately, European
leaders decided that U.S. political domination did not necessarily hurt their
economic and financial interests in the region.[11] Indeed, the United States
came to be seen as the guarantor of stability in Latin America. That trend
reached its culmination with President Theodore Roosevelt's articulation of
his famous corollary to the Monroe Doctrine, which declared that "in the
Western Hemisphere the . . . Monroe Doctrine may force the United States,
however reluctantly, in flagrant cases of . . . wrongdoing or impotence, to
the exercise of an international police power."[12]

At the beginning of the 1890s, the American policy that did the most to
reshape power relations in the Caribbean was commercial reciprocity. Since
the early 1880s, Secretary of State James G. Blaine had envisioned a Western
Hemisphere system organized under American leadership but demanding
little in the way of responsibility from Washington. The components were
to include a customs union, arbitration agreements to settle disputes among
the American republics, and an isthmian canal, preferably across Nicaragua,
to open the way for interoceanic commerce.[13] At the first Pan-American
Conference in Washington in 1889–90, a majority of participants, led by

Argentina, vetoed a customs union because Latin American governments relied on customs receipts for much of their revenue. In addition, Argentina, Chile, and Brazil objected to exposing their infant industries to direct competition with goods from the United States. After Blaine's plan failed to win support, he turned his attention to a series of bilateral commercial treaties.[14]

Reciprocity was not a new idea. In fact, the United States had signed reciprocal treaties with Hawaii and Mexico in the 1870s.[15] But Blaine made reciprocity the linchpin of his hemispheric system with the United States at its center. Reciprocity was, in effect, selective free trade, lowering tariff barriers only to nonindustrial nations with few manufactured exports. The policy promised the benefits of free trade, especially reduced prices for raw materials and tropical crops, without substantially increasing competition for American manufacturers. "We should confine our reciprocity negotiations," President Harrison told Blaine, ". . . to the admission to our markets of non-competing products, as much as possible."[16]

At Blaine's insistence, Congress made a last-minute change in the tariff bill of 1890 giving the executive branch the discretion to allow the free entry of tropical products in return for lower duties on American goods. Eventually the United States perfected treaties with Brazil, Guatemala, Costa Rica, Nicaragua, Honduras, and the Dominican Republic, as well as with Great Britain and Spain for their Caribbean colonies. If reciprocity disappointed Republican leaders by only slightly increasing U.S. exports to the region, the policy did dramatically reshape Caribbean trade. In fact, the new economic pattern created by U.S. trade policy was a major factor in the region's defining crisis of the 1890s — Cuba's struggle for independence.

In Cuba, the immediate effect of reciprocity was an upsurge in exports to the United States. Sugar exports to the United States leaped from $54 million in 1890 to $79 million in 1893. By 1894, the United States was buying almost 90 percent of all Cuba's exports. When Congress ended reciprocity and stopped the free entry of Cuban sugar in 1894, the Spanish colony plunged into an acute economic crisis, "creating a favorable atmosphere for a new rebellion."[17] While the renewed outbreak of an armed independence struggle in February 1895 obviously reflected the internal dynamic of Cuban politics, it also underscored the political repercussions of Washington's trade policies.

In the Dominican Republic reciprocity also had important economic and political effects. The United States was already the republic's main trading partner, supplying 37 percent of the island's imports and taking 58 percent of its exports, mostly sugar, in 1891.[18] With reciprocity, the Caribbean republic allowed the duty-free importation of a wide range of American agricultural and manufactured goods in return for the free entry of its sugar, hides, molasses, and coffee into the United States.[19] Soon after the treaty went into effect, on September 1, 1891, the Dominican government suffered a loss of revenues due to the reduced tariff on U.S. goods. A report by the Dominican customs director calculated lost revenue at more than $100,000 for one twelve-month period.[20] Since government income was at the time only about $1.4 million annually, the reduction was significant.[21]

The American attempt to use commercial treaties to recast trade and power relations in the Caribbean was understood and opposed by Europe, above all Great Britain, still dominant in Latin American trade despite growing competition from American goods.[22] One British mercantile house, "shippers of English manufactured goods in considerable quantities to Santo Domingo," complained to the Foreign Office in early 1894 that "our trade for the last year or two has been seriously interfered with by the preferential tariffs given to the United States."[23] The Foreign Office noted that the Dominican Republic "was a small market but it is of course important not to lose it." British officials worried that reciprocity with the United States threatened to throw "Santo Domingo entirely into the hands of the United States which I believe we are anxious to avoid."[24]

Recognizing the larger policy behind reciprocity, Britain, France, Germany, and Italy vigorously protested the new treaties, claiming that the special treatment given American goods violated the most-favored-nation articles in their commercial treaties with the Dominican Republic. European consuls in Santo Domingo worked in harness to press for tariff reductions for their respective nations.[25] Germany, the main buyer of Dominican tobacco, was in a strong position to retaliate if the Dominicans did not comply.[26] The German foreign ministry "knows by experience that small Republics are not to be trusted," the British ambassador in Berlin reported, and was especially assertive in its demand for parity.[27]

The European protests put the Dominican Republic in an untenable position. The Dominicans could not grant European demands for equal treatment under the most-favored-nation clauses of their commercial treaties. To do so would be to commit financial suicide, since the government's budget came mainly from import duties, already reduced by reciprocity with the United States. Frantic diplomatic correspondence between Santo Domingo and Washington shows the Dominicans desperately holding off European retaliation while calling on the United States to take a strong stand against European pressure.[28] As time passed with no clear statement from Washington, the Dominican vice president pleaded with American minister John S. Durham: "But what does the United States purpose to do? We have been driven to the wall. We can argue no longer."[29]

Durham kept Washington fully apprised of the European threats against the Dominicans. At one point, acting Secretary of State William F. Wharton blithely advised that if Germany's "action is confined to tariff reprisals, it is within the power of the Dominican Republic to defend itself by counter action." The assumption that the Dominican Republic could defend itself in a trade war with Germany showed scant appreciation of that nation's relative weight in the world economic order.[30] In contrast to the view from Washington, Dominican president Ulises Heureaux's perception of global power was starkly realistic.[31] Independent but small, poor, and weak, the Dominican Republic could hardly expect the fiction of "sovereign equality" among nations to be taken seriously.

> The United States invites us to a reciprocity arrangement. We desire to save our sugar market, but we fear the Europeans and the most favored nation clause. The United States answers us that we need not entertain such fear. We accept the assurance and send our Envoy to Washington, where the treaty is made. The European nations protest. We . . . ask what the United States purposes to do for us. We receive a reply four months later in which we are made friendly promises. In the meantime Germany threatens an ultimatum which will shut out our tobacco from its only market.[32]

In the end, the reciprocity conflict was settled, in part because the United States at last issued a forceful statement of support for the Heureaux regime.[33] But that was not the only reason why the European powers backed off from the confrontation with a tiny Caribbean nation. In these same months, the pending U.S. lease of Samaná Bay and the SDIC's acquisition of the Dominican foreign debt had been reported by the European press. The British ambassador to Washington, Lord Pauncefote, reported on European concern that the takeover of Dominican finances by an "American Syndicate . . . might enable the U.S. Government to put such pressure on the Dominican Government as to amount almost to a control of the affairs of the country."[34] Together these events demonstrated to Europe that the Dominican Republic had passed under the protective wing of the United States, making further protests pointless.

By 1890, American attempts to acquire Samaná Bay had a long if not venerable history. The notorious filibuster William Cazneau had won a lease on the bay in the 1850s. Later, under the Grant administration, the United States negotiated another treaty for the lease of Samaná. Both plans failed.[35] The next cycle of diplomacy began with a heavy-handed effort to lease Haiti's Môle St. Nicolas, in 1890. That overture too ended in failure, thwarted in part by Frederick Douglass, U.S. minister to Haiti at the time.[36] Efforts to acquire Samaná began again at about that time. With the United States embarked on an ambitious program of naval construction, and with the isthmian canal in Nicaragua actually underway in the early 1890s, the United States wanted coaling stations and naval bases at strategic sites in the Caribbean.[37] In 1890 the American consul in Santo Domingo, John S. Durham, took the initiative to suggest the lease of Samaná to Dominican President Ulises Heureaux. Not surprisingly, the naval base was discussed at the same time the two nations were discussing the reciprocal trade treaty. Dominican President Ulises Heureaux apparently hoped to profit from the ambitions of his northern neighbor.[38] Negotiations began in earnest in May 1891, when the Dominican government sent Manuel Galván to Washington to sign the reciprocity agreement.[39] A draft lease was drawn up, but the document remained secret, and Heureaux took no action at that time.

In early 1892 Durham, who had succeeded Douglass as U.S. minister to Haiti and the Dominican Republic, complained to the Secretary of State that Heureaux had "attempted a change of base in his negotiations looking towards the lease of Samana Bay."[40] Heureaux's dilatory tactics suggest that he was carefully weighing the consequences of alienating part of his nation's territory. The dictator fully expected a rebellion to follow the lease of Samaná. Nevertheless, he was prepared to push the lease through a special session of congress, on condition that the United States pay $200,000 immediately upon ratification of the treaty. Told by the American minister that the money had not yet been appropriated, Heureaux snapped: "I cannot ask insurgents to wait until I receive money from the United States with which to fight them."[41]

By May 1892 other factors had complicated the Samaná negotiations. That month, SDIC officials notified the Dominican government that the country's external debt now belonged to them, and in August the *New York*

Herald publicized the transfer. As noted, the pending lease of Samaná encouraged the SDIC's interest in the Dominican Republic. "The New York syndicate knows this Samaná story," Durham informed Secretary of State John W. Foster, who was no doubt already aware of that fact from his dealings with company representatives in Washington.[42] Durham warned Washington that news stories "about the transfer of the Dutch loans to the United States through the agency of a private corporation has raised a storm of excitement" in Santo Domingo. At just this moment, the Dominican quarrel with Europe over reciprocity was also reaching the boiling point. Samaná, reciprocity, the national debt — suddenly the country's future seemed to be mortgaged to the United States. As crowds held "indignation meetings," Heureaux was forced to declare that he would not permit the transfer of the external debt to American capitalists. Even to a battle-hardened opportunist like Heureaux, the situation seemed perilous.

Despite the dictator's new-found nationalism, Durham reported a few weeks later that "Heureaux is threatened from all sides because of his friendly attitude toward the United States."[43] To many Dominicans, the dictator's "friendly attitude" toward a foreign power must have smacked of treason. Ordinary Dominicans did not make nice distinctions between private projects, like the Improvement Company, and official policies, like reciprocity and the lease of Samaná Bay. The prospect of rebellion was real, especially in the country's north, where tobacco farmers depended on the German market and trade reprisals by that country would mean economic disaster.[44]

By the summer of 1892, the convergence of American designs on the Dominican Republic proved too much for Heureaux to manage, and the dictator tried desperately to backpedal. Despite clear evidence that the dictator's pro-American policy was destabilizing his government, the State Department stepped up its efforts to clinch the Samaná deal. In August, Secretary of State Foster told Durham confidentially that "the money is now at the disposal of the President of the United States." Foster urged Durham, who usually resided in Port-au-Prince, to sail at once for Santo Domingo. There he was to offer the payment to Heureaux and see to it that the Dominican congress ratified the treaty for the lease of Samaná.[45]

At this difficult juncture, Durham believed a new tactic was needed to put the Samaná lease back on track. In early September, he advised the State Department that the missing element was a U.S. warship stationed in Dominican waters. "It is difficult to explain to the Department just what assistance can be had from the presence of a man-of-war, but I am sure that I make no mistake when I say that our chances for success will be increased by the attendance of such a vessel." The department, however, had found that a similar display of force backfired in its dealings with Haiti over Môle St. Nicolas. Secretary Foster cautioned Durham that sending a warship to Santo Domingo was a delicate matter and that "the continued presence of a naval vessel would not tend to promote the important interests that you had in hand." Nevertheless, Foster urged Durham to keep the pressure on Heureaux and to stay, "until further directed, at San Domingo."[46]

It soon became evident that creation of the SDIC had changed the balance of power in Santo Domingo. Durham, still bargaining hard for the lease of Samaná Bay, was puzzled when Heureaux put off further negotiations by feigning illness. "I cannot learn his motive for deferring action except it be to secure money from the Syndicate in New York which has been interested in the transfer of the Dutch loan." The conduct of the SDIC's agent in Santo Domingo irked Durham. "Unfortunately the New York syndicate sends telegrams almost daily instructing its agent to inform the managers at New York concerning my Samaná negotiations. . . . It is astonishing to me that the people in New York know my instructions to the letter." Durham was beginning to realize what his superiors in Washington presumably knew already: by taking control of the country's finances, the SDIC had preempted normal diplomatic channels between Washington and Santo Domingo. Ironically, the SDIC's takeover of the Dominican debt had undermined the Samaná deal, the opposite of what policymakers had expected, and an unheeded warning that even small, poor, tropical nations cannot simply be commanded from afar.[47]

Early in 1893, with SDIC officials in Santo Domingo to negotiate their contracts with Heureaux, the secretary of state sent a cipher cable to Durham in Port-au-Prince: "San Domingo business much more important now. If you have good reason to believe your presence in San Domingo will bring about success you should go without delay." The secretary's hopes were soon dashed.[48] Heureaux, who was about to force the SDIC contracts through congress, understood the limits of public tolerance. Adding the Samaná lease to the reciprocity accord and the SDIC contracts was impossible. Soon after the Dominican congress approved the SDIC's contracts, Heureaux's foreign minister denounced him and fled the country on a Spanish warship. The rebellion that followed was easily repressed. Still, the lesson was plain. In the overcharged atmosphere of Dominican politics, the lease of Samaná was too explosive even to discuss publicly.

For the time being, at least, the Samaná lease was dead. In March 1893, the commander of the *Kearsarge* advised the secretary of the navy that public uncertainty about the lease served only to undermine Heureaux. "If it is not the intention of the Department to push the matter of the lease of the coaling station," A. S. Crowninshield wrote, ". . . the sooner that fact is made known here the better; opposition to President Heureaux would thus largely cease."[49]

As it happened, Heureaux's retreat from the lease coincided with political changes in Washington. On March 4, 1893, Democrat Grover Cleveland was inaugurated President for the second time. For Smith M. Weed, the second coming of his "warm personal friend" to the presidency must have been a welcome event.[50] The SDIC could, and would, count on its close relations with Cleveland in moments of need, as will be seen. At first, however, contemporaries expected Cleveland to pull back from the aggressive expansionist policies of Harrison and Blaine. The new president's refusal to support the annexation of Hawaii, where American planters had overthrown the hereditary ruler a few months earlier, seemed to confirm these expectations. "The return of President Cleveland to power was most opportune and effective in checking the designs of the late cabinet," British ambassador Pauncefote reported with evident satisfaction. "His first executive act, on returning to Power, has been to withdraw from the Senate the Treaty with the provisional Government of Hawaii hastily concluded by President Harrison. It may be hoped therefore that the Samana Bay question will sleep for awhile."[51]

The predictions regarding Samaná were correct, but Cleveland was hardly opposed to expansion. He firmly supported the rapid naval build-up that had begun in the 1880s. In 1895, Cleveland's secretary of state, Richard Olney, astonished Britain with a vehement declaration of U.S. supremacy in the Western Hemisphere. The occasion was a dispute between Venezuela and Britain over the border of British Guiana. "Today the United States is practically sovereign on this continent," Olney boomed, "and its fiat is law upon the subjects to which it confines its interposition." Although the provocative declaration nearly led to war, Cleveland warmly supported Olney's belligerent position.[52]

To ambassador Pauncefote and some American historians since, however, the United States "lost" Samaná because the Cleveland administration was anti-imperialist. Yet the United States bid seriously for the base from mid-1891 through March 1893, Congress secretly appropriated $250,000 for Samaná, and the lease was never consummated not because "every administration resisted the pressure to take Samaná," but because Heureaux delayed its ratification for nearly two years.[53] For eight months of that time the United States stood ready, money in hand, to make the deal. The decisive factor in the breakdown of negotiations was Heureaux's fear that the transfer would spark a popular revolt, not the forbearance of Washington.

American ambitions had converged too quickly upon the Dominican Republic, with little regard for the Dominican people as actors in their own right.[54] Heureaux was a dictator, but he maintained the forms of republican rule and could not oppose the unified opinion of the Dominican people. "Heureaux will never carry through to the point of signing the lease," Crowninshield said, ". . . as he is well aware of the very great opposition which exists among all classes of San Dominicans" to the plan. Giving up Samaná would "increase his unpopularity to a point of bringing about a revolution."[55]

As later events would show, when Heureaux tried and failed to "modernize" Dominican agriculture by undermining peasant subsistence farming, the dictator was far from omnipotent. Economic chaos would lead Heureaux to seek to lease Samaná again at the time of the Spanish-Cuban-American War, but once more the threat of popular opposition kept him from clinching the deal. Moreover, by the summer of 1898, the United States had gained Puerto Rico and Guantanamo Bay in Cuba, making the Dominican harbor redundant.[56]

The events of 1891–93 were a turning point in United States–Dominican relations. Reciprocity, the Samaná lease, and the SDIC's takeover of the debt together represented a coordinated projection of American commercial, financial, and geopolitical power in the Caribbean republic. By the mid-1890s, however, a new combination of events overtook and largely erased Blaine's legacy. At the time of Cleveland's election in 1892, the Democratic Party also took control of Congress. That political realignment, combined with the economic crisis that began in 1893 and the challenge posed by the Farmers Alliance and Populists, led to an inward-looking revision of the tariff in 1894 that nipped reciprocity in the bud. By 1895 the original conditions that had induced the creation of the SDIC had vanished, and only one of the three pillars of the aggressive U.S. policy toward the Dominican Republic remained, SDIC control of finances.

For Heureaux, Washington's retreat came too late. The Dominican leader had already decisively cast his lot with the Americans.[57] The showdown over reciprocity, pitting the United States and the Dominican Republic against Europe, was a watershed.[58] American naval officers confirmed that Heureaux "is doing all in his power to further American interests" and therefore "felt he should receive in return the support of the United States Government."[59] The dictator took his forced marriage in earnest. He stayed abreast of events in the United States, corresponding with several former American consuls who had returned to the States and who kept him up to date about political currents and trade policies. The Dominican chargé d'affaires in New York reported on the attitudes of Congress and the President, and Dominican newspapers regularly carried wire stories about American political developments. In sum, Heureaux was able to stay well informed about his northern neighbor, as shown by his familiarity with the platforms of the two major parties in the 1896 presidential election.[60]

Heureaux's new reliance on the United States did not, however, mean assuming an utterly passive role. In fact, the Dominican ruler looked for ways to turn the embrace of the United States to his advantage. Preeminent among the instruments at hand was the Improvement Company itself. If Washington believed that the SDIC's contracts gave Americans informal control over the island republic, Heureaux saw the connection in a different light. He strained to reverse the flow of influence by making the SDIC serve his interests. As he well knew, the company directors had solid connections in Washington. The company's president, Smith M. Weed, was a personal friend and long-time political associate of Grover Cleveland. From Heureaux's point of view, the SDIC was not another spike in the boot of U.S. imperialism. The very informality of the company's Washington connections made it an instrument congenial to Heureaux's way of doing business. When it came to the merger of private and public interests, Heureaux could play schoolmaster to Weed.

Once the presence of the SDIC was a fait accompli, Heureaux lost no time in seeking to profit from the relationship. He tried to convince the Americans that they stood shoulder to shoulder against a hostile world, reminding them that Europe would react jealously to U.S. inroads in the Caribbean. "The European is a foe to the American," he counseled SDIC vice president Charles W. Wells on one occasion. During a diplomatic confrontation between France and the Dominican Republic in 1894–95, Heureaux warned of a French "desire to humiliate a weak nation as punishment for our relations with the United States."[61] On another occasion, the dictator warned the commander of the *Kearsarge* that France, Germany, Italy and Spain "were opposing any extension of American influence or American interests in the island."[62] American officials readily agreed that Europe was hostile to U.S. designs in the region.[63] Calling on the United States to protect its Caribbean interests was another way for Heureaux to influence Washington. Structurally a lackey, the dictator assumed the posture of an ally of both Washington and the SDIC.

Beyond seeking to unite his interests with those of the SDIC and the U.S. government, Heureaux made a modest attempt to move Washington toward a specific goal in 1894, when he asked President Cleveland to upgrade American diplomatic representation in Santo Domingo. He argued that having a minister resident in Santo Domingo would encourage the "growing commercial traffic" between the two nations. Heureaux asked Weed to hand deliver the request to the White House. Weed conferred with the President, Secretary of State Walter Q. Gresham, and Senator John Tyler Morgan of Alabama, the powerful chairman of the Foreign Relations Committee. Despite Weed's good offices, however, the State Department did not raise the mission to embassy level until 1904.[64]

Ironically, Weed's close ties to the White House might have argued against the diplomatic upgrade he and Heureaux sought. Weed communicated regularly with Cleveland, usually about patronage, and could evidently see the President whenever he wished to travel to Washington.[65] The company accomplished Washington's primary goal simply by preventing European financial or strategic encroachments in the republic. Chronically tight-fisted, the department was content with the informal supervision of Dominican affairs that the SDIC provided at no cost to Washington. The decentralized American state had neither the will nor the infrastructure to exert rigorous control over the Dominican Republic.[66]

After U.S. interest in the Dominican Republic retreated from the high-water mark of 1893, it left behind the SDIC as informal *intendant* of the Caribbean nation. The Improvement Company neither took orders from Washington nor dictated policy to American officials. Indeed, Washington's foreign policy apparatus was still too small to oversee the operations of a private company in a foreign country, even if there had been the political will to do so. In moments of crisis, however, the SDIC could expect diplomatic and even military backing from the United States: more than once American warships appeared in Dominican waters at the SDIC's request.[67] The channels of influence between Wall Street and Washington, in the persons of Smith M. Weed and Grover Cleveland, were real enough. But the collaboration did not require tight coordination because it followed from interests that, in the largest sense, coincided. At a time when the State Department staff was minuscule, it was easy for the SDIC to assume the role of a private, parallel diplomatic instrument. The company's intimate ties to the Dominican dictator and its control of the republic's finances — at least on paper — seemed to make it a safe, cheap, convenient champion of American interests in the Caribbean. The weakness of this primitive forerunner of Dollar Diplomacy emerged only after Heureaux's assassination in 1899 and the advent of regimes hostile to the SDIC. In the meantime, the SDIC seemed to be an adequate instrument for safeguarding American influence in Hispaniola at a time of aggressive European territorial and economic expansion.

Heureaux had no illusions about the significance of his nation's independence in a world of great powers.[68] At the height of the reciprocity dispute, Heureaux noted that the laws of nations had been created by Europeans and were ultimately imposed by superior force. Since Britain, France, Germany, and Italy "are those who have fixed and are able to determine the character of positive international right," Heureaux noted, "it would be ridiculous on our part, a fatal oversight, because we believe ourselves to be in possession of the truth, to resist that which they may decide and are able to sanction as the principle of these times."[69] Nor did the willingness of the United States to defend the sovereignty of Latin American nations impress Heureaux. After Secretary of State Olney's blustery note to Britain during the Venezuela crisis, he observed that "President Cleveland has gone too far" and that "the Monroe Doctrine has been getting respectful approval, which I don't see as very promising for the future of the small nations, even though in the case of Venezuela there may be some immediate benefit."[70]

The net result of U.S. overtures toward the Dominican Republic in the early 1890s can be summarized as follows: A private American company had taken over the country's foreign debt, its investment guaranteed by income from Dominican custom houses, which accounted for nearly all of that government's revenue. The lease of Samaná Bay by the United States had fallen through, and commercial reciprocity between the two nations had lapsed by 1894. In other words, two important props for the Improvement Company's investment in the Dominican Republic had disappeared. Despite these reversals, the founders of the SDIC counted on their contacts in Washington to secure the venture in case of problems with European interlopers or the Dominicans themselves. Presumably, the sovereignty and independence of the Dominican Republic would prove to be polite fictions. Apparently, the Americans were in control. So at least Smith M. Weed and his fellow entrepreneurs must have hoped.

3   Peasants in the World Economy
The Dominican Republic in the Late 1800s

The hopes which were entertained a few years ago, as regards
the future welfare of this Country, after the introduction of
foreign Capital, and its investment in agricultural purposes, have
not unfortunately been realized. There has been a total absence
of honesty, among those who have the management of the public
funds, and to whose hands has been blindly confided the money
proceeding from the loans, which loans in fact have only resulted
in the awakening among a part of the people of ideas of cupidity,
and of luxurious habits hitherto quite unknown.
— British vice consul, Santo Domingo[1]

A visitor might land at Puerto Plata having in his possession
$10,000 and, chartering a mule, ride into the heart of the
country alone and unprotected, and be in no more danger than in
the average Connecticut town.
— Smith M. Weed[2]

From Washington's point of view, the project of the SDIC
was essentially geopolitical: preventing European encroachment in the Dominican Republic. Yet, lending money to the Dominican state and admin-
istering the country's custom houses naturally involved the SDIC in the
internal dynamic of Dominican society. The New York attorneys and polit-
icos who had organized the Improvement Company probably had very little
knowledge of the country they were setting out to "improve."[3]

The SDIC had tied itself to a nation that was both like and unlike its
Caribbean neighbors. Like Cuba, Haiti, Jamaica and many of the smaller
islands, the Dominican Republic was a post-emancipation society: slavery
had ended with Haiti's invasion of eastern Hispaniola in 1822. On the other
hand, it was one of only two sovereign states in the Caribbean, having won
its independence not from Spain but from Haiti, in 1844. While the plan-

tation economies of its colonial neighbors were in decline, large-scale sugar production was a new phenomenon in the Dominican Republic in the late 1800s. It was upon this distinctive social and economic terrain that Ulises Heureaux and the SDIC struggled to extract revenue and impose their vision of order and progress.

In size, at least, the Dominican Republic must have seemed manageable to the directors of the Improvement Company. About equal in area to Vermont and New Hampshire combined, the Dominican Republic has a notable variety of terrain and weather. Mountain ranges running from east to west across the island have long separated the country into distinct northern and southern zones. In the North, the vast, well-watered, fertile valley of the Cibao was by the mid-1800s the country's preeminent agricultural region. The flatter, lower-lying terrain along the southern coast was less populated than the Cibao and, before the 1870s, had not developed into an important agricultural area.

In the 1890s the Dominican Republic was still overwhelmingly rural and, compared to Haiti, Puerto Rico, and Cuba, underpopulated.[4] An 1887 survey gave the country's population as 382,312, which by 1908 had increased to 638,000, an annual growth rate of 2.4 percent.[5] Relative underpopulation allowed Dominican peasants access to arable land, which was crucial in the evolution of the Dominican economy.[6] The racial makeup of the population was of keen interest to SDIC officials. "There are about 600,000 people in the republic," Smith M. Weed told the New York Times, "many of them descendants of Europeans, some with a mixture of colored blood in their veins."[7] The census conducted by American occupying forces in 1919, which categorized Dominicans as blanco, negro, mestizo (mulatto), and amarillo (Asian), gave a different portrait. The population of Santo Domingo city, according to the Marines, was 39 percent white, 22 percent black, 39 percent mestizo, and less than 1 percent amarillo, although these figures count nearly 3,000 foreigners. In rural areas of Santo Domingo province, however, those classified as black and of mixed race made up 95 percent of the population.[8]

Dominican cities retained many features of small towns. The Puerto Rican scholar Eugenio María de Hostos, who lived for many years in the Dominican Republic, wondered in 1892, "Does the country really have cities?" and replied: "It would be better to retain the colonial term and call them towns." In 1892, the capital had roughly 14,000 inhabitants, which by 1908 had reached 18,626; as late as 1919 Santo Domingo had only 27,000 inhabitants. The other important towns in the 1890s were Santiago, capital of the Cibao, with about 30,000 residents, and Puerto Plata, the Cibao's leading port, with some 15,000.[9]

Nearly all Dominicans were farmers, and most were campesinos, or peasants. Some owned land; others held shares of *terrenos comuneros*, or undivided communal properties, and still others were *jornaleros* or day laborers. In towns and villages an array of artisans plied their trades.[10] Merchants were a small but influential segment of the population, of which an even smaller group dedicated themselves to shipping goods overseas. They lent money to peasants producing cash crops, bought their crops at harvest time, and shipped the product to Europe or the United States.[11] Many were foreign-born — Italian, Spanish and German — who retained foreign citizenship as a hedge against disputes with the Dominican government.[12] Before the rise of sugar plantations late in the century, these merchants were the wealthiest people in the country and often provided loans both to the government and to revolutionary movements.[13]

The mountain ranges that divided the country into distinct regions had historically made overland travel difficult. When SDIC officials arrived in January 1893, Frederick William Holls was appalled to find a road system ill suited to export agriculture. "Puerto Plata has . . . grown considerably and is now the most important sea port in the Republic," he noted, "but there is not even a carriage road from there to Santiago. . . . All freight and passengers must be transported on horseback at a cost of $30. a ton for the transportation of 40 miles."[14] The president of the SDIC, after visiting Santiago in 1894, observed that "the commerce of the city is dependent on the pack mules. Long trains of them, numbering hundreds, are constantly to be seen coming and going in the vicinity." Bad roads hampered the growth of export agriculture, since the muleteers who conveyed tobacco, coffee, and cacao to market charged high fees.[15]

As elsewhere in Latin America, improving the transportation network was a key concern of Dominican modernizers. During the early years of Heureaux's rule, from 1882 to 1887, Scottish railroad magnate Alexander Baird had built a line from Samaná Bay to La Vega, an agricultural town in the Cibao. By lowering the cost of freight the new road encouraged farmers to raise coffee and cacao for export.[16] Not until the SDIC completed the Central Dominican Railroad in 1897 was there an alternative to the mule teams that picked their way over the mountains between Santiago and Puerto Plata. In the south, by contrast, the only railroads were narrow-gauge private lines constructed by more than a dozen sugar plantations, another indication of the country's regional bifurcation.[17]

The Heureaux regime's contracts with the SDIC fit a larger pattern of granting concessions and franchises to build the republic's infrastructure. Major improvements required the investment of capital that was scarce and dear in the Dominican Republic. One Dominican newspaper complained that "here there are only the crumbs of the capital that is plentiful elsewhere."[18] As a result, the government granted concessions for bridges, wharves, telephone and telegraph systems, railroads, steamship lines, and even the national bank.[19] The largest concessions went to foreigners. William Clyde, an American who resided in Brooklyn, had a monopoly on shipping between the republic and the United States that exempted his ships from duties and port fees.[20] The telegraph services, which linked the republic's main cities and connected it to Europe and the United States, were operated by French companies.[21] The Banque Nacionale de Saint Domingue, another French concession, opened in 1889 with an initial capitalization of 2 million pesos in gold (about $2 million) and a monopoly on the issue of currency.[22]

Concessions usually gave monopoly rights to companies and sometimes guaranteed a subsidy if earnings fell below a fixed minimum, as in the case of the SDIC-owned Central Dominican Railroad. If a concession proved profitable, citizens often complained that the operator was charging too much.[23] On the other hand, if a contract was not profitable, the government was obliged to make contributions or grant exemptions from taxes. Since the state was inevitably involved in any dispute with a foreign concessionaire, quarrels with foreign companies often escalated into diplomatic confrontations, as foreign ministries came to the defense of these private but nevertheless national interests.[24]

At the time of the Improvement Company's arrival, the United States dominated trade with the Dominican Republic, encouraged by regular steamship service to New York.[25] In 1891, the United States supplied 37 percent of the republic's imports and took 58 percent of its exports. For the years that the reciprocity treaty of 1891 was in effect, the importation of Dominican sugar and coffee into the United States increased significantly. The republic's other main trading partners were Spain, Great Britain, France, the Dutch Antilles, and Germany, the latter being the main market for Dominican tobacco.[26] With the exception of a small mining industry, the Dominican economy was almost wholly based on agriculture. As late as the 1870s agriculture remained diverse, small-scale, and regionalized, with no large-scale plantations. The country was still "almost a virgin frontier," with abundant land, scarce population, and only a fraction of arable terrain under cultivation.[27]

The first region to produce crops for export was the northern Cibao valley, which from the 1840s on led the country in production of tobacco.[28] Merchant export houses lent money to farmers, then bought, classified, and shipped the leaves to Bremen and Hamburg. Tobacco prices declined steadily in the 1870s and finally collapsed in 1884; thereafter it was a crop of marginal profitability. At the same time, a growing demand for cacao, the source of chocolate, encouraged many small and medium farmers in the Cibao to switch to the new crop. By 1888 some 5 million new cacao trees had been planted, and cacao surpassed tobacco in export earnings in the 1890s.[29] Because cacao, like tobacco, was usually raised on small farms and marketed through local merchants, the new crop did not change the structure of rural society. Coffee, another cash crop in the Cibao, was of secondary importance.

Before the 1870s, the main economic activities in the south were raising livestock and harvesting natural hardwood trees, above all mahogany. By the 1870s, the wood industry was in decline as cutting zones retreated further from rivers and the seacoast, making export difficult and costly.[30] But the fertile, sparsely populated lowlands proved inviting to a new form of agriculture: large-scale sugar production. Cuba's ten-year fight for independence from Spain (1868–1878) propelled many Cuban planters into exile. Some settled in the nearby Dominican Republic, attracted by the low cost of land and the familiar climate, terrain, language, and culture. The newcomers brought capital, modern technology, and intensive production methods based on large plantations. Other foreign investors, especially Italians and Americans, followed the Cuban pioneers. The areas around Santo Domingo and San Pedro de Macoris, some 80 kilometers east of the capital, became the centers of the sugar industry. The new sugar estates engrossed thousands of acres of land and in time built their own railroads, wharves, electric plants, and water systems. Production grew rapidly: from 7,000 tons exported in 1880, to 24,352 in 1890, and 48,169 in 1905. Sugar quickly overtook tobacco and cacao to become the country's leading export.[31]

Sugar was destined to reshape the Dominican economy, but it took years for the industry to assume its modern organization. In the early days, from the 1870s to the mid-1880s, relatively high wages lured Dominican peasants

from their *conucos*, or small farms, to cut cane. By the early 1880s Dominican intellectuals were commenting on the effects of this partial transition
to wage-based, commercial agriculture. The changes included the tendency
to raise land values, detach peasants from the soil, create a workforce dependent on wages, and reduce the supply of food crops. "The sugar mills
came," noted Eugenio Maria de Hostos, "and with them the offer of work,
so that the peasants abandoned their small plots and their livestock, so strong
was their desire to earn in a few days what before they had earned in weeks
or even months, and as paradoxical as it may seem, the country became
poorer as the state got richer."[32] Dominican sociologist Pedro Francisco
Bonó put the issue even more bluntly: "Before even poor peasants owned
land, but now the poorest have been reduced to proletarians. What progress
does that show?"[33]

Despite the fears of intellectuals, many Dominican peasants stubbornly
resisted becoming wage laborers on the sugar estates. Although newspaper
articles by Hostos and Bonó probably did little to keep peasants on the land,
the crash of sugar prices in 1884 and the subsequent wage cuts on the
plantations did.[34] After a series of violent clashes between workers and *azucareros*, Dominican peasants largely withdrew their labor from the plantations and returned to their *conucos*. This created a labor shortage just as
planters faced plummeting profits due to the fall in the world price of sugar.
In contrast to the preceding decade, the ten years after 1885 saw the founding
of only two new sugar *ingenios*; many more failed as the still-infant industry
was roughly shaken out. The crisis led to a concentration of holdings and
increased foreign ownership of new, larger estates called *centrales*.[35] By 1893
seven large mills in the region of San Pedro de Macoris produced 67 percent
of the country's sugar exports. Of these mills, six were largely or entirely
foreign owned by 1899.[36]

As the sugar sector grew, labor proved to be its most vexing problem.
Planters complained constantly of the scarcity of labor and the unwillingness
of Dominican peasants to work on sugar estates. William Bass, a New Yorker
who had moved his sugar business from Cuba to the Dominican Republic
in the 1870s, stated the issue frankly in a long letter to President Heureaux
in 1897:

> The feature of retaining all the employment for the few inhabitants of
> the country in order that they may profit by abnormal wages, creates
> that condition where the value of a product is not sufficient to cover

the expense of labor and yield satisfactory returns. . . . When I was in the country I saw the difficulty . . . and was a strong advocate of importing ordinary able-bodied working men. . . . It being almost impossible to reduce the price of labor, the next best thing is to contrive such means as will afford an abundance.[37]

As Bass foresaw, sugar planters eventually solved the problem of peasant intransigence by importing unskilled labor to work as field hands on the sugar estates. Planters first brought in contract laborers from the British West Indies in the 1890s and later turned to Haiti for their supply of *braceros*.[38]

The question of what most Dominicans did for a living would become a major issue for Heureaux and the SDIC. In the Dominican Republic, slavery ended long before a plantation economy had become established.[39] Plentiful land allowed former slaves and other peasants to farm and raise animals on land they owned or, more commonly, held jointly with others.

In the absence of a nervous planter class to complain about the peasantry, Dominican historians have disagreed about the extent to which peasants outside the sugar industry dedicated themselves to cash-crop production. Roberto Cassá believes that by the 1890s nearly all peasants were producing cacao, tobacco, or coffee along with traditional foodstuffs. Pedro San Miguel's careful study of Santiago province in the Cibao similarly emphasizes that peasants "participated actively in market production" from the late 1800s onward.[40] Jaime Domínguez and Raymundo González, on the other hand, find intermittent market contact to be the norm in most regions, especially those far from ports, railroads, and towns. Domínguez asserts that low sugar and tobacco prices from the mid-1880s through the turn of the century actually pushed some peasants back to subsistence. Gradually, however, capitalist agriculture penetrated the countryside, as noted by a Dominican official in 1897: "We are now in a period of transition from household to industrial agriculture. One part of the country, lacking transportation, produces only what it consumes, but coastal areas and places with access to transportation, grow valuable crops of sugar, cacao, and coffee and have made the switch to commercial agriculture."[41]

Reports from provincial governors in the 1890s leave little doubt that cash-crop production, on sugar estates but also on smaller holdings of coffee, cacao, and tobacco, was expanding rapidly. In 1897 the governor of Santiago reported that "while previously this province didn't export anything but tobacco, now it produces regular harvests of coffee and cacao." In the region surrounding the capital, "in many parts where only yesterday there was nothing but virgin land, they have built up coffee, cacao, and tobacco farms as well as fields of the tropical fruit that are so plentiful here." A newspaper report in 1894 asserted that in La Vega, in the heart of the Cibao valley, "not a single farmer can be found in this province who doesn't grow cacao and coffee."[42]

Among reports praising the industry of Dominican farmers, however, are hints that not all peasants responded alike to the lure of the market. Some governors complained about the indolence of campesinos, especially those who raised livestock instead of tilling the soil. In 1892 the governor of La Vega province called for the appointment of agricultural inspectors who would root out "vagrancy and laziness," and so "strengthen the vagrancy law that has become a dead letter." Another governor called for new inspectors "with enough power to prosecute vagrancy, which does so much damage to the society that tolerates it." In Puerto Plata, the governor took pains to convince campesinos "that a man who doesn't cultivate a piece of land can't truly be independent," and reinforced his view by arresting peasants who did not cultivate at least ten *tareas* (about an acre and a half) in a six-month period.[43] Assuming that complaints about laziness and vagrancy reflected elite disapproval of peasants who were happy enough with a self-sufficient lifestyle, these provincial reports suggest that many peasants did not rush to sow cash crops, though it is less certain that the government persecuted these peasants in any systematic way.[44] As will be seen in chapter 4, the Heureaux regime attempted to undermine peasant self-sufficiency through the reform of grazing laws, but the effort failed because of strong popular resistance.

At the time of the SDIC's arrival in the Dominican Republic, then, the country was undergoing rapid agricultural change, but along distinct regional axes. In the north, tobacco gave way to cacao as the leading export crop, yet a social and economic structure based on small producers and export merchants accommodated the change. In the south, falling sugar prices brought concentration and foreign control. Large investments in sugar *centrales* substantially altered the social and economic organization of the region, as plantations grew into vast, semi-autonomous enclaves. In both regions, non-market peasants retreated before cash-crop producers, leading to the creation of an "internal frontier" along which market-oriented farmers and *azucareros* confronted campesinos living more or less outside market relations.[45]

The shift toward commercial agriculture affected the economy in significant ways. As peasants turned to cash-crop production, became *braceros* on sugar plantations, and worked on railroads and other projects, food production declined.[46] In the Cibao, "there is evidence that many peasants stopped growing food crops and dedicated themselves exclusively to producing cacao."[47] In the sugar regions of the south, "a relatively large market for foodstuffs and consumer goods was suddenly created in a region that hitherto had provisioned only small urban populations," according to Michiel Baud. "In the urban centers of the Dominican Republic," he notes, "food prices soared sky high from the 1890s onward. Crops that had been abundant for centuries were virtually disappearing."[48] As food crop production declined, imports of foodstuffs, mainly from the United States, increased. Foodstuffs made up a substantial part of the steadily growing quantity of products imported into the republic.[49]

For the Dominican government and the SDIC, the transformation of the Dominican economy was of primary importance.[50] Progress and modernization became synonymous with the production of cash crops for export. In the long term, they envisioned the creation of a prosperous republic made up of hardworking small farmers, rather than what they saw as lazy peasants. But the steady march of commercial agriculture also promised more immediate and concrete rewards to the government and its American allies. At the time, nearly all government revenue came from customs receipts. Roughly 80 percent came from levies on imports (charges that importers routinely passed on to consumers), with the balance derived from export taxes on sugar, cacao, tobacco, coffee, and other crops.[51] Thus, every step away from subsistence agriculture and toward commercialization of the economy had a double benefit. First, farmers who raised cash crops for sale overseas had to pay a duty on these exports. Second, by switching to cash crops, farmers raised less food for their families and often bought imported meat and grain. As a result, the commercialization of agriculture increased the sources of revenue that sustained the Dominican government and guaranteed the SDIC's loans. Statistics for the 1890s confirm that the volume of both imports and exports rose significantly, and customs revenue increased steadily during the SDIC's tenure as well.[52] As will be seen, Heureaux and the SDIC actively pursued policies to make the country hospitable to foreign investment, increase government revenues, and accelerate the commercialization of agriculture.

The SDIC's tenure in the Dominican Republic coincided with an unusual period of political stability. The agent of order, who became known as the

"Pacificador del País," was Ulises Heureaux. Before Heureaux, weak and cash-starved Dominican governments invited rebellion: for example, 13 regimes rose and fell between 1874 and 1879. Heureaux centralized power in his own hands and strengthened the repressive arm of the state.[53] To survive the dictator needed an organized system of bribery and coercion, and to bribe and coerce he needed cash. As a result, Heureaux borrowed heavily from local capitalists and also looked abroad for new sources of revenue.

Even before Heureaux's long dictatorship began, however, Dominican leaders had depended on short-term loans from local merchants to oil the wheels of government.[54] Although the funds of local merchants had limits, the Dominican state was too weak, and the economy insufficiently commercial, for governments to impose direct taxes on the peasant majority. As a result, Dominican leaders looked abroad for fresh sources of capital.

In 1869, the administration of Buenaventura Báez, desperate for money after several years of civil war, contracted what became known as the "Hartmont loan" with an English banking house. An 1875 House of Commons investigation of the London stock exchange partially revealed the machinations behind the floating of the loan. The Hartmont loan is the starting point for understanding how Dominican finances had reached such a desperate condition by the time the SDIC arrived on the scene nearly 25 years later. The infamous loan is also an illuminating case study of the ways that metropolitan stock brokers, bankers, and middlemen dealt with non-European borrowers.[55]

On May 1, 1869, Edward Herzberg Hartmont agreed to provide £420,000 (at the time, about $2,100,000) to the Dominican government, of which £50,000 was to be paid immediately, and £270,000 by the end of the year. The remaining £100,000 ($500,000) was to go to Hartmont for his commission, outlays, and risk. In return, the Dominicans agreed to pay £58,900 annually for 25 years, making the total cost of the loan some $7,500,000, for an annual interest rate of nearly 20 percent. As a guarantee, the republic pledged all its assets, including the customs receipts of the two leading ports, Santo Domingo and Puerto Plata.[56] In London, Hartmont issued a prospectus for a loan with a nominal value of £757,700 ($3,788,500), to pay 6 percent interest annually, and offered to the public at 70 percent of par — that is, at a discount of 30 percent. If the bonds had actually been sold at that discount, the issue would have raised not £420,000 but £530,000. When investigators later asked Hartmont what he would have done with the half-million-dollar difference, he replied, "I would have kept it undoubtedly; not for myself alone, but for all those who were interested."[57]

As was often the case in Latin American finance, political events complicated the loan. Even before the Dominican bonds went on sale in Europe, President Buenaventura Báez negotiated a draft treaty with the United States allowing annexation of the entire republic. The United States had no intention of annexing the Dominican debt, however, and Secretary of State Hamilton Fish made clear that he would not push the treaty unless Báez canceled the loan.[58] Báez assured the Americans that Hartmont would not be able to deliver the money on time and would thus default.[59] The Dominican bonds went on sale late in 1869 but were "very badly received by the public." Investors bought only £15,000 of the Dominican bonds at 70 percent of face value. Hartmont then organized a group of stock brokers to buy the remaining bonds at a discount of from 50 to 55 percent. Eventually, Hartmont and his allies unloaded the bonds on the European market.[60]

At this point, the Dominican government had received $250,000 of a loan for which it had promised to repay $7.5 million. In February 1870, Hartmont sailed to Santo Domingo, allegedly to offer the balance of the loan (£211,100) to Báez. When asked if the Dominicans refused the money, Hartmont replied:

No, they did not refuse at that time; they had concluded annexation treaties with the United States . . . and President Báez told me that I should either stay there until the treaties were ratified, or I could go to Washington and work for annexation, and pay the balance of the loan then over to the United States Government, because it would belong to them as soon as they were annexed.[61]

The U.S. Senate defeated the annexation treaty on June 30, 1870. In July, the Dominican senate repudiated the loan on the grounds that Hartmont had issued bonds far in excess of the amount needed to raise £420,000, and that most of the loan had not been paid.[62] Hartmont later contended that he had not learned of the repudiation until more than two years later.[63] To keep the loan from going into default, Hartmont used the undistributed proceeds to pay bondholders interest during 1871 and 1872, even though the Dominican government made no payments on the repudiated loan.[64] In August 1872, a new Dominican minister to England informed Hartmont that he had been stripped of all powers and published his country's repudiation of the loan in the London press.

Despite Hartmont's questionable business practices, the House of Commons investigation faulted the Dominicans for the Hartmont disaster. "It is

clear," the report stated, "that the Republic found the loan to be an impediment to the scheme of annexation to the United States, and felt the im-
providence of a bargain by which in return for a sum of 320,000 L. they
were to pay . . . the total sum of 1,472,500, or in other words more than 18
per cent. per annum for 25 years." Hartmont insisted that he was the injured
party. "During three or four years I have worked very hard indeed in this
business," he protested, yet the Dominicans "played fast and loose with me."
The Dominican government owed him damages that he put at $450,000
"for robbing me of my concession."[65]

The Dominican government's first foray into foreign borrowing could not
have been a more complete disaster. Having presided over the defeat of
annexation and the loss of almost the entire Hartmont loan, Báez was de-
posed in 1873. The catastrophe cannot simply be laid at Hartmont's door-
step, however unsavory he may have been. The Dominican loan operation
involved some of the largest and most respected brokers in London, including Bischoffsheim, J. S. Morgan, and Morton, Rose & Company. The Hartmont loan may have been a bad one, but it was not an anomaly.[66] It also
foreshadowed later events in that U.S. strategic interests decisively influenced the ostensibly private transaction. The republic paid dearly for pin-
ning its hopes for the future on annexation by the United States.

In the years after the Dominican Republic defaulted on the Hartmont
loan, bondholders in Britain and on the continent closed ranks to keep the
country from obtaining further credit. The vigilance of the bondholders,
organized in groups like London's Corporation of Foreign Bondholders, was
unrelenting. Not until 1888, when President Ulises Heureaux at last reached
terms with the bondholders, did the Dominican government once again win
the chance to hazard its fortunes in Europe's capital markets.

By the late 1880s Heureaux was desperate for new sources of money.
Pacification was expensive, and while he was an eager consumer of local
capital, merchants and planters had their limits. Heureaux was careful not
to kill the geese that occasionally provided him with gold. He also realized
that, under existing conditions, he could not create the fiscal machinery
needed to sustain his regime. The situation was particularly desperate in
1888, since the country was in the grip of an economic depression brought
on by low sugar and tobacco prices. Irresistibly, he looked abroad for new
credit.[67]

A new loan, contracted with Westendorp & Company of Holland in 1888,
bore many similarities to the ill-fated Hartmont loan. Its nominal value,

£770,000 ($3,850,000), was nearly identical to that of the earlier issue, and it bore the same interest rate of 6 percent. After commissions, other charges, and the expected discount, the government was to receive only £442,610, about 57 percent of the nominal sum. In return, the government pledged to pay £55,645 annually for 30 years — £1,669,350 in all.[68] Because of the country's less-than-perfect credit rating, the loan was offered to the European public at discounted rate of 83.5 percent of face value, while Westendorp was allowed to buy notes at 75 percent. Holders of the unpaid Hartmont notes would receive new bonds, but at a steep discount.[69] Heureaux destined the rest of the new loan to pay back local lenders and inject money into the economy, both steps to relieve political pressure on his regime.[70]

One clause of the Westendorp contract dramatically undermined the republic's financial independence. The clause gave Westendorp the power to place its own employees in Dominican custom houses to collect export and import taxes alongside Dominican officials. Officially called the Caja General de Recaudación de Aduanas, but known universally as the Regie, the new institution was designed to give an ironclad guarantee to investors. The Regie verified all customs receipts and withheld the amount needed for interest payments before turning the surplus over to the Dominican government. Not surprisingly, the Regie was frequently at odds with Heureaux, who at least on paper had surrendered the source of 95 percent of his government's revenue to foreign creditors.[71]

The infusion of funds from the 1888 loan did not long satisfy Heureaux's need for money. Despite regular conflicts with the government, in 1890 Westendorp arranged a second emission of bonds, for £900,000, this time to fund the construction of the Central Dominican Railroad from Santiago to Puerto Plata. The railroad, it was hoped, would give peasants an outlet for cash crops, thus promoting commercial agriculture. Sale of the bonds began in London on November 11, 1890. The next morning, telegraph lines buzzed with news of the imminent failure of Baring Brothers, England's largest investor in Latin America. The panic paralyzed the sale of Dominican bonds at a stroke. The second Westendorp loan was a dismal failure: the government received only £36,977, the balance being retained by Westendorp for the cost of building the railroad (estimated at £540,000), to pay off the internal debt once again, to make interest payments on the 1888 loan and the new loan, and for commissions and fees.[72]

Soon after the second Westendorp loan was floated, the country's financial situation became critical. Continued low prices for the republic's commodities were an important factor, as was the rapidly declining value of silver, the country's main currency. The reciprocal trade agreement with the United States that went into effect in September 1891 reduced customs revenues significantly.[73] Debt service had grown to £79,645 (about $400,000) annually, while yearly customs receipts declined from $1,635,412 in 1890 to $1,429,390 in 1891 and $1,087,395 in 1892.[74] Loan payments consumed 40 percent of government revenue, leaving only about $57,000 a month to cover all other outlays.[75]

Europeans in the Dominican Republic recognized that the reciprocity treaty with the United States would reduce the revenues that guaranteed the foreign debt. Even before Heureaux signed the reciprocity treaty with Washington, Westendorp and the French concessionaires who controlled the Banco Nacional had fought against it. "The French and Holland bankers" opposed reciprocity because "they want a large revenue to pay them for their loans at large interest."[76] Although the United States unilaterally abrogated the treaty in 1894, reciprocity had by then played a decisive role in the transfer of financial control from Europeans to Americans, helping the SDIC root itself in the Dominican treasury.

By 1892, Heureaux was feeding his patronage system from an ever-thinner trickle of funds turned over by the Regie. Somehow, the dictator convinced the local representative of Westendorp to reduce the portion of this revenue dedicated to debt service to only 35 percent, leaving the lion's share for Heureaux. Westendorp's home office rejected the unauthorized action of their employee and protested to the Dominican government, but to no avail.[77] It is likely that the European financiers had at last seen the writing on the wall. Rumors of the pending lease of Samaná Bay no doubt added to Westendorp's perception that Washington would brook no competition with its interests in the Dominican Republic. By early 1892 the Dutch company was shopping for an American buyer of its Dominican holdings.

On the eve of the SDIC's arrival in Santo Domingo, Ulises Heureaux had imposed a fragile political stability on the country paid for with money borrowed both at home and abroad. The surface stability masked rapid social change, as the country moved from subsistence farming to export agriculture. That transition sparked tensions between self-sufficient peasants and commercial farmers, but it advanced too slowly to supply Heureaux with the income he desperately needed to stay in power. Government spending had spun out of equilibrium with economic growth, as the dictator borrowed in Europe to buy peace at home. Moreover, the new loans brought onerous conditions, including foreign supervision of nearly all revenue collection.

For Heureaux, the replacement of European capitalists by American investors in 1893 offered opportunities as well as risks. If the arrival of the Americans meant that foreign capital would flow once more, Heureaux could look forward to holding onto power for a few more years. Even more promising, Heureaux's partnership with a progressive American company dedicated to "improving" the tropical republic suggested that the business of modernization — turning peasants into cash-crop farmers — would push forward with new zeal. The SDIC-Heureaux years would indeed prove to be historically significant, but their legacy would not be one of progress.

4 Dictating Development

Ulises Heureaux and the SDIC Remake the Dominican Republic

> Like all Spanish-American countries, the politics are generally of the kind in which individuals, rather than principles, are the prominent factors, sometimes called 'personal politics,' and, naturally, there is a feeling between the "ins" and "outs" which occasionally becomes so bitter as to make trouble. . . . but the administration of President Heureaux in San Domingo has been so wise and able that he has reduced disturbances from such causes to a minimum.
> — Smith M. Weed[1]

> The two peoples who live in this beautiful part of the Antilles had better not dream, or sleep, or rest! There is a price on their head: either they organize themselves for civilization, or civilization will absorb them brutally, as it has already started to do. . . .
> The verdict of the times is final: Civilization or death.
> — Eugenio María de Hostos[2]

Before the Improvement Company, the foreign creditors of the Dominican Republic had done little more than take the money and run. Unlike the British and Dutch lenders who came before them, however, the Improvement Company became an intimate partner of the Dominican government. The Dominican national archive holds more than a hundred long and detailed letters from President Heureaux to Improvement Company officials in New York City. These letters document a complex relationship that ultimately led the Dominican government toward bankruptcy and financial chaos, but that included genuine efforts to remake the Dominican Republic in the image of a modern, capitalist society.

From 1893 to 1897, the Improvement Company and Dominican President Ulises Heureaux pursued the classic nineteenth-century ideal of progress, promoting ambitious reforms that promised to remake Dominican society. These included the completion of the Central Dominican Railroad, the adoption of the gold standard, and the reform of grazing laws to promote commercial agriculture by discouraging peasant self-sufficiency.[3] To understand the allure of the idea of progress, it is helpful to look at one episode that captures the master themes of the Heureaux regime.

In August 1894 Heureaux made a rare trip to the northern cities of the Dominican Republic. Undertaken mainly to bolster support for the dictator in the often-hostile Cibao region, on one level the excursion showed Heureaux's eagerness to preempt any political opposition. Yet the visit also had more ambitious goals. In each city Heureaux staged an elaborate procession that used symbols and pageantry to underscore the fundamental ideas of his regime. The most important message was that peace, whether voluntary or coerced, was the foundation of prosperity and progress. That argument underlay the modernizing project of Heureaux and his partners in the San Domingo Improvement Company.[4]

Since the overland route to the Cibao amounted to little more than a network of mule paths, Heureaux traveled north aboard one of the Dominican navy's two small warships. He disembarked in Puerto Plata, the city of his birth and residence of many foreign merchants involved in the coffee, cacao, and tobacco trade. His reception there was typical of the response to his visit throughout the region. Although newspapers accorded Heureaux the republican title "citizen president," his visit had all the trappings of a royal progress. Local notables and resident foreigners received the honored visitor with shows of fawning devotion.

The route that Heureaux and his retinue followed to the city center had been painstakingly decorated. Banners strung from the municipal buildings proclaimed a reign of Honor, Justice, Law, and Light. As the president passed through one street, thirty girls in white dresses threw flowers at his feet. The popular poet Juan Antonio Alix composed several lyrics for the occasion:

> *Everyone is getting ready*
> *to welcome the leader of our nation*
> *gladly and with unequaled enthusiasm;*
> *He is visiting us today,*
> *because of his love for the people.*[5]

The Spanish, Italian, and British colonies in Puerto Plata competed to offer the best welcome, erecting allegorical arches along the procession's route that proclaimed an era of Progress, Peace, and Order. Heureaux took care to return the compliment to the Europeans, who played a key role in the country's rapidly growing export economy. Responding to a profuse welcome from British residents, Heureaux "formulated in proper English a warm reply."[6] The dictator's command of both English and French made communication with foreigners easier and showed his outward-looking orientation. Later in his stay the president would attend a formal dinner at the "Club de Comercio" made up largely of foreign merchants, including a Dutch employee of the SDIC, Den Tex Bondt. Heureaux's respectful attention to the European colony in Puerto Plata underscored his embrace of foreign investment and commerce.[7]

According to local newspapers, the highlight of the welcome came when the entourage reached Heureaux's family home. Four young women, probably daughters of local merchants and politicians, stood atop pedestals in symbolic representation of the Nation, Peace, Agriculture, and Commerce. The figures saluted the president and thanked him for pacifying the nation, from which, they declared, flowed a "newborn agriculture" and "flourishing commerce."[8]

Peace and its benefits, the topic that dominated the speeches, toasts, and benedictions offered during Heureaux's visit, had long been central to the dictatorship's ideology. The Dominican congress formally recognized peace as the greatest public good by granting Heureaux the title "Pacificador del País," or pacifier of the nation, in 1888. In public discourse Heureaux proclaimed peace the nation's most precious resource, the "fundamental base of public wealth" and "seed of the riches that are increasing every day in the country."[9] The regime celebrated public order not merely as the absence of rebellion, but also as an active good that allowed progress in both the public and private sectors.[10]

The theme of peace, or more to the point, pacification, was not merely rhetorical. For a dozen years, Heureaux successfully suppressed both rival candidates and armed rebellions. The dictator enjoyed the longest tenure in office of any president from the time of independence in 1844 until Rafael Trujillo's accession to power in 1930. The project of pacification succeeded in part because Heureaux spent large sums of money to modernize the armed forces and to purchase warships that deployed troops quickly around the island. Equally important was his practice of neutralizing opponents with

bribes and sinecures or — for the less malleable — prison, exile, and summary execution.[11] For the country's elites, at least before the economic crisis
that paralyzed the nation after 1895, maintaining public order justified
Heureaux's repression and violence.[12]

Heureaux's choreographed visit to Puerto Plata shows that the ruler invested time and effort to fortify his regime with republican symbols.[13] Yet
the argument that Heureaux manipulated "the routines and rituals of rule"
as part of a cultural project of state building can easily be carried too far.[14]
Heureaux did manipulate language and imagery to charge the ideas of
peace, progress, and prosperity with symbolic weight. But the regime could
not even extract the minimum revenue it needed to survive, much less reg-
ulate the nation's cultural forms. Within the limits imposed by a weak and
cash-starved state, Heureaux did attempt to mold the political vision of his
countrymen. When he undertook controversial projects like agrarian reform
or paper money issues, he had provincial officials hold public meetings to
sell the government's position to the people.[15] Nevertheless, what Paul J.
Vanderwood has noted of Porfirio Díaz is also true of Heureaux: "He made
no effort . . . to mobilize mass support or even to develop a political party
among elites."[16] Heureaux's statecraft could not have penetrated very far into
the many small villages of an overwhelmingly rural nation. Nor did the
dictator prepare the public for the reforms he implemented: he imposed
them from above. Only when these reforms threatened the lifestyle of the
peasants did their opinion about modernization become clear.

In fact, Heureaux was more anxious to impress national and foreign elites
than the Dominican masses. To those elites, he presented himself as the
only leader able to hold the country's chaotic politics in check. With the
mortgaging of his country's finances to foreign investors, pacification took
on new importance. Since the SDIC, like Westendorp, raised money by
selling bonds in Europe, the country's fate turned to a significant degree on
its public image abroad. That fact put a premium on the appearance, if not
the reality, of peace and stability. Any hint of a revolution that might cause
a default on interest payments would lower the value of Dominican bonds
and undermine future borrowing. Heureaux spoke candidly about the problem. "I promise," he assured SDIC vice president Charles W. Wells in 1894,
"that I will redouble my efforts to make sure that no political disturbance
damages the confidence that peace brings to the foreign bondholders."[17]

The internationalization of Dominican finances, then, encouraged the
government to maintain a public facade of peace and prosperity and carried

with it the absolute need to pacify dissidents. Heureaux's attention to foreign merchants and his conscious projection of the image of *pacificador* reflected those imperatives. To the SDIC he presented his northern tour as proof that the people had rallied around his core ideas. "Everywhere I was received as the mainspring of public well-being," Heureaux told the New Yorkers, "and the ovations that greeted me are clear evidence that a single feeling now unites the entire country: the desire for Progress."[18]

Heureaux's paeans to progress must have struck a sympathetic chord on Wall Street, where the Improvement Company had its offices. The SDIC's modernizing goals had been stated eloquently at the time that company officials visited the island republic in early 1893. Frederick William Holls, the lawyer who helped negotiate the SDIC's contracts with Heureaux, linked economic progress with increasing levels of "civilization" that would eventually democratize the Dominican political system. "With frequent and regular communication" Holls explained

> and especially with railroads the whole state of affairs in San Domingo would be entirely changed and a species of Republican form of Government which would not be out of harmony with our system, though not in all respects identical with the Government of Vermont and Ohio. I see no reason why the building of railroads in all Spanish American Republics should not have a similar effect as in Mexico, where revolutions are practically unknown.[19]

As Holls' unfortunate reference to Mexico suggests, the themes of order, progress, and prosperity that undergirded the Heureaux dictatorship also shaped the discourse and programs of other Latin American elites. Above all, modernizing elites favored the expansion of export agriculture. "The true wealth of a nation," declared one Dominican newspaper, "lies in the production of export crops."[20] In the 1890s, Heureaux and the Improvement Company undertook a program of development to move a largely self-sufficient peasant society toward market relations and export-crop production. Their plans for root-and-branch modernization, with the basic social changes that such a process demanded, failed to materialize but are worth analyzing in detail.[21]

In the late nineteenth century, progress was an obsession of the ruling elites throughout Latin America, and the Dominican Republic was no exception.[22] As the twentieth century approached, the upper strata of Dominican society talked constantly of progress and modernization. The concept embraced not only technical, industrial, and agricultural advancement, but also the idea of moral, political, and educational improvement.[23] In an over-whelmingly rural society like that of the Dominican Republic, the partisans of progress necessarily turned their eyes to conditions in the countryside. They did not like what they saw. Peasants who had not made the transition to cash-crop production were a major preoccupation of the modernizing elites. Liberals denounced the "indolence of the campesino" and charac-terized peasants as "drunks" and "thieves."[24] The terms of derision applied to peasants in the Dominican Republic echoed those employed by elites in other peasant societies.[25]

Dominican modernizers displayed special hostility toward two time-honored institutions that sustained the self-sufficient lifestyle of the peas-antry. A system of *terrenos comuneros*, or undivided communal properties, made it difficult to sell land in many areas.[26] These jointly owned properties were the dominant form of landholding until the end of the nineteenth century, and even in the twentieth century gave way only slowly to full private ownership.[27] Tradition also favored *crianza libre*, or the unrestricted grazing of livestock.[28] Dominican law absolved herders of liability for the damage done by their foraging animals, placing the cost and labor of build-ing fences on farmers who wished to protect their crops. As one newspaper put it, *"la crianza* impedes or kills the prosperity of agriculture."[29]

Dominican liberals tended to be pessimistic about imposing "civilization" on the rural majority without outside help. The modernizers believed "it was necessary to import the ideas, the tools, the technology, and even the men to make progress viable."[30] As a result, they supported a sweeping mod-ernization program to transform the countryside by attracting foreign loans and investment, promoting immigration, granting concessions for infrastruc-ture projects, and in general emulating Euro-American society.[31]

For the most part, Dominican aspirations coincided with the hopes of other Latin American modernizers.[32] In some respects, however, the country was distinct. Dominican modernizers tended to define their "progressive" vision in contrast to the "backwardness" of neighboring Haiti. In his first contacts with the SDIC, Heureaux manipulated the image of Haitian "oth-erness" to present the Dominican Republic as an outpost of Western civili-zation, deftly closing the racial and cultural gap that divided him from his guests.[33] "President Heureaux told me," SDIC attorney Frederick William Holls recorded, "that in his travels in Hayti he had several times attended

religious voudoo services and had actually been invited to partake of a stew
in which he recognized the hands and feet of a baby. His ambition as he
frequently avows is to conquer Hayti and to be a new and enlightened
Toussant," referring to Toussaint L'Ouverture, who defeated white colonists
and British and French troops in the 1790s and opened the way for Haitian
independence in 1804.

The Americans, who did not visit Haiti, accepted Heureaux's depiction
of Haitian barbarism and his self-promotion as "a new and enlightened
Toussant." Heureaux's plan for an unprovoked attack on Haiti won their
enthusiastic support. Indeed, the dictator went so far as to convince Holls
that "the hope of reestablishing the credit of San Domingo with our help
sufficiently to be able to buy more men-of-war was unquestionably a leading
motive in making the bargain with us." Heureaux encouraged his guests
to see their investment in the Dominican Republic as part of a *mission
civilisatrice* in which Heureaux was an ally, not a debtor.[34]

Heureaux's anecdotes of cannibalism and voudoo found a willing audi-
ence because they shared in a larger discourse about the hierarchy of Caribbean societies in which white metropolitans and elite Dominicans could
find common ground.[35] At the time, it was a commonplace of both Euro-
American travel literature and Dominican writings on national identity that
the "Brown Republic" of Santo Domingo was qualitatively distinct from the
"Black Republic" of Haiti.[36] One element of this comparison had to do with
openness to foreign influence. Rafael Abreu Licairac probably spoke for
many Dominican liberals when he wrote: "We are far, very far, from having
reached the level of culture and civilization appropriate to the age we live
in, but in the scale of civilized peoples we occupy a position much higher
than the Haitian people." In Haiti, "the white foreigner is a constant night-
mare: whence come their extraordinary laws of exclusion and their resistance
to any action that might liberalize their absurd legislation."

Abreu Licairac was referring to Haiti's constitutional prohibitions on foreign investment and landownership. In the view of Dominican elites and
foreign visitors, these impediments to foreign penetration at once symbolized
Haiti's barbaric isolation and guaranteed its continuation. Outsiders agreed
that Haiti's resistance to foreign control was a matter of racial hatred rather
than an effort to safeguard national independence. Dominicans, in contrast,
welcomed the civilizing influence of European and North American capital.
Abreu Licairac straightforwardly equated civilization with government concessions to foreigners. "What effort would it cost us to show our moral,

political, and social superiority to the Haitians?" he asked rhetorically. "Can there be any doubt after comparing our laws, which are expansive, cosmopolitan, and full of concessions to foreigners, with the prohibitive, narrow, and ridiculously exclusionary Haitian laws?"[37]

American visitors to Hispaniola made the same point. After meeting Ulises Heureaux in 1894, SDIC president Smith M. Weed told the *Times* that Dominicans were "especially considerate toward foreigners, in which respect they differed very much from the Haitian at the other end of the same island." J. Laurence Laughlin, an economist who helped the SDIC introduce the gold standard in the Dominican Republic, noted that "the color line in Haiti is drawn against the white man; in Santo Domingo it practically does not exist." Even Frederick Douglass, U.S. minister to Haiti and the Dominican Republic from 1889 to 1891, observed that "Santo Domingo, more liberal than her contiguous neighbor, Haiti, does not refuse to foreigners, but encourages in them, ownership in her soil."[38]

Demonizing Haiti made sense for Heureaux. Against the Haitian backdrop, his program of alliance with the SDIC, foreign borrowing, and granting of concessions — which could be seen as wounding the nation's sovereignty — became emblems of the republic's march toward civilization. Dominican liberals were not far from Heureaux and the SDIC in their view of progress, linking openness to financial and commercial penetration with social and political betterment. The readiness of liberals, including opponents of Heureaux's dictatorship like Abreu Licairac, to frame relations with foreigners in such terms was of no small utility to the Dominican president and the SDIC. It meant that the most articulate and influential Dominicans were disposed to favor Heureaux's policies and that the general belief in progress took immediate and concrete meaning in contrast to the radical nationalism of Haiti.

For Heureaux, as for Latin American modernizers from Domingo Sarmiento to Porfirio Díaz, development was more than a matter of economic growth. In fact, the dictator promoted modernization with an eye toward specific political goals. Construction of the Dominican Central Railroad in the Cibao, the regime's premier infrastructural project, is a case in point. The rail line promised to give small farmers greater access to national and international markets by dramatically lowering shipping costs. The project, Heureaux believed, "implies the agricultural and commercial development of the entire Cibao, which is rich enough to guarantee incalculable returns."[39] From that benefit others would flow: "The project is of utmost political importance since it will not only vastly increase the resources of the government, but will also secure peace for the republic, which it is necessary to preserve at all costs to complete other worthwhile plans."[40]

The new rail line, then, promised to pacify restive northern farmers by giving them new economic opportunities. At the same time, it would increase exports and thus benefit merchants in Puerto Plata and other cities of the Cibao. As more and more peasants planted cash crops, the government would collect more taxes on both imports and exports. Foreign creditors, entitled to a share of all customs revenue, also stood to gain. The railroad would secure the peace in a more direct way, too, by permitting the rapid deployment of troops into the heart of the often recalcitrant Cibao.

The constellation of advantages brought by the railroad shows that the dictator understood "progress" as an economic process embedded in a social and political milieu. In his speech inaugurating the Central Dominican Railroad in 1897, Heureaux frankly acknowledged economic growth as the complement of political repression. "I could not go to my grave quietly if the task of pacification which I have taken on were limited merely to its political and military aspects," he declared. "Beyond the project of repression which has eliminated insurrections, the happiness of the people demands that we substitute works of progress for the causes of discontent and rebellion that existed earlier."[41]

Heureaux's "works of progress," especially the railroad, encouraged the spread of capitalist agriculture but did not give rise to the discontents brought by modernization in other parts of Latin America. As Pedro San Miguel has shown, the coming of the northern railroad did not radically change the structure of peasant life in the Cibao.[42] It is true that commercialization of agriculture raised prices for food and land. Nevertheless, the change took place within a durable social system of small producers. The boom in the Cibao's export production reflected the fact that peasants were planting new crops and not the spread of plantations, concentration of landownership, or proletarianization of the peasantry.[43] This unique economic structure saved Heureaux from facing the kind of popular uprising that brought down Mexico's Porfirio Díaz in 1910. Similarly, the expanding sugar enclaves in the south relied on foreign workers for the labor-intensive task of harvesting the cane. Imported workers, first from the British Caribbean and later from Haiti, spared the Dominican peasantry a direct encounter with the hard logic of the sugar plantations. At least in the short term, there was no necessary collision between Heureaux's fomentation of capitalist agriculture and the traditional independence of the peasantry.[44]

While peasants were insulated from the worst effects of capitalist agriculture, Heureaux was scarcely happy with the way most rural Dominicans lived. The Central Dominican Railroad may not have revolutionized the peasant economy of the Cibao, but Heureaux hoped that changing the country's agricultural laws would. As already mentioned, the traditional practice of *crianza libre* had been the bête noire of Dominican modernizers for many years. The issue burst into the public arena in 1894, when a detailed critique of the practice by Emilio Tejera, future minister of foreign relations, rallied elite support for a change in the law. Tejera's scathing broadside blamed *crianza libre* for the large-scale importation of foodstuffs, violence between farmers and herders, and even the abandonment of land by farmers who preferred to become day laborers than see their crops destroyed.

> The truth is, one must be a supreme optimist . . . to launch the most insignificant agricultural project here, knowing that CRIANZA LIBRE exists, and that the pig with his powerful snout intact enjoys the right to go and eat wherever he pleases. . . .
>
> In fact we have two classes of property owners, the herdsman, who possesses his own property and that of his neighbors, and the farmer, who in fact controls only a tiny part of the land that belongs to him, and that precariously.[45]

Tejera's critique found an echo in the complaints of commercial farmers. One group of coffee planters in the province of Baní detailed their sufferings in a long and articulate petition to the Dominican congress. The petitioners, who held extensive unfenced lands planted with coffee, astutely framed their argument in terms of the state's loss of revenue as a result of *crianza libre*. "There is no greater source of wealth in the region than coffee," they averred, but "because of a few pigs, which bring no benefit to the town, nor to commerce, nor to the government, all this positive wealth is being destroyed." The pigs "can easily be moved to other areas, but not so our coffee bushes." The beleaguered farmers asked congress to declare Baní an agricultural zone so that the herdsmen would be forced to fence their stock.[46]

The importance of the issue is confirmed by the government's unusual effort to conduct a national census to determine how much land was dedicated to agriculture and how much to herding. The Ministry of the Interior had provincial governors submit surveys showing how many *secciones* were in each category and also how much area separated the two zones, on the false assumption that agriculture and herding zones did not overlap. The responses did little to clarify the issue. Nevertheless, Heureaux threw his weight behind the proposed reform, which restricted in various ways the practice of free-range husbandry.[47] By securing the property of farmers and eliminating the need to fence croplands, the law would stimulate cash-crop agriculture. The reform had the support of commercial farmers, especially sugar planters, whose large holdings were particularly vulnerable to the depredations of unfenced livestock.

Congressional debate over the reform exposed the fracture lines of two antagonistic economic and social systems.[48] While a small elite of wealthy ranchers owned huge herds of cattle, most herders had a few dozen animals at most. Often these impoverished campesinos were shareholders in *terrenos comuneros* as well. Argument over the reform centered on the violation of property rights by these peasants, who routinely grazed their animals on land they did not own. During the debate, one angry legislator exclaimed, "A man cannot raise animals unless he has land on which to raise them." When an antireform colleague asked, "And what of the tolerance that has existed for centuries?" the first replied frankly, "That is what must be destroyed."[49] It was no use for opponents to argue that the new law would undermine traditional agrarian life — that was precisely its aim.

After the law was adopted in May 1895, Heureaux took steps to ensure its enforcement. The dictator proclaimed that the reform was beneficial to herders as well as to farmers, but he clearly understood that the law would undercut the legal basis of the subsistence economy. "While herdsmen enjoy an exaggerated property right," he wrote, "for farmers there is only a restricted and mutilated right of ownership." Moreover, Heureaux hoped to chip away at the widespread practice of communal landholding, a perpetual obstacle to land sales and thus to commercialization of agriculture. The new law "will contribute to the measuring and marking of the *terrenos comuneros* which . . . is another problem that has weighed on property holding and whose solution matters to the whole nation."[50]

Despite Heureaux's propaganda campaign, the agrarian reform was widely recognized as a frontal attack on the peasantry's way of life. Opposition was swift and widespread, coming both from wealthy ranchers and small pastoralists.[51] One provincial official reported that he had held ten meetings with farmers in his area "but despite my efforts and explanations, in the end nearly all the inhabitants openly refused to comply with the new law."[52] By September 1895 an insurgent movement had broken out, taking the new grazing law as the focus of its protests. The *pacificador del país* faced a revolutionary movement that, unlike many others, was not launched by a rival faction of the Dominican elite, but was in fact a mass movement. Thus threatened, Heureaux was savvy enough to retreat quickly. Only a few months after the law's passage, he suspended its enforcement, in effect annulling the law.[53] In the Cibao Heureaux personally met with officials charged with enforcing the law, explaining that he "believed the new law would be good for the country. . . . but the peasantry had not understood it that way."[54] It would be more than a decade before the Dominican congress took up the volatile issue once again.

The failed effort to end *crianza libre* shows the political danger of a modernizing scheme that touched the quick of peasant self-sufficiency.[55] The difference between railroad construction and agricultural reform is instructive. The railroad opened new commercial outlets for small as well as large farmers and did not directly injure any social group, except the muleteers who had carried coffee, tobacco, and other products to market. Reforms that threatened the practices of *crianza libre* and *terrenos comuneros*, on the other hand, although cloaked in the language of progress, implied a radical restructuring of the peasant economy. The government's retreat from the attack on *crianza libre* demonstrates that the popular will constrained Heureaux's apparent absolutism, at least when the issue was of real concern to the agrarian majority. In addition, the incident fixes the boundary of the dictator's commitment to modernization. Heureaux promoted commercialization of agriculture, knowing that growing commerce meant more revenue for his government. But the dictator was no ideologue, and his enthusiasm for change stopped well short of laying the groundwork for his own overthrow.[56]

While the Dominican government did attempt to undermine *crianza libre*, it made no direct move against the equally retrograde practice of communal landholding. The government's timidity cannot be explained by indifference, since Heureaux himself condemned common lands, as has been noted. Nor were suggestions for reform lacking. William Bass, the American planter quoted in chapter 3 on labor shortages, proposed a general survey of *terrenos comuneros* in 1893. The plan required peasants to show good title to land and then pay an annual tax of $2 in gold on each *cabellería* they owned. Peasants who could not produce a title or pay this hefty fee would forfeit their land to the government, which as Bass well knew, would almost certainly have made the land available to sugar planters. The plan was never adopted, nor did the government mount any other direct attack on the *terrenos comuneros*, perhaps because the issue was too explosive politically even to broach.[57]

The most ambitious reform promoted by the SDIC in the mid-1890s was adoption of the gold standard. This reform alone entitles the SDIC's project in the Dominican Republic to be considered a precocious version of Dollar Diplomacy. As Emily Rosenberg has shown, the creation of a gold-based monetary system was the trademark reform promoted by American financial advisors in underdeveloped territories, protectorates, and even independent nations after 1900.[58] Years before Jacob H. Hollander revamped the monetary system of Puerto Rico and Charles A. Conant created a gold-based currency in the Philippines, however, the Improvement Company experimented with a similar reform in the Dominican Republic. In the words of one SDIC official, the effort was "a new feature in monetary science."[59]

The gold-exchange system was a way for less-developed countries to stabilize their currencies at a time of rapid silver inflation.[60] At the same time, by pegging the value of these currencies to the U.S. gold dollar, the plan would not incidentally give American commerce an advantage like that enjoyed by the nations associated with Britain through the sterling union. "An Americanized gold-exchange standard would simplify international transactions and create a gold dollar bloc, centered in New York, to rival the *de facto* sterling standard that had prevailed in most of the world since the late nineteenth century and proved a competitive advantage for British businesses."[61]

The goals of the SDIC in pushing for monetary reform probably were not so global. The company and Heureaux stood to benefit in very concrete ways from the switch to a gold-backed currency. The circulating medium in the Dominican Republic was the Mexican peso. Since merchants and planters paid customs duties in silver, the steady drop in silver's value effectively cut government revenues. Moreover, interest payments on the country's foreign debt had to be made in gold, so that the decline of silver threatened the "inevitable loss of public credit and domestic bankruptcy." Since the Improvement Company collected a share of the government's revenue on behalf of foreign bondholders, the gold standard obviously favored the company's interests as well. In addition, by ensuring price stability, the gold standard was widely seen as an incentive to foreign investment.[62]

To help move the Dominican Republic onto a gold footing, the SDIC turned to J. Laurence Laughlin, one of the leading American economists of the late 1800s. Laughlin, who had taught for a decade at Harvard before moving to the newly founded University of Chicago, was a prominent spokesman for the gold standard during the debate between hard money and silver advocates in the 1890s. He later played an important role in shaping the Federal Reserve Act. As the SDIC contemplated reforming the Dominican currency, *New York Post* editor Horace White recommended Laughlin to help promote the reform. In February 1894 Laughlin traveled to Santo Domingo with SDIC officials. His "assistance and advice" helped convince the Dominican congress to adopt the reform the next month.[63]

As a theoretician of hard money, Laughlin promoted the shift to the gold standard as a master reform that would unleash the republic's economy. "The credit of the country," he wrote, "the value of the bonds, the means to build railways, the improvement of harbors and rivers, the increase of military and naval protection, the building of forts, the carrying on of internal improvements, — all these were concerned in the question of gold and silver."[64] Laughlin's innovative solution was for the government to mint a new silver coin whose value would not depend on its silver content but would simply be fixed at one gold dollar. The silver dollar was to be held at par with gold by the guarantee of redemption on demand for gold from the Banco Nacional de Santo Domingo. In this way, silver would remain the republic's currency, but without fluctuating in value relative to gold. "Convertible paper is always at par," Laughlin pointed out. "Why not have convertible silver?"[65]

Charles W. Wells, vice president of the SDIC, presented the reform as a universal panacea, at least for the social groups that concerned him. "The bankers, the sugar planters, and all classes, in short, were suffering from the great fluctuations in exchange arising from the decrease in the price of silver," Wells explained to the *New York Times*.[66] In reality, the gold standard promised different consequences for several powerful groups in Dominican society. Exporters of sugar, cacao, coffee, and tobacco sold their commodities for gold overseas, but paid workers and suppliers in depreciated silver. Paying wages in gold or its equivalent would in effect double the salaries of workers, a result that was not lost on those who hired labor. Laughlin argued that the reform polarized social classes around conflicting interests. "It was no wonder that the agitation for reform secured a strong support among . . . the working and trading classes," Laughlin noted, while "the sugar-planters and exporting classes, who were largely foreigners, should be inclined to look unfavorably upon monetary reform."[67] Since customs duties that had been paid in devalued silver would now have to be paid in gold, exporters and planters would be doubly injured by the reform. Wells later admitted that "employers of labor" agitated against the reform and that "the opposition of the sugar planters became serious."[68] The government, on the other hand, stood to profit not only from collecting taxes in gold, but also from seigniorage amounting to 50 percent of the nominal value of the new coins.[69]

The gold-exchange system depended on public confidence that their government could, and would, redeem silver coins for gold upon demand. "Central banks were the harness that would naturally maintain price stability," writes Emily Rosenberg, in effect "putting government in control of the amount of circulating silver coinage." The government of Ulises Heureaux was not sufficiently solvent and credible, however, to inspire much confidence among ordinary Dominicans. "At the very beginning, of course, tests of the ability to redeem may be more or less frequent," Laughlin had predicted optimistically, "until confidence is firmly established."[70] In practice, tests of the government's ability to redeem silver for gold were incessant. Heureaux struggled for years to keep the Banco Nacional solvent, at times resorting to impromptu bank holidays to avoid bankruptcy. The refusal of Dominicans to put their faith in the new money was another example of the popular will asserting itself tacitly against the modernizing designs of the government and the SDIC.

As Laughlin presented the issue, the gold standard aligned the working classes, the government, and the SDIC against plantation and commercial interests, many controlled by foreigners. Perhaps if the reform had worked effectively, confrontations among these different interests would have become manifest. In fact, there is little evidence of a political struggle over monetary reform like that which surrounded the issue of *crianza libre*. One newspaper commented obliquely that since only England, the United States, and a few other wealthy nations were on the gold standard, "it could be said that gold is the currency of bankers while silver is the money of the people."[71] Nevertheless, to placate planters, the government softened the blow by lowering customs duties.[72] More important, the reform itself proved ephemeral. Within a year the government had resorted to issuing unbacked paper currency to cover its day-to-day operating expenses. As a result, planters and import-export merchants returned to paying customs duties in one of several depreciated currencies.[73]

The retreat from the attack on *crianza libre* and the failure of monetary reform raise basic questions about the modernizing drive of Heureaux and the Improvement Company. In the mid-1890s, wholesale restructuring of the Dominican economy was beyond the reach of the Dominican government and its American allies.[74] The Dominican state was too weak, the SDIC too poor, to wage the long twilight struggle required to launch genuine modernization. Their failure can be usefully compared to later, successful examples of Dollar Diplomacy. When Puerto Rico and the Philippines became American territories after 1898, American financial advisors could muster resources far beyond those available to the SDIC in order to impose monetary reform. The SDIC might call on the U.S. government for gestures like the sending of an occasional warship, yet the company commanded neither the capital nor the coercive power needed to remake Dominican society.

The legacy of SDIC financial stewardship was unmitigated disaster — a disaster that convinced President Theodore Roosevelt and his advisors that leaving Dollar Diplomacy to a private company without substantial U.S. government supervision was a recipe for future fiascoes. The failure of the Improvement Company's proto-Dollar Diplomacy, in fact, created the crisis that led to Roosevelt's redefinition of that policy. As Emily Rosenberg notes, effecting financial reforms that created political stability "was an objective that found implicit expression in the Theodore Roosevelt Corollary to the Monroe Doctrine and then in the government policy that came to be known as dollar diplomacy."[75]

As late as 1895, the collapse of the Dominican economy still lay in the future. In the early years of the SDIC's operation in the Caribbean republic, Smith M. Weed and other company officials had room for optimism. Development was what the Improvement Company was all about. Weed had, after all, built his career opening the remote Adirondack region of upstate New York to railroad and mining interests. Superficially, the Heureaux regime's concessions for infrastructure development and borrowing were similar to the government subventions and monopolistic contracts that Weed had milked so profitably back in the States. The SDIC's attorney, Frederick William Holls, saw no conflict between progress for the Dominican Republic and windfall profits for the SDIC. "Altogether I think the scheme will bear the closest scrutiny," he wrote of the SDIC's contracts with Heureaux, "both as a good commercial enterprise for us and as a just and highly desirable arrangement for the development of San Domingo." Private vices would be the engine of public benefits.

The Caribbean context was, however, radically different from anything the SDIC's organizers were acquainted with. Even remote areas of New York State were integrated into the world's fastest growing industrial economy. The Dominican Republic, on the other hand, remained underdeveloped even by the standards of the Caribbean. Equally important, Dominican peasants had enough control over land to hold in check "reforms" that would have left large numbers of them landless.

The problem emerged clearly in an interview Smith M. Weed gave after visiting the Dominican Republic for the first time in the spring of 1894. The country's agriculture was "productive beyond all comparison," Weed told the *New York Times*, and the people seemed "happy and contented." Weed then recalled a conversation in which President Heureaux had said: "'We have not the wealth, nor the wealthy men, that you have in the United States, but I can say truthfully what I do not think you can say of it or of any other wealthy country in the world, and that is that for years and years no one of my people has ever gone to bed hungry.' "[76]

Weed evidently intended the anecdote to embellish his portrait of a tropical Garden of Eden. Yet, to a rigorous modernizer, the realization that no Dominicans went to bed hungry should have been a cause for concern. The fact that most Dominican peasants had access to land and produced their own food, making wage labor unnecessary, would prove to be a nagging problem for promoters of Dominican progress. Indeed, many Latin American landowners "believed that without hunger or the need to cover expenses, the ordinary rural inhabitant simply would not work for another person."[77]

The Americans, like Heureaux, were arrogant in their expectation that they could reshape Dominican society virtually overnight. Whatever modernizing ideals Laughlin and Holls may have had, however, the SDIC's principal officers were, in the end, hard-headed businessmen.[78] Their dealings with Heureaux suggest that the New Yorkers did not count on windfall profits accruing from the slow progress of Dominican agriculture, the country's basic source of wealth. The SDIC's vice president acknowledged as much in 1901. "We never hoped when we went to Santo Domingo to realize anything from managing the finances of the country," Charles W. Wells said. "Where we did hope to make our money was from the sale of the country's bonds which we took, some at 50 and some at 60 [percent of par value]. We hoped that, by a conservative management of the finances of the country, we could find a market for the bonds and realize a very satisfactory profit."[79]

The company, in other words, hoped to make money from the spread between the market price and the insider price for Dominican bonds, plus the usual commissions and surcharges.[80] That source of money had little to do with the progress of the Dominican Republic, economically, politically, or otherwise. The statement, made after the company had been expelled from the Dominican Republic by Heureaux's successors, no doubt reflected the bitterness of hindsight. Moreover, political stability and economic growth would obviously have made it easier for the company to sell Dominican bonds, collect customs revenue and make interest payments. But the statement does suggest what would become the SDIC's bottom line — modernization was not necessary to insure profits. Big money could be had in Europe, where savings sought profitable outlets, but not from meager accumulations in the Caribbean. In the long run, the SDIC would prove to be little different from Hartmont and Westendorp, which also looked to make money through dubious bond sales.

As for the political liberalization Holls foresaw as a result of economic growth in Santo Domingo, the company, like Heureaux, had a strong vested interest in the containment of disorders that might discourage potential buyers of Dominican bonds in Europe. In practice this meant keeping Heureaux in power at whatever cost — and the cost for ordinary Dominicans was high indeed. For the dictator himself, modernization, far from leading to political liberalization, promised to generate the resources needed to keep his grip on power. Crudely put, progress meant more revenue for a needy state, period.

Popular resistance to reform of grazing laws and the gold standard undermined two key planks in the long-term development strategies of Heureaux and the SDIC. Hidden within the word progress were social dislocations that the Dominican state, even when fortified by the SDIC, was too weak to face down. If Heureaux and the SDIC failed to reshape Dominican society along lines congenial to modernizers, however, they did radically alter the international financial position of the country through a series of loans secured in Europe. Those schemes required the collusion of bankers and stockbrokers in Europe, not the reordering of Dominican society. Whatever the de facto limits on Heureaux's control of the Dominican people, the dictator and the SDIC could trade on the sovereign independence of the Dominican Republic to secure new loans. Foreign loans and paper money emissions were a tempting alternative to genuine modernization. Neither the dictator nor his American allies would resist the temptation.

5 The Cash Nexus

Economic Crisis and the Collapse of the Heureaux-SDIC Regime

— But this situation is intolerable! . . .
— Don't believe it, friend. Lilís is sharper than the whiteys who run the Imprúven. He'll get more cash out of them.
— But in the end, it's you and me and the rest of the country that will get stuck paying the bills.
— Tulio M. Cestero, *La Sangre*[1]

A government cannot let itself die of inanition.
— Ulises Heureaux[2]

The defining acts of the Heureaux-SDIC era were a series of foreign loans engineered by the Improvement Company from 1893 to 1897. The loans raised the outstanding debt of the Dominican Republic from under $5 million to over $35 million, yet aside from the completion of the Central Dominican Railroad, the country was left with little to show for the borrowing spree. In fact, the questionable nature of the loans, as much as the failure of the modernizing schemes of the SDIC and Heureaux, would within a few years convince Secretary of State John Hay and President Theodore Roosevelt that upholding a private company's unregulated control of another nation's finances was a poor way to achieve American strategic goals. The financial catastrophe that the SDIC oversaw in Santo Domingo would move Roosevelt to innovate a more successful version of Dollar Diplomacy, in which the U.S. government played a much greater role.

The Dominican loans of the 1890s came well after the Latin American lending boom that had ended abruptly with the near-failure of Baring Brothers, England's principal lender to Argentina, in 1890. In terms of global financial trends the loans may have been out of season, but they were in perfect harmony with Ulises Heureaux's ideology of progress and modernization. Any project, Heureaux declared, that "helps bring new capital into the country, to develop our industries and to increase our production and our commerce, deserves my staunch support."[3] Nevertheless, Heureaux's public discourse made little mention of borrowing money. For one, the loans were private contracts about which there was virtually no public debate. Moreover, with the exception of the first loan of 1893, the government made no pretense that the moneys were to be dedicated to public works or other productive uses. Nearly all the capital obtained by the SDIC went to four ends: (1) to convert bonds outstanding from earlier loans; (2) to pay off local capitalists who had lent money to the regime; (3) to pay the government's operating expenses and to buy guns and a new warship; and (4) to pay the fees and commissions charged by the SDIC and other middlemen. Given the uses of the loans, great fanfare would have been unwise.

Despite the deliberate secrecy of the SDIC and Heureaux, the pattern of Dominican foreign borrowing in the 1890s is clear enough. All the SDIC-sponsored loans, like those of Westendorp before them, were based on the sale of bonds on the stock exchanges of Europe, principally Paris and Brussels.[4] "The only limit on the issue of such bonds," David Landes has written, "was the confidence of the public."[5] The company's first contract with the Dominican government, approved by the Dominican congress in March 1893, provided for the issue of £2,035,000 (about $10 million) in bonds bearing 4 percent interest. Most of the loan (£1.61 million) was earmarked to pay back the 1888 and 1890 Westendorp loans on which the government had defaulted, a feature typical of Latin American loans of the time.[6] The balance of the loan, £425,000 (about $2 million), went to the SDIC to pay for completion of the Central Dominican Railroad, of which only 11 miles had been constructed by Westendorp.[7]

At the time of this first transaction, a separate, additional loan of $1.25 million was issued in the form of 66 year notes also bearing 4 percent interest. The entire loan was turned over to the SDIC in order to pay Heureaux's debts to five leading merchants living in the Dominican Republic. The SDIC disbursed the $1.25 million in bonds to settle debts that totaled $438,000 in gold, the bonds selling at 30 to 35 percent of their nominal value. Less than a year later, in 1894, the SDIC arranged for a third loan, again for $1.25 million. Once more, this loan was dedicated to the repayment of internal debts that had accrued in the previous year, a clear sign that foreign borrowing did not cover the regime's upward-spiraling outlays. The local loans refunded by the 1894 issue totaled $538,000 in gold.[8]

The next transaction arranged by the Improvement Company had an

origin and purpose different from those of earlier loans. It grew out of a
conflict between Heureaux and the National Bank of Santo Domingo, a
French concession with its main office in Paris. In 1895 the dispute blew
into a full-scale international conflict, with both France and the United
States sending warships to Santo Domingo. The incident was settled dip-
lomatically, but in its aftermath Heureaux persuaded the SDIC to take over
the bank, whose total assets comprised only $20,000 in cash and the value
of several unpaid loans to the Dominican government. The SDIC claimed
that it paid $750,000 to acquire the bank from its French owners. In return,
the company arranged a new loan for the Dominican government, totaling
$1.75 million, which was turned over in its entirety to the SDIC. Of that
amount, the SDIC accepted $925,000 in bonds to settle the government's
debt to the bank. Most of the balance, $750,000, canceled $300,000 owed
directly by the government to the SDIC.[9]

Even a brief summary of the geometric expansion of the Dominican debt
suggests a conflict at the heart of the SDIC's business. Legally the New York
firm was the trustee of the bondholders, nearly all of whom were European.
As such it pledged to safeguard their investment by overseeing the collection
of custom duties and ensuring that the Dominican government paid interest
and amortization on the loans. In practice, the SDIC conducted itself as a
sort of private financial agent to the Dominican leader. The loans of 1893
and 1894 were undertaken to rescue Heureaux from his local creditors. The
1895 loan to purchase the Banco Nacional placed a formerly independent
institution under Heureaux's direct control. Since the bank had exclusive
rights to issue paper money, the dictator gained a new device to stave off
bankruptcy. The Improvement Company collaborated in each of these measures, which made more sense as tactics to keep Heureaux in power than as
steps to defend the interests of the bondholders.

In 1895 the SDIC spun off two sister companies. The San Domingo
Finance Company handled the purchase and sale of bonds and acquired
all the securities of the original company. Later the Company of the Central
Dominican Railroad was created to manage the railroad project. The "sole
office" of the original company became that of "trustee in the collection of
the Government Revenues and their disbursement," in such capacity acting
as "Trustee of all the holders of the foreign debt." By separating the collection of revenue from the sale of bonds, the SDIC may have sought to
disguise the incompatibility of the roles of trustee for the bondholders and
de facto fiscal agent for Heureaux. Since the directors and personnel of all

1. Santo Domingo harbor in 1901, with colonial-era buildings used as residences in foreground.

2. Smith M. Weed, president of the San Domingo
Improvement Company.

3. Dominican President Ulises Heureaux.

4. Commercial street of a provincial Dominican city in the early 1900s.

5. A Dominican peasant and his daughter, early 1900s.

6. Rural home or *bohio* near Puerto Plata, early 1900s.

7.1 & 7.2. A two-peso note and a one-peso "silver" coin, both issued by the SDIC-owned Banco Nacional de Santo Domingo in the last years of the Heureaux regime.

8. John Bassett Moore, advisor to the State Department and attorney to the SDIC, in a portrait by Edwin Burrage Child.

9. The U.S.S. *Bancroft*, a small, steel-hulled gunboat, often patrolled Dominican waters while assigned to the Caribbean squadron from 1902 to 1906.

10. From left, U.S. Minister Thomas C. Dawson, Dominican President Carlos Morales Languasco, and Dominican Minister of Foreign Affairs Juan P. Sánchez, in Santo Domingo, 1904.

11. Soldiers marching in Santo Domingo in 1904 or 1905.

12. Jacob Hollander, architect of the refunding of the Dominican debt after 1905.

13. President Theodore Roosevelt with U.S. naval officers and other officials during a naval review, 1906.

three companies were identical, however, the underlying contradiction remained.[10]

Far from playing the role of advance agent for Yankee imperialism, then,
the SDIC served Heureaux as a boon companion. "Since the Improvement
took charge of the Regie, I have never found Mr. Wells anything but well-
disposed to help me," Heureaux wrote of the company's vice president. "He
has never shown the slightest hesitation in making special efforts on my
behalf, and overburdened though he may be, I always find him accessible
and eager to show his willingness to help me. Of course, I understand that
by helping me he helps himself, but it is unreasonable to expect him to
ignore or abandon his own interests."[11] If at times the dictator showed irri-
tation with the company, in general he saw it as another weapon in his
struggle for survival.

Working together, Heureaux and the SDIC managed to keep up interest
payments on the loans for several years. By 1896 the government was once
again in desperate straits, and Heureaux and the SDIC failed to meet the interest payment that fell due on January 1, 1897 — the first but not the last such
failure. When news of the default spread across Europe, the value of Dominican securities plummeted. Despite this reversal, the SDIC and Heureaux
mounted one more scheme to resurrect the nation's credit. The 1897 loan
was the largest of all, having a nominal value of £4.23 million (about $21
million). Although the most doubtful of all the SDIC-sponsored loans, it was
the first to be listed on the London Stock Exchange.[12] Most of the loan —
some $15 million — rolled over outstanding debt from earlier loans.

The flotation did not fare well.[13] Of the amount not absorbed by the
conversion, the SDIC itself had to buy £277, 980 of bonds, paying about 32
percent of face value for them. The balance of the loan went to fees and
commissions, leaving a small sum, perhaps $450,000, to pay off new debts
to local creditors. The near failure of the 1897 loan at last convinced
Heureaux and the SDIC that no further credit could be squeezed from
credulous European investors. Thereafter Heureaux embraced the politically dangerous alternative of paper money emissions to keep his government
from collapsing in complete insolvency.

In only four years the SDIC had orchestrated the issue of some $35
million (nominal value) in new loans, almost none of which was dedicated
to productive purposes such as infrastructure development. Nearly all the
bonds had been purchased in Europe, mainly in Belgium and France. They
had not even been offered for public sale in the Dominican Republic or the

United States. Even so, the SDIC had become the holder of a large amount of Dominican paper from the loans of 1895 and 1897. Many of those bonds made their way into the hands of important British banks, creating a constituency in London that would find it easy to get the ear of the Foreign Office.[14] After the 1897 default, French and Belgian bondholders created committees of defense that dogged the SDIC and the Dominicans for repayment. Thus, the resort to borrowing in Europe internationalized the debt of the Dominican Republic and pushed forward the contradiction between the SDIC's political strength, emanating from Washington, and its financial power, concentrated in Europe.

While SDIC officials knew that the country's previous creditor, Westendorp, had faced chronic collection problems, the Improvement Company nevertheless remained sanguine about this vast new debt. The SDIC evidently believed that control of Dominican custom houses, reinforced by State Department support, gave them adequate guarantees. When the arrangement moved to daily practice, however, the company found that Heureaux had an arsenal of fiscal weapons that stopped short of breach of contract. Heureaux's maneuvers had little to do with the fine print of contracts and everything to do with his control of the republic's political and economic system and his ongoing access to other sources of credit, both in Europe and the Dominican Republic. For the dictator, the SDIC was no more than the brightest star in a constellation of financial agents. These parallel instruments included Dominican merchants and sugar planters as well as banking and mercantile houses in New York and Europe. Heureaux handled these alternative sources with some discretion, always avoiding an outright confrontation with his American allies. The SDIC was, after all, a political asset, not least of all because European powers saw the firm as a veiled instrument of U.S. foreign policy.

Ironically, if the SDIC struck Europeans as a stalking horse for Washington, Heureaux himself did not regard the company as an agent of American finance capitalism or a proxy for the State Department. If anything, Heureaux was disappointed that the company did not have closer ties to Wall Street and Washington. After meeting with SDIC officials in 1893, the Dominican leader showed no fear of concentrating financial power in the hands of the New York company. On the contrary, he encouraged the SDIC to extend its ownership to include the national bank. "If Wells finds himself mixed up in the bank business today," the dictator boasted, "it is my doing. He has obliged me by eliminating obstacles that the earlier bank directors had put in my path, damaging our political and economic interests."[15] As noted in chapter 2, the dictator also sought to use the company as a conduit to Washington, ignoring the metropolitans' assumption that influence could flow only from North to South.

The SDIC contracts defined a simple and apparently secure mechanism to effect repayment of the loans. SDIC-approved agents in each of the country's custom houses would supervise and verify the collection of duties by Dominican officials. An SDIC employee served as director of the Caja de Recaudación, or Regie, and in that post approved the record of collections submitted from each port, withholding the sums needed to pay interest and principal on the loans. The contract obliged the company to pay the government 90,000 pesos a month in silver for its budget.[16]

Once the presence of the American company was a fait accompli, Heureaux insistently identified his interests with those of the SDIC.[17] Despite that posturing, the Dominican government and the SDIC were as much rivals as allies, competing to control the same revenue stream. Historically, customs receipts had been the principal resource not only of the central government but of local creditors and provincial officials as well. The revenues of Puerto Plata, for instance, paid the expenses of that province.[18] Local demands on the custom houses did not end simply because the national government pledged these duties to foreign lenders, beginning with Westendorp in 1888. Instead, the customs houses became an arena of conflict between the local and foreign lenders to the regime. Much of Heureaux's financial maneuvering resulted from conflicting promises made to local creditors on the one hand, and to the SDIC and foreign bondholders on the other.

That conflict pushes to the foreground the role of local capital in Heureaux's financial system. A dearth of local capital has been assumed to be the fundamental condition of the Dominican Republic, as of other nations in Latin America. Dominican historians have noted the role of merchant lenders such as Juan B. Vicini and Cosme Battle, but they have tended to emphasize the overriding predominance of foreign capital after 1888. Jaime Domínguez, the most meticulous historian of the era, has written that "the dictatorship of Heureaux was essentially a dictatorship of foreign loans and foreign investments," emphasizing the dictator's submission to foreign, especially American, financiers. Nevertheless it is clear that trade and sugar production generated surpluses that were essential to the viability of the national treasury.[19]

Foreign loans did not dwarf the capital generated in the Caribbean re-public.[20] The leading merchant lender, Juan B. Vicini, made large loans to the Heureaux regime. From 1893 to 1898, contracts show that Vicini lent from $178,000 to $352,278 annually to the government, while in 1899 the figure jumped to $1.36 million.[21] Cosme Battle and other local merchants also extended credit to the government in the same period.[22] Despite their much greater nominal value, the SDIC's loans sometimes yielded as little as $250,000, meaning that there was not an order of magnitude of difference between the local and international capital tapped by Heureaux. Nor was it true that foreign capital was always used to pay off local lenders; money flowed in the opposite direction as well. Heureaux used money from local merchants to pay interest on European loans and settle accounts with Eu-ropean banking houses.[23] National and international borrowing, then, far from being either mutually exclusive or distinct stages of Dominican eco-nomic development, took place simultaneously and symbiotically.

It is nevertheless true that Heureaux preferred to borrow abroad than to borrow locally.[24] Not only were interest rates lower and the sums available at least nominally larger, but also the collection of international debts was a slow process, even in an age when the great powers stood ready to send in gunboats for their "moral effect" on delinquent debtors. Even though Heureaux preferred to seek credit abroad, however, he often found himself obliged to borrow locally. From the time of the SDIC's arrival in the repub-lic, local capitalists were essential to the government's survival.[25] In fact, the SDIC itself signed contracts with Cosme Battle for "the provision of funds."[26]

The importance of local capital is underscored by Heureaux's eagerness to repay local lenders promptly. Given the perpetual shortfall in government revenues, day-to-day expenses were often paid by short-term loans from local planters and merchants.[27] An embargo on new credit by these men threat-ened to bring down the elaborate house of cards that kept Heureaux solvent and in power. Already in 1894 Cosme Battle had suspended payment on government notes, an action which caused a "noticeable slowdown in the government administration."[28] Heureaux was elaborately courteous to these figures and never sought to intimidate or harass them as he did his political opponents.[29] He courted the merchant elite and presented himself as the champion of their interests, yet he was more dependent on local capitalists than they were on him.[30] Although many of the leading local merchants held foreign citizenship, they were not about to flee the country.[31] Staying put was their best guarantee of repayment, since over time Heureaux learned that the merchant capitalists could be counted on to supply new credit, provided he made some arrangement to pay back earlier loans. Foreign lenders, by contrast, could easily be seen as absentees and transients.

Access to local credit gave Heureaux a measure of freedom in dealing with the SDIC. The dictator used national credit, and the demands made by local capitalists, to manipulate his American allies. When merchant lenders froze further credit, Heureaux pleaded that only the SDIC "in the present circumstances can solve the conflict we face."[32] The availability of local capital became a lever to extract more money from the Americans.[33]

Thus, as it tried to enforce its apparently airtight contracts, the SDIC faced a battle-tested bloc of local capitalists as well as a willful dictator. It should not be a surprise that the Americans never gained real control over Dominican finances. First, throughout its tenure the Improvement Company was essentially an absentee agent, never maintaining an officer of the company in the Dominican Republic.[34] Unlike Minor Keith in Central America, who drank, swore, and fought with the workers building his railroad lines, the directors of the SDIC managed the construction of the Central Dominican Railroad, as well as the collection of customs revenue, from New York.[35] The company employed agents, both Dominicans and foreigners, to handle its day-to-day business. Apart from brief annual visits to Santo Domingo by Charles W. Wells, the company relied on sea mail and occasional cables to oversee its operations on the Caribbean island. In practice, this meant relying on Heureaux's administration, usually to the detriment of the company.

The regime, in collusion with local merchants, used several tactics to thwart SDIC control of customs without openly violating the company's contracts. The most common device was for Heureaux to grant the merchants *concesiones*, or exemptions, from custom duties in exchange for loans.[36] Merchants simply presented proof of the exonerations to port officials when their ships docked in Dominican harbors. For large merchants, the *concesiones* were the surest way to recover moneys they had lent to Heureaux.[37] Since the merchants evaded paying taxes at the ports of entry, the Regie had no chance to deduct the SDIC's share of them.[38]

Heureaux skirted SDIC control in other ways as well. The company had the right to approve all appointments to the Dominican customs houses, and Heureaux observed the letter of the contract by clearing his nominees with the Americans.[39] Since the SDIC relied on the dictator's choice of officials, however, it allowed his patronage needs to undermine honest ad-

ministration. In 1896, Heureaux admitted that corrupt officials were reducing government income, since "for the political interests of the Government
I was obliged to employ in the Custom houses . . . some important persons"
who had proven dishonest. Customs declarations in several ports had been
found to be "wholly false."

In fact, patronage was the heart of Heureaux's political system, yet to the
SDIC he made a show of crusading against corruption. The dictator asked
for SDIC permission to dismiss corrupt officials who "all are rich enough,"
warning that otherwise "I could not remain in power, for next year the
proceeds of the Customs will not be sufficient to cover the most perentory
[sic] necessities."[40] Heureaux's promises that a general reform of the customs
service was underway became formulaic. "I am dedicating all my attention
to the custom houses, from now on we won't appoint as inspectors men
whose political importance forces us to tolerate abuses."[41] Eventually he
admitted that the Regie was an ineffective instrument of control.[42] The problem rested on an underlying contradiction of Heureaux's regime. To stay in
power, he systematized corruption, yet corruption sapped state revenues and
thereby undermined the regime. Neither the dictator nor the SDIC would
find a way out of that vicious circle.

The SDIC never succeeded in effectively supervising Dominican customs, much less in dominating the nation's finances. It is hardly surprising
that Heureaux sought to evade foreign control. More significant is the fact
that, early on, the company itself gave up the hope of enforcing its contracts
and became in effect a prop of the regime. Dealings between the company
and the Dominican government quickly took on the character of private
deals.[43] As early as 1894, the SDIC's second year in the republic, the approach of the deadline to pay interest on the loans spurred frantic letters
between New York and Santo Domingo.[44] The letters speak not of money
owed by the Dominican government to the bondholders, but by Heureaux
to Wells. More than once Heureaux complained that he had exhausted his
own resources to support the company, blaming the SDIC for its inability
to collect sufficient revenue at the ports. "Thoug[h] I am always most perfectly willing to help even with prejudice to my own interest," Heureaux
warned Wells in 1896, "I have come to the end of my resources and it is
impossible for me to do more. . . . I repeat to you that this is really the last
time that I can be of any material help to you."[45] By personalizing his dealings with the SDIC, the dictator could assume the role of benefactor on the
occasions when he actually did forward money to the company. The failure

of the SDIC to raise sufficient revenue was the company's problem, Heureaux implied, having nothing to do with his administration. By using the SDIC's nominal control of the custom houses against it, the Dominican leader was able to mask and to an extent neutralize the apparently stubborn opposition of creditor and borrower.[46]

The willingness of the SDIC to sacrifice its duty to the bondholders in favor of an unflinching support of Heureaux has several explanations. As the country's finances became more and more problematic, the company must have anticipated that Heureaux's overthrow would plunge the nation into political and economic chaos. By this logic, it was imperative to keep Heureaux in power even if he was the one who destabilized the country's finances. No doubt equally important was the fact that, despite Heureaux's maneuvering, the Dominican business was profitable to the SDIC, if not to the bondholders.[47] In any event, the company made no effort to sell its assets, as Westendorp had done. A final reason may well have been the SDIC's certainty that, in the last instance, it could count on official U.S. support if Heureaux's maneuvers went beyond bilking the bondholders to cheating his ostensible ally, the SDIC.

An 1895 incident involving the Banco Nacional de Santo Domingo suggests that the company's confidence was not misplaced. For some time Heureaux had urged the New Yorkers to buy the Banco Nacional from its French owners. As the government's financial position deteriorated, the bank's exclusive right to issue coins and paper money naturally attracted Heureaux. The right of coinage, he said, "is the equivalent of a long-term, interest free loan with very low emission costs."[48] In 1893, Heureaux forcibly collected a sum of money from the bank. Later, the murder of a French national led France to sever diplomatic relations and demand a large indemnity.[49]

As the conflict heated up, Heureaux took pains to emphasize that American interests were at risk. The Dominican legation in Washington sent Secretary of State Walter Q. Gresham a memorandum detailing their version of events and pointing out that the French claims conflicted with the rights of the SDIC. A "forcible attempt" to extract the indemnity "would seriously injure the large interests of citizens of the United States, and furnish a basis for just complaint."[50] The SDIC's control of finances served as a tripwire to draw the U.S. government in on the side of the Dominican Republic. With a French warship steaming toward Santo Domingo to back up an ultimatum, Heureaux wired New York, urging the company to secure Washington's intervention. "It is very important that you convince the U.S. government to protect the interests of the San Domingo Improvement Company" he wrote, merging the company's interests with his own. The SDIC responded by bringing the issue before Secretary of State Gresham. Smith M. Weed's letter of protest was forwarded to the U.S. ambassador in Paris, where the company's interests were vigorously pressed.[51]

Meanwhile, the New Yorkers sent Heureaux a long-winded reply demanding details about the crisis: "Whence comes your information? What is the nature of the French ultimatum? Why are they using force if as you say France has accepted arbitration?" Heureaux lost patience with the SDIC's hand-wringing. He did not even bother to answer because it was "pointless to continue spending money on cables of this sort." A short time later the SDIC advised Heureaux that Gresham had indeed intervened and forwarded a tentative plan to end the crisis. The dictator was unimpressed. "French Government has offered me a better proposition," was his terse reply.[52] The feuding nations eventually agreed to have the conflict settled by arbitration, which ended with the Dominicans being forced to pay France the substantial indemnity of $50,000.[53]

Heureaux had used his own channels to end the confrontation with a leading European power. Nevertheless, the United States did send three warships to Santo Domingo, overcalling the French display of force.[54] The triumph of American interests became even clearer some months later, when the Improvement Company bought the National Bank from its French owners. By that time, Heureaux's attitude had changed, and he thanked the SDIC profusely for orchestrating Washington's help during the crisis. Smith W. Weed, in turn, thanked Secretary of State Gresham for "the manner in which you have treated us and defended the rights of our company — an American company, and composed of American citizens."[55] European powers evidently took the Franco-Dominican incident seriously, viewing it as a confirmation of U.S. support for the SDIC's project in Santo Domingo.[56]

This show of official support for the American company illustrates that United States and SDIC interests still ran in the same channel. Washington responded energetically, it can be assumed, not only because of the close personal ties between President Cleveland and Weed but because United States strategic interests were being redefined to discourage European intervention in the Caribbean. The vigorous policy on behalf of the SDIC preceded by only a few months Secretary of State Richard Olney's aggressive assertion of U.S. hegemony in the dispute between Britain and Venezuela mentioned in chapter 2. The incident can also be seen as a dress rehearsal for events a decade later when the threat of European intervention would trigger forceful United States action and the articulation of a new policy in Latin America.

When the chips were down, the United States backed the SDIC and Heureaux against France. Nevertheless, Washington took little interest in the disastrous consequences of SDIC stewardship on the Dominican Republic itself. By bringing the bank under SDIC control, the 1895 French-Dominican crisis cleared the way for a new and catastrophic stage in the company's financial trusteeship. By 1896, the government's financial situation was dismal. The 1895 loan that had paid for the SDIC's purchase of the Banco Nacional had injected scant money into the nation's economy. Desperate for cash, Heureaux found in the bank a philosopher's stone that could transform mere paper into currency. For a time, the company evidently tried to restrain Heureaux's plan to emit large amounts of paper money.[57] Whatever doubts the Americans had about the plan evaporated, however. As directors of the bank, they were instrumental in unleashing the flood of fiat currency that pushed the Dominican economy beyond instability toward chaos.

As an astute politician, Heureaux knew the danger of printing paper money. Doubtful bond issues may have eroded the republic's credit in the eyes of European bankers and foreign ministries, but those sources of censure were far away. Flooding the republic with adulterated coins and unbacked paper money, on the other hand, threatened to create a financial panic that would quickly redound on the political arena.

At first Heureaux was cautious. In 1896, for example, he hesitated to put $275,000 pesos in circulation "as long as the establishment here doesn't have enough specie to guarantee it."[58] Before the SDIC finalized the loan of 1897, the dictator held the line against a large paper emission, claiming it would "perhaps irremediably wound our credit and faith in the public administration."[59] Only a month later, however, dissatisfied with the results of that loan, he decided that the country could absorb a $1.5 million emission.[60] Yet by December he had become convinced that "the moment has passed" to emit that quantity since "already the harvest of coffee and cacao is half completed in the Cibao, for which the circulating medium was needed."[61] Although the effects of the issues were ultimately devastating, Heureaux did not undertake them lightly.

From 1897 to 1899, the National Bank put 3.6 million pesos of paper money and 2.2 million pesos of debased silver coins into circulation.[62] At first the notes traded at a ratio of two to one with gold, but soon declined to 20 to one. As the dictator himself had feared, the paper emissions paralyzed much of the economy, eventually forcing merchants and ordinary citizens to revert to *trueque* or barter. For years the domestic market had been largely quarantined from Heureaux's disastrous fiscal policies, but now the full force of the regime's errors was felt from coastal cities to the smallest villages. Many Dominicans refused to accept the *papeletas,* or bills, at any rate of discount. The depreciated paper further reduced government revenues, since import and export taxes were payable in national currency at the official rate of exchange. Importers and exporters alike could pay customs duties in depreciated currency, in effect reducing their tax burden. When the SDIC asked Heureaux to make customs be payable partly in gold, the dictator explained that "the bills . . . are not redeemable when presented at the Bank; in compensation, it is necessary for them to keep the only real guarantee they have, which is their acceptance for the payment of all classes of national and local taxes."[63]

To prevent general panic in response to the swelling quantities of unbacked paper, Heureaux urged his provincial governors to hold public meetings and explain the regime's monetary policies. The dictator provided these officials with detailed justifications of the paper issues based on something like a quantity theory of money. He argued that the new emission "isn't even large enough to cover the country's monetary needs" and therefore "the value of Dominican coins can't depreciate" because "whatever is scarce appreciates in value."[64] In his 1899 message to Congress the dictator noted that "this limitation, in itself, constitutes a solid guarantee" of the currency and blamed the "baseless panic" on "the lack of economic understanding among most of our people."[65] Privately, however, Heureaux was quite sober in analyzing the public's aversion to the national bank and its money. "As long as the establishment is not a subsidiary of a powerful and creditworthy European bank, it will continue to stumble and be shunned by the public. That's only natural. It is Mr. Wells and myself who have had the most to do with the Bank's operations, and our present situation is not likely to surround it with all the confidence it requires."

For the Bank to serve as a source of instant if artificial revenue, Heureaux would have to keep its doors open — a tactic that demanded regular infusions of specie and discreet declarations of bank holidays. Despite these burdens, Heureaux was unwilling to allow the bank to fold. "I am only keeping up the institution," he confessed in 1896, "in the hope that in a short time the

Bank will get its capital back in cash . . . [in] order to prevent that by a general distrust of the public in the Bank . . . the possibility of emitting paper money should be lost for ever."[66]

As the country's finances spiraled out of control, Heureaux continued to declare his optimism about the country's future. The opening of the Central Dominican Railroad in August 1897, an event celebrated with "dances, civic processions, banquets, and public inaugurations," encouraged Heureaux. So did the favorable reception of the Dominican pavilion at the international exhibition in Brussels the same year, which reportedly drew positive comments from King Leopold II himself.[67] Heureaux took pride in both accomplishments, although neither could be enjoyed for long. Complaints about the high cost of shipping on the railway soon reached the dictator. The success of the Belgian exhibit was tarnished by an ironic notice in a Brussels newspaper: "The Dominican Republic has generated favorable comment at our Exhibition. . . . Only one thing is missing from the Dominican pavilion: a specimen of a paid interest coupon."[68]

Despite the barbs, Heureaux founded his optimism on the hope that good harvests, growing investments in sugar, and increasing commercialization would rescue the nation from its sharpening crisis.[69] At least one element of this sanguine outlook was not illusory: Dominican exports did continue to grow in spite of the ongoing disaster in public finances. Statistics for the period show that exports increased from $3.6 million pesos in 1892 to $11.5 million pesos in 1898. In the same period, the value of imports also rose, although not as rapidly, going from $2.4 to $3.39 million pesos.[70] For sugar planters and other exporters, economic conditions were reasonably favorable. They could pay workers in inflated paper currency while earning gold or its equivalent for their commodities.[71] "One good result of the crisis has been that an impetus has been given to exports," reported the British consul to Santo Domingo in 1899. He attributed that growth to the fact that "practically the only way of transacting business with other countries during the past year has been by the exchange of commodities."[72]

The export boom, however, did little to obscure the general misery that had spread across the land. Reports of widespread suffering reached Heureaux from all sides. From Cotuí a letter told of the "hunger that reigns in this area." Another warned that the rapid currency devaluation injured Dominican peasants and workers: "Those most affected are the working classes, who are completely devastated, since one who holds paper money can't buy what he needs to survive."[73] The last years of the Heureaux regime were a grim confirmation of Pedro Francisco Bonó's rejection of the liberal idea "that the happiness of a people consists entirely in the increase of imports and exports, at whatever cost."[74] Exports increased, yet misery reigned.

Although the larger merchants may have been able to ride out the economic crisis, smaller ones were squeezed by runaway inflation and falling consumption. Many of these retailers hiked their prices so high that protests erupted in different cities. Heureaux was forced to treat the economic disturbance as a political danger. He responded by threatening to punish profiteering merchants. "This must not continue," he told one provincial governor. "Call together the merchants and make them understand that, either they hold themselves to rational profits, or the government will be forced to defend itself."[75]

The fact that Heureaux found himself bullying merchants, probably his most loyal constituency, shows the fatal pass he had come to. The short-term goals of the regime — liquidity at any price — had at last collided with the private sector's need for a stable currency and a non-predatory state. Government workers, the backbone of the regime, went unpaid for weeks, even months.[76] Worse still, Heureaux was driven to cut municipal and provincial budgets, a blow against the very patronage system that kept him in power. "The cutbacks contained in our budget, " warned one governor, "have considerably affected economic life here. . . . the police . . . can't even feed themselves on 30 cents a day."[77]

As economic prospects dimmed, Heureaux kept up the front that the crisis would not have political consequences. "As far as politics are concerned everything is in very good condition," he wrote to Wells, adding "not the same can be said about the financial situation." But the distinction between political and economic realms was untenable. Privately, Heureaux admitted that the economic collapse nourished political discontent. "The devaluation of the currency has caused great apprehension and serves as a weapon in the hands of our enemies," he confided to one ally.[78] Despite Heureaux's disastrous policies, the SDIC did not abandon its ally. The company made no attempt to turn control of Dominican finances over to an international commission of creditors, as its contracts allowed. "That great remedy," the SDIC later explained, should only be applied in "extreme cases."[79]

With the default on interest payments in January 1897 and the printing of paper money the same year, the delicate mechanism that supported Heureaux's dictatorship at last began to break apart. Once-complementary elements of his financial system — local merchants, European bondholders, and the Improvement Company — squared off against one another. The first fracture appeared when, immediately after the default, the French and Belgian bondholders formed committees to defend their Dominican investments. While the committees did not openly renounce the trusteeship of the SDIC, they signaled their discontent by naming a *Controlador General* to serve alongside the SDIC's employee in the Regie to verify custom receipts.[80]

Meanwhile, in Europe, Dominican financial agent Isidor Mendel and Charles W. Wells worked separately to put together the "combination" that would shortly take the form of the SDIC's last and greatest loan, the disastrous bond flotation of 1897. The negotiations ran up against an unexpected obstacle. Local merchants refused to release the *apartados*, or special taxes, pledged to them and which the Europeans insisted on having as additional guarantees for the pending loan.[81] To free up these revenues, Heureaux increased all import and export taxes 10 percent and granted the proceeds to the local lenders.[82] "This arrangement conflicts with certain clauses of the guarantees given to the bondholders," Heureaux admitted, asserting that the government had no other choice.[83]

With negotiations still bogged down, Heureaux suggested to Mendel that, if necessary, he could strip the Improvement Company of its role as trustee of the bondholders.[84] The Dominican leader and his fiscal agent soon got a rude awakening. The SDIC made it clear that it had no intention of being elbowed aside, and in short order Heureaux was reassuring Wells that "my government has not repudiated, nor will it ever repudiate, its obligations to the San Domingo Improvement Company." Heureaux even reprimanded Mendel for ignoring the company's influence and legal rights. The dictator was ready to play fast and loose with the SDIC until the company made clear that it would defend itself. He eventually backed the loan arranged by the SDIC, which obtained "a million pesos, rather than the 800,000 that the earlier project" of Mendel had promised.[85]

The events of 1897 marked a turning point. Heureaux saw that the Improvement Company could do little more to help him, and he began seeking a new group of lenders in Europe to buy out the company's interests and redeem the country's paper currency. At the same time, Heureaux attempted to capitalize on the slow-burning crisis in neighboring Cuba that would shortly erupt in the Cuban-Spanish-American War.

Since 1895, the Cuban insurrection had stoked tensions between the

United States and Spain. To Heureaux, the situation offered both risks and
opportunities. "The United States and Spain are like the wheels of a gigantic
mill," he wrote in early 1898. "One false step and we will fall between those
two cylinders, and adios republic."[86] Officially the regime pledged strict neutrality.[87] Nevertheless, Heureaux sought to profit from the turmoil on the
neighboring island, pursuing policies that promised material benefits without running material risks. The dictator encouraged the flow of wealthy Cuban refugees to the Dominican Republic by arranging for Santo Domingo-
bound steamships to stop for passengers in Santiago de Cuba. To placate
Spain, he claimed that Cubans residing in Santo Domingo would remain
culturally Spanish, and possibly even loyal to Spain, while those who went to
the United States and Jamaica were lost entirely.[88] Later Heureaux would try
to buy military supplies from a defeated Spain at fire-sale prices.[89]

Heureaux carefully watched the tortuous unfolding of American policy
toward Cuba. A year into the conflict Heureaux took the bold initiative of
devising a plan to reach "a humane and just solution to the armed conflict
in Cuba." The plan, transmitted to Grover Cleveland in April 1896, called
for arbitration of the dispute by a commission. It was received and dismissed
with little fanfare. Precisely what Heureaux sought to gain from the peace
plan is not clear, although had the proposal been accepted it certainly would
have raised the country's diplomatic profile and perhaps earned it favorable
consideration in the realm of commerce and trade, possibly even the renewal
of reciprocity. The proposal was another example of Heureaux's desire to
reverse the flow of influence between the Caribbean and the United States.[90]

Heureaux's understanding of American attitudes toward Cuba and Spain
turned on material interests. For all the bluster of American interventionists,
Heureaux could scarcely imagine that the United States would actually go
to war with Spain. "Having large amounts of money at stake makes nations,
like individuals, skittish and conservative," he wrote. "The threat of war will
slowly modify the excesses of the Americans, unless the whole thing is inspired by a goal greater than the apparent ones, which are commercial."[91]
Since Americans loved dominion less and dollars more, he assumed they
had no good reason to risk their extensive holdings in Cuba by fighting a
war with Spain.

Economic determinism did not, however, prove the best guide to Amer-
ican policy in Cuba. When Spain granted limited autonomy to Cuba in
November 1897, Heureaux predicted that peace would be restored and
American intervention forestalled. "Already in the outward signs of U.S.

policy one can see the results of the new effort by the Spanish government," he said. By January 1898, Heureaux, once more reflecting the shifting mood in the States, concluded that American intervention was imminent. The interests of Spain and the United States in Cuba had become so antagonistic, he believed, that "even settling the current difficulties, the force and nature of these differences will immediately put them in conflict again."[92]

The Dominican Republic remained neutral during the brief U.S. phase of the war, appropriately given the nation's "infinite weakness."[93] But Heureaux seized the opportunity that open belligerency afforded to once again open negotiations for the lease of Samaná Bay.[94] Captain A. S. Crowninshield sailed to the republic in February 1898 to survey Samaná and other possible sites for coaling stations. He met with Heureaux several times to discuss the lease of Samaná, reporting that "the President seemed quite ready to consider my propositions." Heureaux suggested several locations less populated than Samaná, pointing out that "the leasing of them by the United States would less attract the opposition of that faction in Santo Domingo which is inimical to the project." Crowninshield, however, insisted that Samaná was "by far the best location for a naval and coaling station."

In return for the lease of Samaná, Crowninshield reported, "Heureaux distinctly disclaimed any wish for a payment in money, preferring, in lieu thereof, an arrangement of reciprocity by which Dominican products would be admitted to the United States free of duty." The naval officer urged his superiors to open negotiations as soon as possible "for the purpose of obtaining, through a reciprocity treaty, a lease of Samaná Bay."[95] Crowninshield knew that the Dominican leader sought optimal terms of trade for his country's exports, especially sugar, cacao, tobacco, and coffee, a crucial need for a nation moving from subsistence to export-oriented agriculture.[96]

The State Department took Crowninshield's advice. The Dingley Tariff of 1897 had included provisions for commercial reciprocity, and John A. Kasson became William McKinley's reciprocity negotiator.[97] Exactly how negotiations with the Dominican Republic unfolded in the spring of 1898 remains mysterious, but it is clear that Kasson met with both Smith M. Weed and Heureaux, probably in Puerto Rico. The commissioner evidently enticed Heureaux to lease Samaná with the promise of a new commercial treaty. Once again, Heureaux backed away from the offer, fearing popular outrage at the violation of national territory.[98] But he suggested an alternative: allowing American warships to seize Samaná on the pretext that Spain planned to do the same. "As the popular prejudices of the Dominican people are strongly against the alienation of a foot of their territory to any foreign nation," the American consul in Santo Domingo reported, " . . . he wishes our Government to aid him by taking the initiative by seizing the Bay."[99]

Secretary of State William Rufus Day rejected this intriguing offer, but the issue did not end there. Heureaux was concerned about the fate of his country in light of American intervention in Cuba. His chief concern was "the fate of our products, whose principal market is the United States," adding

> situated between Cuba and Puerto Rico, and having the same con-
> ditions of soil and climate, the problem that arises before us is to avoid
> indirect or accidental discrimination that would result against us if
> these two neighboring islands . . . enjoy privileges in the U.S. market
> superior to our own.
>
> We cannot compete unless we come to terms with the United States
> commercially.[100]

The Dominican leader cabled President McKinley that he had authorized U.S. consul Archibald Grimké to speak for him regarding reciprocity and Samaná. In July 1898 Grimké reported to Heureaux from Washington that he had had "a long and satisfactory conference" with Secretary of State Day "regarding the acquisition of Samaná." The consul also spoke with John A. Kasson, who explained "that the Samaná Bay matter has not received ear-lier attention of the government owing to the pressure of war business." Heureaux continued to hope that his country would be put "on the same footing commercially as the other islands of the Antilles," and that negoti-ations regarding Samaná would continue. In September, however, the Do-minican president told Grimké that his government was so hard pressed economically that he could not even pay the latter's expenses while in the United States. The negotiations sputtered out soon afterward.[101]

Fusing the reciprocity negotiations with the cession of Samaná Bay was a fatal error for Heureaux. The Spanish-Cuban-American War shifted power relations in the Caribbean dramatically. Harrying Spain from the Caribbean meant that an important counterpoise to U.S. influence had been lost: Amer-ican economic dominance would no longer be mediated by Spanish sov-ereignty in Cuba and Puerto Rico. The American acquisition of Puerto Rico and Guantánamo Bay in Cuba meant that Samaná Bay had lost its value as a chit in the great power game. Similarly, the new lines of filiation between the United States, Cuba, and Puerto Rico did not bode well for Dominican commercial parity.

Faced with an economic crisis at home, Heureaux realized he could not afford to pin his hopes on obtaining reciprocity with the United States. In the summer of 1898 he moved to shift his political and financial allegiances away from the United States and the SDIC. Heureaux proposed to the French chargé d'affaires in Santo Domingo that "a respectable bank or a French syndicate . . . buy on behalf of the French government, the entire external debt of the republic."[102] Soon after he sought to reach a commercial treaty with Spain, hoping thereby to secure for the Dominican Republic "a position of dominance among the independent nations of the Antilles." A treaty with the Dominican Republic could compensate Spain for what Heureaux delicately referred to as "the new situation created in the Antilles." Heureaux commented, "I don't think that Spain will renounce her Latin American trade, and to that end will need to reach an accord with an absolutely friendly nation that occupies a strategic position and offers secure ports for her traffic." Such a treaty might be the basis for "a new international policy for Spain."[103]

Heureaux was clearly desperate. Fortified by its absorption of Puerto Rico, the Philippines, and Guam, the annexation of Hawaii, and the effective protectorate exercised over Cuba, the United States was in no mood to submit to Heureaux's demands. During the war, the instant of greatest opportunity, the dictator had misplayed his hand. His trump card, Samaná, had lost nearly all its value. In light of the new situation in the Caribbean, the United States might not even tolerate new commercial ties between the Dominican Republic and Europe. Heureaux cautioned his ambassador in Madrid to negotiate discreetly since "the United States is very jealous of its commercial preponderance in the Americas and might not look kindly on us using our sovereignty to do what to us seems appropriate."[104] Meanwhile, domestic conditions could hardly be worse. The economy was in ruins. The end, it seemed, was near.

Astonishingly, Heureaux had not yet reached the end of his rope. He astutely if cynically understood that a new infusion of cash required a switch in great power loyalties. The disaster of the 1897 loan made clear that another conversion of the bonds by the SDIC was virtually impossible. The republic's credit was in tatters, and only by offering his nation as collateral could Heureaux hope to borrow again. By early 1899 Heureaux had found a British investor, F. H. Morris, willing to buy out the SDIC and attempt one more conversion of the Dominican bonds. By this time the directors of the SDIC had become convinced that it was time to part with their Dominican holdings.[105]

As Heureaux scrambled to reposition the Dominican Republic geopolitically, he also took steps to ease the economic crisis. To slow inflation, he began retiring paper money from circulation. It was toward that end that Heureaux traveled to the Cibao in July 1899, where he met with local merchants to arrange new loans to the government. On July 26, after one such meeting in the town of Moca, the son of a man whom the dictator had executed many years earlier shot and killed Heureaux.[106] Throughout his reign, Heureaux had insisted on divorcing economic turmoil from political discontent. But folk wisdom joined the two by giving Heureaux the epitaph, "la papeleta mató a Lilís" — the paper money killed Heureaux.

The Improvement Company has often been presented as the culmination of U.S. financial domination of the Dominican Republic.[107] But a simple formula of domination and submission does not do justice to the complex relationship that evolved between the SDIC and Heureaux. It could even be argued that, while Heureaux's tactics led to disaster, his manipulation of the New York company constituted a form of resistance to foreign control, the deployment of economic "weapons of the weak." Louis A. Pérez, Jr., has written that "through wile and cunning, with resourcefulness and ingenuity, dependent societies learn to exploit vulnerabilities of the metropoles."[108] Heureaux's machinations are classic examples of this survival strategy.

Despite Heureaux's subversion of SDIC control, the relationship never became overtly adversarial. The company could have refused to broker the increasingly desperate conversions of Dominican bonds in Europe. And, after the default of January 1897, the SDIC could have forced the creation of the international committee foreseen in its contracts.[109] But the Improvement Company did none of those things. Instead, it opted to collect commissions and fees as the broker of new loans, whatever the consequences for the Dominican people and the European bondholders. Since the company stood to profit from any flotation in Europe, no matter how foolhardy, the Americans did not simply blink at Heureaux's profligacy but worked actively as his agent abroad to gather new resources. "Unproductive borrowing," as Albert Fishlow has observed of Latin America debt at this time, "was . . very profitable lending."[110]

In the end, of course, Heureaux was the debtor and the SDIC the creditor, or at least the creditors' trustee. The relationship was hardly a collaboration of equals: Heureaux hazarded all, surrendered his nation's future, and paid with his life, while the principals of the SDIC managed to pull their chestnuts out of the fire through U.S. government intervention, indirect and direct. The SDIC landed on its feet, but that fact should not be read backward in time to assert that the company controlled developments in Santo Domingo from 1893 to 1899. After Heureaux's death, the SDIC made itself out to have been the victim of the dictator's dishonesty and guile, but this does not explain why the company played along for so many years.

At the moment of Heureaux's death, the Dominican Republic seemed more marginal than ever to Washington's regional goals. After the defeat of Spain, the new American relationship with Cuba and Puerto Rico crowded out commercial and strategic needs that might have given some leverage to the Dominican Republic. Events moved in an unexpected direction, however. Ironically, the SDIC's overt control of finances, so reassuring to Washington, had created more problems than it solved. The loans floated by the SDIC from 1893 to 1897 brought local capitalists and foreign creditors into increasingly sharp conflict. They also changed the position of the Dominican Republic in the world financial system, making the Caribbean nation an unlikely player in the geopolitical rivalries of the great powers. When European bondholders turned to their foreign ministries for help in recovering their Dominican investments, the stage was set for the clash of financial and geopolitical interests that led, in 1905, to the Roosevelt Corollary and direct U.S. intervention.

As Heureaux had foreseen, by 1902 both Cuban and Puerto Rican products had privileged access to the American market, while Dominican commodities went toe to toe with those of other tropical producers.[111] Meanwhile, the financial structure created by Heureaux and the SDIC proved to be almost literally a house of cards, a system based on printing discredited bonds in Europe and unconvertible paper money at home. Yet there was nothing ephemeral about those paper documents. However irresponsible the actions of Heureaux and the SDIC, the debts they incurred had the standing of legal contracts backed by the force of international law. After July 26, 1899, the dictator was gone. The debt remained.

6   Old Wine in New Skins

The U.S. Government Champions the SDIC, 1899–1904

The American Improvement Company is spoken of in a mysterious manner — It is said to be but the agent of foreign bondholders . . . that the late President Heureaux was one of its members; that it owns or is, the National Bank, and has flooded the country with worthless money which has produced the financial crisis and destroyed confidence and credit; that all the custom receipts of the country, with small exceptions, are paid over to it; and it is said by planters and merchants that it opposes their interests — It is jocularly referred to as the American Destruction Company.
— U.S. naval officer[1]

Like the people in a majority of such countries as Santo Domingo, the Dominicans like foreigners until they get their money, and then the latter are regarded as public enemies, and the slogan is "Drive out the foreigners."
— Smith M. Weed[2]

The death of Ulises Heureaux in July 1899 opened a new chapter in the history of Dominican-American relations. Contemporaries saw the end of the long tyranny not simply as another regime change, but as the dawn of a new epoch. The "Revolución de Julio" created a consensus in favor of political liberty and freedom of expression. In the four months after Heureaux's assassination six newspapers were launched. Their titles, including *Bandera Libre, Popular, Redención,* and *Nuevo Régimen,* suggest the optimism of the moment.[3] The death of Heureaux also marked a new, more problematic relationship between the SDIC and the Dominican government. The firm, which had kept a low profile under Heureaux, emerged after his death as a powerful force in Dominican public life.[4] This led to conflicts between the SDIC and the post-Heureaux governments and, in turn, to greater U.S. military and diplomatic intervention in the Dominican Republic.

From Washington's point of view, the hostile attitude of the Dominican government toward the Improvement Company threatened American influence in the Caribbean. When Dominican President Isidoro Jimenes expelled the SDIC in 1901, the company lost its hold over the country's finances, and the door swung open to new levels of European influence in the Caribbean. The bold Dominican move against the company, however, belied the actual geopolitical situation of the republic. The Spanish-Cuban-American War had reshaped the Caribbean in ways not especially propitious for the Dominican Republic. Sandwiched between Cuba and Puerto Rico (both of which would soon enjoy privileged access to the U.S. market), with agricultural products no different from those of its neighbors, and having its strategic trump card, Samaná Bay, made largely irrelevant by the new bond between the United States and its two sister islands, the Dominican Republic found itself in a weaker position to confront an increasingly powerful American presence in the Caribbean.

After Heureaux's death, most Dominicans hoped to build a stable political system, one that would end both dictatorship and revolution.[5] They also hoped to free themselves from foreign financial control. Heureaux was gone, but the Improvement Company was still abroad in the land. Dominicans saw the New York firm as the dead hand of the past that held back a brighter future. In the post-Heureaux era, however, the Dominican Republic achieved neither political stability nor financial independence. The anti-dictatorial consensus that flourished after 1899 collapsed in the face of unpalatable economic choices and the resurgence of civil strife. From 1899 to 1905, five provisional governments and three constitutional regimes came to power. The drive to achieve financial autonomy fared no better. The republic briefly threw off the SDIC's control of national finances, only to have the company return, this time vigorously championed by Washington.

Tensions between the SDIC and the Dominican government emerged quickly. Late in 1899, the company dismissed all its Dominican employees from the custom houses and replaced them with foreigners. In December 1899, a new figure appeared in Santo Domingo to champion the interests of the SDIC. John T. Abbott, former American ambassador to Colombia, arrived in Santo Domingo aboard the U.S. warship *Machias*.[6] Like other SDIC officials, Abbott brought political clout to his private interest in the company.

The conflict between the SDIC and the new Dominican leaders took shape in the political vacuum left by Heureaux. Two new political groupings emerged. One formed around Isidoro Jimenes, a wealthy merchant who had lived in exile during the dictatorship of Lilís. The other coalesced around Horacio Vásquez, a young politician who had taken part in Heureaux's assassination.[7] After a brief provisional government, Jimenes and Vásquez alternated in power until 1903, when a stalemate between them allowed the accession of a mutual enemy, Alejandro Woss y Gil. A Heureaux stalwart, Woss y Gil clung to power for only seven months, when he was overthrown in turn by Carlos Morales Languasco, a compromise candidate between the *Jimenistas* and *Horacistas*. By cooperating with U.S. military and diplomatic officials eager to keep him in office, Morales remained in power from November 1903 until January 1906.

All these ephemeral governments faced terrifying economic prospects. The first months of the new era saw the denouement of the economic crisis prepared in the dictator's last years. Besides confronting the insistent demands of foreign creditors, who had been paid nothing since 1898, the government needed to retire the paper money that had disordered the economy for years.[8] Moreover, to improve the country's economy and carry out political reform, the government had to end the system of sinecures and bribes that Heureaux had used to stay in power. Jimenes, who formed the first constitutional government of the new era, did at first reduce bribery. Threatened with political fragmentation, however, later governments returned to the costly old policy.[9]

Like Heureaux, Jimenes was overwhelmed by the task of structurally reforming the Dominican state. Instead of basic reform, the new president believed that the key to economic recovery was striking a bargain with the SDIC. Given the country's ongoing default on the foreign debt, obtaining fresh credit was impossible. The government could not meet its obligations to creditors and maintain its budget from the $60,000 in gold allowed it each month by the American firm. Nor could it hope to launch public works that might satisfy the high expectations of the long-suffering Dominican people. "No government which may be elected," the British vice-consul informed London, "can do anything unless they can negotiate a new loan or are assisted by their creditors the 'Santo Domingo Improvement Co.' " An interim government that had preceded Jimenes tried to obtain a larger share of the custom receipts from the SDIC, but the company refused to cooperate. That tight-fisted policy seemed short sighted even to European observers sympathetic to the SDIC. "It is very unfortunate," reported the British vice-consul, "that this company does not find it convenient to come to the country's aid as there is actual starvation and distress everywhere. . . . Even as a matter of business sense it would seem that the Improvement Co. could with great benefit to themselves give their aid to the Government."[10]

In the new era, the SDIC's policies no longer enjoyed the power of financial fiat they had under Heureaux. Instead, the company itself became a burning public issue. "The question of the Improvement," wrote Francisco Henríquez y Carvajal in *La Lucha*, "is one that raises the hackles of the entire nation." For the first time, Dominicans could openly express their opinion of the company.[11] A few months after Heureaux's death, an American naval officer discovered marked hostility toward Americans, which "seems to be due somewhat to the influence and action of the American Improvement Company, and also probably because the most valuable properties in the island belong to Americans."[12]

The directors of the Improvement Company were aware that their firm had become a pariah. Naturally, they saw events through their own lens. "The Dominican people" the company observed later of the post-Heureaux era, "especially the press and the politicians, denounced the companies daily and loudly called for their withdrawal from the republic. . . . Altogether, a state of public feeling existed which threatened the destruction of the companies' interests then and there."[13] To the Americans, the Dominican government had fallen into the hands of political incompetents "unfamiliar with administrative duties" and "unacquainted with the contracts of the government and the rights, duties, and powers of the American companies."[14]

Despite the anxiety of the SDIC, the Jimenes regime at first followed a moderate policy. Pressed by strong anti-SDIC sentiment among the people, it moved to free the nation from its contracts, but first tried to ascertain the strength of the company's ties to the McKinley administration. Jimenes asked the Dominican consul in New York to "ascertain with as much precision as possible to what extent it is true that the members of the Improvement enjoy influence over the American government, or at least certain officials, and how far that government's support of the company would go in showdown with the Dominican government should we decide to liberate ourselves from that company's dominion."[15]

Jimenes concluded that taking radical measures against the company would be risky. Many Dominicans were shocked when, instead of expelling the company and seizing its assets, their leaders announced a new contract with the SDIC in March 1900. The contract increased the revenue of the

Dominican government at the expense of the bondholders. It postponed the payment of interest for three years and allowed the Improvement Company to use customs receipts for its own expenses and to pay the internal floating debt.[16]

The willingness of Jimenes to come to terms with the SDIC ignited a controversy that dominated the Dominican press for months. "The contract is bad," one editorial argued, "because it recognizes the right of the Improvement to meddle in our internal affairs, thereby wounding our honor, . . . but most of all because it echoes the deeds of the old regime, defeating the noble work of redemption begun by the revolution of July." Dominicans had hoped the death of Heureaux meant release from the SDIC's grip, but financial independence remained elusive. To the SDIC, on the other hand, the public debate proved that "a campaign had been begun, the *sole object* of which was the *expulsion of the American Companies* from the *Regie* and the country without any compensation whatsoever."[17]

As the debate raged in Santo Domingo, news from Europe embarrassed the SDIC. One clause of the new contract required the company to gain the consent of a majority of the bondholders. But European investors had little reason to embrace a moratorium on interest payments.[18] As a result, a group representing a majority of Belgian bondholders withdrew power of attorney from the SDIC and rejected the contract.[19] The rejection encouraged Dominican opponents of the SDIC, but the company insisted that it remained trustee for all the bondholders and, as such, continued to collect its share of the customs revenues. "This action on the part of the Improvement Co.," reported the British consul in Santo Domingo, "is generally considered very weak in business circles here."[20]

Faced with public outrage and an ambiguous legal situation, the Jimenes government moved decisively against the SDIC in January 1901. Asserting that the company no longer represented the majority of bondholders, it ordered SDIC employees to vacate the customs houses. The decree "was read to the Public at all important street crossings and was received with the greatest enthusiasm." Crowds flooded the streets of Santo Domingo and other towns celebrating victory over the "intangible phantom" and the "Octopus with a hundred tentacles."[21] At last the republic seemed to have broken free of the SDIC's grasp.

With the expulsion of its employees from the custom houses, the SDIC had lost its best weapon against the Dominican government — physical possession of the country's revenue. That fact boded ill for future negotiations over the debt, which were inevitable given the disastrous state of Dominican finances. In the United States, the company immediately assumed a public posture of wounded innocence. "There is no doubt that the people would be glad to be rid of us," SDIC vice president Charles W. Wells explained to the *New York Times* a few days after Jimenes expelled the company. "It is a case that often happens to a man — that of legally incurring an obligation and then wishing he were free from it."[22] Company officers naturally made no reference at all to the years of shady loans and mismanagement under Heureaux.

Though few people realized it at the time, the expulsion of the Improvement Company would win for the Dominican Republic a moment of unwanted attention on the world's geopolitical stage. The republic was no longer under the "trusteeship" of private American interests, and henceforth Washington would play a more active role in resolving the problems faced by the SDIC. The vast debt left behind by the Heureaux regime ensured that even the most able Dominican leaders would face a financial crisis that fed internal discontent and prompted calls for intervention by European creditors. Growing political and economic instability from 1901 to 1905 would also prompt increasing U.S. attention to the Caribbean nation, signaled by stepped up diplomatic pressure and the naming of a full ambassador in Santo Domingo. When political turbulence threatened payment of the SDIC's claims, President Theodore Roosevelt sent the U.S. Navy's Caribbean squadron to patrol Dominican waters and discourage rebellion. By 1904, American naval and diplomatic officials were playing a decisive role in deciding who would rule the Dominican Republic. The stage was set for the final step toward American domination of the republic, which came in 1905 with the proclamation of the Roosevelt Corollary to the Monroe Doctrine and the U.S. government takeover of Dominican custom houses that would last 35 years.

At this early date, the Dominican government was aware that the SDIC had taken its grievances before the State Department. President Jimenes moved swiftly to head off American intervention in support of the SDIC, sending one of his ablest statesmen, Francisco Henríquez y Carvajal, to Washington. In meetings with Secretary of State John Hay, Henríquez y Carvajal pointed out the SDIC's dubious operations under Heureaux, particularly the loan conversion of 1897, about which the company had not "up to now given any account." The minister assured Hay of his government's eagerness to reach an agreement with the Improvement Company and offered "to submit the question to a Court of the United States rather than to one of its own, in spite of its indisputable jurisdictional right." In essence, the Dominican government was voluntarily offering extraterritoriality to the American company.

In the talks, Henríquez y Carvajal insisted that point the SDIC present its accounts prior to reaching a settlement so that "the Government may understand the true economical situation of the country."[23] The company's failure to present its accounts had emerged earlier as a contentious issue in the Dominican Republic, where *las cuentas* were often the topic of irate editorials.[24] Nevertheless, the Dominican demand to see "a complete statement of the receipts and expenditures of Government funds" for the years the SDIC had controlled the customs revenue was roundly rejected by the company, the State Department, the Corporation of Foreign Bondholders in London, and the British Foreign Office.[25] The Improvement Company and its allies argued that the rendering of accounts was immaterial to reaching a settlement with the company and that, in any case, the SDIC stood ready to present its accounts at any time.[26]

During the years of Heureaux's alliance with the SDIC, no complaints about the company had been allowed to reach Washington. Now, however, the Dominican government had articulate spokesmen in the North American capital. Caught between the protests of the Improvement Company and the arguments of the Dominican government, the State Department avoided official intervention.[27] Washington hoped that the SDIC itself would be able to extract a satisfactory settlement from the Jimenes regime, and the State Department urged Henríquez y Carvajal to come to terms with the company.[28] Indeed, after only a few weeks of discussion, the Dominican reached a tentative agreement with the SDIC under which the company agreed to sell all its holdings — bonds, the Central Dominican Railroad, and the Banco Nacional. The SDIC agreed to accept a sharply reduced annual payment from the Dominican government. The agreement did not set a price on the SDIC's assets, leaving that and other details to be decided by arbitration. Since the Improvement Company no longer represented a majority of the bondholders, Henríquez y Carvajal next went to Europe, where he reached an accord with the French and Belgian bondholder committees.[29]

The Jimenes government seemed to have made a historic settlement with all its foreign creditors, opening the way to a rationalization of government finances. But years of repressed anger toward the American company bore unexpected fruit. When Henríquez y Carvajal returned to Santo Domingo, he vigorously lobbied for approval of both contracts. The Dominican Congress ratified the European agreement in September 1901, but debate over the SDIC contract dragged on for months amid constant press attacks on the company. In the end the congress rejected the contract "on principle."[30]

Rejection of the 1901 contract convinced the Improvement Company that further dealings with the Dominicans would produce few results. Instead, the SDIC took aggressive steps to rally support for its claims in both the United States and Europe. Central to this new activism was the company's retention of a new counsel, John Bassett Moore. Moore's involvement with the SDIC gave the company a powerful and articulate champion in Washington and, in time, would help to make the Dominican question a defining issue in the foreign policy of Theodore Roosevelt and John Hay.

Like Frederick William Holls, Smith M. Weed, and John T. Abbott before him, Moore fit the pattern of private-public fusion that had characterized the SDIC from its inception. Indeed, from the 1890s through the 1930s, Moore was an important if uncelebrated "servant of power" in the areas of international law and foreign relations.[31] He moved easily between his private legal practice and public service, consulting with secretaries of state Gresham, Sherman, and Day before becoming third assistant secretary of state in 1898. Moore is credited with writing the 1898 peace treaty with Spain after the Cuban-Spanish-American War. During negotiations with Colombia in 1903, Moore, again a private citizen, argued that the Bidlack Treaty of 1846 gave the United States the right to build an isthmian canal without obtaining any further approval from Colombia. Moore visited Theodore Roosevelt at his home in Oyster Bay to discuss this interpretation, which fascinated the President.[32] Through these official and semi-official duties Moore became well known to the State Department as well as to Roosevelt, who in 1905 wrote that Moore was "as high minded a public servant, in or out of office, as I have ever met," a compliment that unintentionally underscored the blurring of public and private interests that Moore embodied.[33]

After 1901, Moore became the key figure in projecting the SDIC's influence within the highest circles of the U.S. government. He gave the company regular, personal, high-level contact not only with State Department officials but with Theodore Roosevelt himself, who became president in September 1901 after William McKinley succumbed to an assassin's bullet.[34] In his new role, Moore corresponded regularly with Charles W. Wells, the SDIC vice president who handled most of the company's affairs from its

New York office. Moore also dealt with John T. Abbott, who in 1899 had become the company's man in the Dominican Republic. Through Abbott and his own contacts at the State Department, Moore kept abreast of reports from the U.S. diplomatic representative to the Dominican Republic.[35] Moore's regular contact with the SDIC and State Department would prepare him to defend the company in the moment of truth that came in 1904.

While actively seeking to shape U.S. policy through the interventions of John Bassett Moore, the SDIC also urged its English allies in the Corporation of Foreign Bondholders (CFB) to seek the support of the British government. In fact, Dominican rejection of the 1901 SDIC contract launched a long collaboration between Washington and London on behalf of the holders of Dominican debt. The British, unlike the French and Belgian bondholders, remained loyal to the SDIC even though the company had failed to pay interest since 1898. At one point the CFB had threatened to sue the American firm, but by 1902 British bondholders saw the SDIC as their only hope to recoup their investment.[36] Not only had British investors bought Dominican bonds, but some had also loaned money directly to the SDIC, accepting Dominican paper as collateral. Much of the paper later passed from individuals to banks, including the London Trust, the National Union Society, and the International Assets Company.[37] In 1902, the CFB estimated that at least $2.5 million of Dominican bonds were held in Britain out of an estimated total of $13 million.[38]

The CFB was, therefore, willing to heed the SDIC's plea for help. Its secretary advised the Foreign Office that, while the ministry may not have been "greatly impressed with the Improvement Company," the CFB believed "that the interests of the British holders of San Domingo bonds will be best protected by keeping under the skirts of the Company." The expulsion of the SDIC by Jimenes convinced the CFB that the Dominican Government simply wanted "to free itself from the control of its revenues by foreigners." The British investors clung to the SDIC in large part because it "certainly enjoys the support of the powerful United States Government."[39] In fact, the CFB's correspondence shows that it saw the SDIC's interests as identical with those of Washington.[40]

The SDIC succeeded in forging an alliance of British and American investors able to influence both national governments. The Foreign Office was more than willing to follow up on the bondholders' request for coordinated action with Washington. Noting that "both U.S. and British Interests are alike prejudicially affected" by Dominican rejection of the SDIC contract, the Foreign Office had the British ambassador in Washington, Lord Pauncefote, inquire whether the United States "would be disposed to take joint-action in support of the claims of the U.S. and British Bondholders."[41]

By 1902, the Improvement Company had brought two powerful new actors into play against the Dominican Republic. John Bassett Moore put his prestige as a leading expert on international relations, as well as his personal contacts in Washington, at the company's service. At the same time, the Council of Foreign Bondholders pushed the Foreign Office to lean hard on the Dominicans by coordinating policy with Washington. These new forces bore fruit in Santo Domingo, where the U.S. Minister, William F. Powell, enthusiastically took up the challenge of forcing the Dominican government to come to terms with the SDIC.

As Powell took up the cudgels on behalf of "our citizen the Improvement Co.," he found that the main stumbling block to a settlement was the issue of the company's disgraceful performance during the Heureaux era, embodied in the SDIC's alleged refusal to present its accounts for those turbulent years. Powell worked tenaciously to overcome the obstacle.[42] The SDIC "nowise refused to exhibit or submit their accounts," Powell insisted, but neither did they "purpose to submit in such a way as will involve their legal rights." In plain English, the SDIC would render its accounts only when the Dominican government was ready to buy out the company's interests; these were "simply parts of one transaction."[43]

Toward that end, Powell pressed the Dominican government to make a flat offer to buy out the SDIC without a prior examination of the debt. "Does your Government desire to be free of the interests represented by the Santo Domingo Improvement Company?" Powell asked the Jimenes regime. "If so, *what compensation does your Government offer to mine for such interests?*" The query suggests the degree to which, for Powell at least, U.S. interests had merged with those of the company. The illogic of buying the SDIC's assets without knowing their true value was pointed out by Henríquez y Carvajal. The Dominican intellectual argued that "the presentation and liquidation of the accounts" was far from "a matter of secondary importance"; in fact, "the first thing to be done is to define the interests at stake."[44] Nevertheless, within a few weeks the Dominican government seemed ready to abandon its demand to investigate the debt before settling with the company. The government agreed buy out the SDIC "for a certain sum (not named as yet)," leaving the accounts to be "considered simply a secondary consideration."[45]

Political events thwarted the pending settlement, however. Not long after a meeting at which, as Powell happily reported, the Dominicans had "waived all consideration of accounts and desired to give the Improvement a certain sum," Jimenes was overthrown by Horacio Vásquez.[46] The new regime found the idea of fixing a price for the SDIC's assets before seeing its accounts to be "a very strange procedure."[47] But Powell, warning of Washington's displeasure, persisted. By January 1903 the Vásquez government had before it two proposals, both drawn up by the State Department, embodying the two roads open to the republic.[48] The first allowed the Dominican Government to "investigate all the transactions that it has had" with the SDIC before making a settlement. Under the second proposal, the Dominican government agreed to pay a flat $4.5 million to buy the company's assets, with no investigation of the debt's origin or amount.

Powell urged the Dominicans to sign the second agreement, which "is more than favorable to your Government." Under it the parties "could come to a solution of the pending questions in a much shorter period of time."[49] The seemingly technical matter of which protocol to sign masked a major issue. If, as the Dominicans had long contended, the SDIC had been party to illegal transactions and had failed to account for millions of dollars in bonds, only a full and impartial audit of the company could determine the amount owed to — or perhaps by — the firm. By accepting a purchase price of $4.5 million for the SDIC's assets, the Dominicans would lose any chance of getting to the bottom of the company's dealings during the Heureaux regime.

Powell manipulated the fears of subsequent Dominican administrations about the consequences of opening the debt to investigation, and the talks that had begun under Jimenes at last yielded an agreement with Horacio Vásquez. On January 31, 1903, the Dominican government signed a protocol agreeing to pay the SDIC $4.5 million for its holdings. The agreement also required the Dominican government to allow an international arbitration tribunal to fix the amount of the monthly payments it would make to the SDIC and to set up the guarantees the company would be given for the $4.5 purchase price. The Dominican Republic was no longer a renegade debtor. On the other hand, Powell had won a signal victory for the SDIC by preventing an investigation of the Dominican debt.

Subsequent events challenged, but did not change, the January 1903 protocol. The Vásquez government was overthrown in April 1903, and the new regime of Alejandro Woss y Gil at first refused to recognize the protocol.

When the United States threatened to break off diplomatic relations, Woss y Gil acquiesced and named the lone Dominican representative to the arbitration tribunal. When Woss y Gil in turn was overthrown by Carlos Morales Languasco, Powell made acceptance of the protocol and arbitration a condition for that leader's official recognition.[50] Morales gave in. Whatever nationalist pretensions the Dominican regimes had, all buckled under unwavering American pressure.

By early 1904, the SDIC had succeeded in rallying both the British and U.S. governments to its cause. American diplomatic pressure had worn down the resistance of successive Dominican regimes, squelched an inquiry into the origin of the SDIC's claims against the Dominican government, and persuaded the Dominicans to accept the company's demand for $4.5 million. For the first time since Heureaux's overthrow, the Improvement Company had reason to be optimistic. Washington's unflinching support for the SDIC had borne out its founders' belief that the success of the private venture depended on strong official backing by the United States. Apparently, SDIC officials had no inkling that their insistent prosecution of the company's interests would soon alienate policymakers, including Theodore Roosevelt himself, and lead to a radical change in the direction of U.S. policy.

7 A Reign of Law Among Nations

John Bassett Moore and the Vindication of the SDIC, 1904

The character of the people of Santo Domingo is worthy of the highest praise. Dominicans are good workers, honest and peace-loving. . . . If they can have peace, there is nothing in the life or character of the Dominican to incapacitate him from paying enough money yearly to provide for an orderly administration of the national finances.
—John Bassett Moore[1]

It is sometimes suggested that, when citizens of a country go abroad and engage in business, they must be held to assume all the risks of disorder and injury in the country to which they go, and can look to the local authorities only, no matter how inefficient or malevolent they may be, for protection; but it suffices to say that no respectable government acts on any such theory.
—John Bassett Moore[2]

The arbitration hearing that took place in Washington in the spring of 1904 was another turning point in United States-Dominican relations. The American case against the Dominicans looked beyond simply winning the minor points at issue before the tribunal. To the lawyers who presented the U.S. case on behalf of the Improvement Company, the tribunal was an occasion to place Yankee efficiency and rectitude in stark contrast against tropical disorder and vice. John Bassett Moore, at once the representative of the State Department and attorney for the SDIC, proposed a radical restructuring of the Dominican government that would make the nation politically stable and financially solvent. Moore's detailed plan for reform tacitly called on the U.S. government to carry out a transformation of the Dominican state that the private company had proven incapable of realizing. By setting forth this ambitious project, Moore pointed the way to

Washington's forceful intervention under the aegis of the Roosevelt Corollary.

The arbitration between the Dominican Republic and the United States seemed to embody the highest ideals of impartiality and due process. The tribunal that would decide the case consisted of three men, one American and one Dominican, chosen by their respective governments, and a second American, chosen by the Dominican government from a list of U.S. federal court judges. The Dominican Republic obtained legal representation from the well-known New York firm of Curtis, Mallet-Prevost & Colt. John Bassett Moore presented the case of the United States.

Moore was the right man for the job. As noted in the preceding chapter, he was not only a well-known international lawyer and advisor to the State Department, but also a pioneer in the field of international law and an advocate of arbitration agreements to settle international differences peacefully. A prolific writer, Moore's first articles on arbitration appeared in the 1890s, the last in 1940. The publication of his 1898 *History and Digest of International Arbitrations* made the principles underlying arbitration widely available for study and citation and thus promoted the institutionalization of arbitration as a solution to disputes between states.[3]

In his writings, Moore promoted arbitration as a mechanism to "displace war between nations" by resorting to judicial methods. In practice, however, arbitration was not usually employed between the great military and industrial powers that became belligerents in 1914 and again in 1939, but instead between industrialized and less-developed nations, especially those of Latin America.[4] The disputes that gave rise to arbitration usually concerned the enforcement of contracts and protection of property rights by Latin American governments. In this sense, the United States-Dominican arbitration of 1904 was typical.

Statistics for the years 1870 to 1914 show that the United States was party to 74 arbitrations that involved Latin American countries. While arbitrations between industrialized states tended to concern boundary, maritime, and territorial questions, those between the United States and Latin America dealt with private claims, including contract, property, and torts.[5] Arbitration among the great powers may have sought, as Moore claimed, to prevent conflicts that could lead to saber rattling or even war. Between the United States and Latin America, on the other hand, arbitration was a way to project the legal standards of industrial capitalism inside the frontiers of less-developed states.[6]

Nationalism, corruption, and other factors at times led Latin American courts to rule against foreigners in ways inconsistent with property laws in the United States and Europe. "If the court of a particular country departs from the general [world] opinion," Moore noted, "there is no remedy but a diplomatic claim, enforceable in the last analysis by war." The obstacle to enfolding Latin America within a global regime of law was "the want of some form of international organization by which a common interpretation and common enforcement of its mandates may be secured."[7] In lieu of an effective world government, arbitration provided a way to overcome the inadequacy of "local remedies" in Latin America.[8] Because it was Americans and Europeans who invested in Latin America, rather than the other way around, metropolitan governments often looked to arbitration in cases of "denial of justice" to their nationals, since the submission of aliens to local laws presupposed "the existence of competent tribunals impartially administered."[9]

Moore's representation of the United States in the Dominican arbitration of 1904 amounted to the practical application of theories he authoritatively advocated. Since he was at once the paid counsel of the SDIC and the State Department's attorney for the same company, however, Moore occupied a peculiar space in the interstices between public and private spheres. The scholar frankly acknowledged that this dual role was problematic. "The Department of State will bear out my statement," Moore told the SDIC, ". . . that they think it undesirable to permit attorneyship for claimants and representation of the Government to be united in the same person, and that they extended special consideration to me in that regard, because of their confidence that I would not abuse their trust."[10]

Moore tried to handle this dual role "responsibly" by doing justice to both the company and the State Department. He explained to Under Secretary of State Francis Loomis that his goal in doing so was to avoid a crisis like that in Venezuela in 1902, when Britain, Germany, and Italy had bombarded towns and briefly landed troops in order to compel payment of outstanding debts and indemnities. Despite concern about European occupation of territory in the Americas, the United States, and President Roosevelt in particular, had tolerated the Venezuelan intervention. The Venezuela case became all the more relevant in February 1904 when the Hague court rendered a judgment that favored the European powers. "I trust that such an award may be made in the pending arbitration here as will render it easy for our Government to . . . avoid such a situation as has resulted in Venezuela," Moore said, referring to European governments' use of force in the Western

Hemisphere. But he signaled his fidelity to the SDIC by adding: "It is entirely feasible, I think, to do this within the limits of the protocol," the agreement between the SDIC and the Dominican Republic.[11]

When the two nations argued their cases before the tribunal in the spring of 1904, the only questions at issue were the amount of the monthly payments to be made to the SDIC, the "mechanisms of payment," and security. The Dominican government expected the evidence and arguments to be limited accordingly. Instead, Moore presented a brief that ran to more than 200 pages and took up fundamental issues such as the origin of the Dominican debt, the reasons for chronic government default, and precedents for a dramatic U.S. intervention in Dominican affairs, with particular emphasis on the creation of the Egyptian *Caisse* by Britain and France.

The case Moore presented had two distinct and seemingly contradictory axes. The first asserted that, despite the Dominican Republic's formal sovereignty, it lacked the attributes that conferred genuine "stateness." "Since July 1901," Moore wrote, "revolution has succeeded revolution until a state of practical anarchy has come to be the unhappy plight of the Dominican people." Not only revolution, but also chronic weakness lay behind the republic's failure to pay its creditors. The government squandered its revenue and did not even fully control its national territory. "The causes of the Dominican Government's financial difficulties," Moore wrote in a summary of the case,

> were revolutions, inefficient and corrupt administration of the revenues, and wasteful and illegal expenditures, including those for the payment of "revolutionary" claims and "asignaciones.". . .
>
> It is upon such things that the public revenues, so far as they are actually collected by the government and not by its enemies, are dissipated, while ordinary expenses are paid by emergency loans or left unpaid, and the public creditor receives nothing.

In essence, Moore felt, the Dominican state was no state at all.

In the context of the arbitration, Moore's allegation of anarchy pointed toward a dangerous conclusion. If the Dominican government had ceased to function, how could it make good on its unpaid debt? Moore anticipated the question and skirted it. "Is the plea that revolution and anarchy are the prevailing conditions to prevent creditors from a reasonable and just enforcement of their debts?" he asked. "The answer must be no."[12]

While acknowledging that "revolutions have occurred in the past and may occur in the future," Moore urged the arbitrators to ignore the republic's chronic turmoil. "Revolutions should not be taken into account" when the arbitrators tried to "measure the 'physical ability' of Santo Domingo" to pay. Moore proposed a tortured formula to determine the country's capacity to pay its creditors: "What the country is able to do when it is in a situation approaching what the normal situation of the nation ought to be." What, then, was "normal" for the Dominican Republic? Anticipating another logical snare, Moore asserted that "normal conditions" could not mean "ordinary conditions," since "the usual or ordinary conditions have never, for any considerable period, even approached what a really normal condition easily might be and ought to be." Normal, apparently, was to mean normative.[13]

Moore's logic required that the Dominican Republic be apprehended not as it was, but as it "ought to be" — a sovereign nation in full control of its territory and possessed of all the attributes of a "normal" state. Actual conditions, which Moore fully described, were to be overlooked and replaced by an imaginary but remediable state of affairs corresponding better to great power notions of solvency and sovereignty. In other words, Moore first assumed the breakdown of the Dominican state, then projected its competence to pay its debts "without improper or undue strain on the people."[14] In defining the republic's ability to raise money, Moore was sensitive to the tenets of international law. He knew that the "honest inability to pay" had legal force and might protect the Dominicans from an adverse decision by the tribunal. It was vital, therefore, to show that the republic's default was in fact willful.[15]

To clinch his argument, Moore excluded two periods of Dominican history as abnormal and hence irrelevant to the arbitration. These were the epochs "prior to the autumn of 1899" and "subsequent to the summer of 1901." That is, in pursuit of the "normal," Moore excluded the entire Heureaux era — indeed, all Dominican history from independence through July 1899 — as well as the period after the SDIC's expulsion in January 1901. What remained was a parenthesis of about two years in which the country "was in a situation more nearly 'normal' than it ever was in before or has been since." Moore saw no reason why that brief span should not "be adopted as the measure of the country's 'physical ability' to produce revenues." Based on that assumption, Moore asserted that the republic could raise "a minimum revenue of $2,000,000 per annum and a probable revenue of $2,500,000," while government expenses could be reduced to $800,000 a year.[16] The country's creditors could be paid from the $1.2 to $1.7 million excess each year.

In its counter-case, the Dominican government argued that it needed at least $1.2 million a year for expenses and that revenue could not be expected to exceed $1.75. In this scenario, the government would be able to dedicate at most $550,000 annually to pay all its creditors, compared to Moore's estimate of $1.2 to $1.7 million. The Dominican figures took into account actual conditions on the island, in particular "the necessity which there will be to expend large sums so as to re-establish peace and order." The Dominican case should have been reinforced by the fact that, as the arbitrators met, President Carlos Morales was fighting — literally — for political survival.[17]

The breach between the reality of internal disorder and the ideal of sovereignty and solvency that Moore projected could only be resolved by the *deus ex machina* of external intervention in Dominican affairs. Not surprisingly, Moore argued forcefully for just such an intervention, asserting that the arbitration itself was a vital first step in disciplining the Dominican state. The republic's creditors had the right to expect a change in existing conditions: "perhaps no better, certainly no more feasible, beginning can be made than by basing the conclusions of this Commission upon estimates which will cure some of the most obvious defects of the present system of appropriations and expenditures."[18]

Moore did not leave the tribunal to imagine what he meant by these "most obvious defects." In fact, the U.S. case included a detailed blueprint for the radical reordering of the Dominican state. Among other reforms, it recommended collapsing or eliminating provincial governments, abolishing cantonal administrations, and doing away with the ministries of justice and public works, the latter "because there are no public works." More important, Moore called for the abolition of both the army and the police force. In their place he favored the creation of an insular force similar to that established not long before in Puerto Rico. Finally, the only remedy to the country's chronic shortage of funds was "collection of the assigned revenues by an independent authority, capable of commanding respect for its own rights. The only such authority, in the present case, is the United States." Moore urged the tribunal "to establish a Caisse . . . whose officers shall be appointed by the United States." Such a step would not "constitute 'annexation' nor establish a 'protectorate,' nor in any sense a 'suzerainty' over the Dominican Government."[19] Rather, it would bring the Dominican Republic into conformity with the principles of advanced states.

Moore's argument embraced some obvious contradictions. He claimed that "to become 'normal' in the true sense," the Dominican Republic needed "a stable peace." At the same time he urged that the insular force be "just large enough to fire salutes to foreign flags." In a country that saw regular challenges to seated governments, how could civil order be kept without an army? Moore explained that "no army which Santo Domingo can clothe and feed would be large enough successfully to oppose . . . a popular revolution." The fact was, "when a revolution is really popular, it always succeeds, because the army itself deserts the Government and joins the rebels."[20] But if revolution was often inevitable, how could the republic achieve the peace it needed "above all"?

The inescapable answer was the presence of U.S. officials and marines in the Dominican Republic. To encourage Washington to intervene, Moore held up British control of Egypt as a pattern for the happy reform of a peripheral debtor. In Egypt, "whose history that of Santo Domingo so much resembles," Britain created an army of only 6,000 men, "one to every thousand inhabitants." That nominal force was able to keep the peace — under the watchful eye of the European powers. Aware that Washington would be reluctant to make a long-term commitment, Moore noted reassuringly that although Britain had been expected "to declare a formal and permanent occupation or protectorate, yet she has persistently declined to do either." In fact, Britain had stabilized Egypt sufficiently to allow her to "gradually withdraw most of her own troops."[21]

As an expert in arbitration, Moore certainly knew that his proposed reconstruction of the Dominican state went far beyond what any tribunal could impose. In light of the minor issues before the tribunal in the Dominican case, Moore's plan was almost comically excessive. But since the United States alone had the prestige and power to get the Dominicans to pay the SDIC, Moore tacitly addressed his argument not only to the three arbitrators but to interested parties in the State Department. By promoting the creation of a modernized, pacified, and solvent Dominican state, Moore gave the company's brief at least the appearance of enlightened self-interest. Washington would intervene not simply to recoup the losses of American investors, but to save Dominicans from themselves.

Moore's recommendations suggest that he looked on the arbitration as a chance to cement the informal union between the SDIC and the State Department by satisfying both the needs of the company and the larger strategic goals of Washington.[22] Nevertheless, his blueprint for reforming the

Dominican state was not purely cynical. On the contrary, it was consistent with his larger vision of the need to foster a global reign of law by imposing norms of fiscal conduct peacefully but vigorously. Moore saw default by successive Dominican governments not as a question of bad faith, but as a structural inability to raise and appropriate money. Like a precocious consultant for the International Monetary Fund, Moore envisioned a streamlined and efficient Dominican state that would at last be capable of meeting its foreign obligations.[23]

Moore's vision of a rehabilitated Dominican Republic also went far beyond what the SDIC could hope to do on its own. By openly calling on the United States to intervene and "fix" the Dominican Republic, Moore tacitly recognized the inadequacy of the private control that the SDIC had exercised in Santo Domingo. Moore ostensibly argued for the SDIC's interests, and those alone, but his master plan for reform pointed the way toward a much more ambitious intervention, one that only the U.S. government could orchestrate. While Moore's case would win the day for the SDIC, his broad vision of the Dominican crisis and its necessary remedy laid the groundwork for Washington to rework its policy toward the Caribbean republic and, only a few months after the tribunal ruled in favor of the SDIC, move the company to the margins of policymaking as a new, progressive form of Dollar Diplomacy replaced the exhausted and ineffectual version represented by the SDIC. Ironically, John Bassett Moore would serve as midwife for the new policy that would bring together the U.S. government, international financial expert Jacob H. Hollander, and the largest international investment banks in New York.

Underlying Moore's case was the premise that the arbitration had lifted the dispute out of the juridical limbo of Santo Domingo to a plane of legality, reason, and order. The United States and the Improvement Company assumed the posture of civilized claimants seeking to deal equitably with a semi-barbarous nation.[24] The Dominican countercase recognized the tactic and burlesqued Moore's representation of the SDIC as "striving always to save, uphold and protect the credit of the Government and the true interests of the Dominican nation," only to be "outrageously despoiled of their property and vested rights by the malicious actions of a wicked and ungrateful people." The Dominicans argued that the United States — "really the Improvement Company . . . it is the hand of Esau, but the voice is the voice of Jacob" — sought to instill in the arbitrators "a prejudice against the Dominican people and their Government." The United States had introduced "impertinent, not to say irrelevant, matter" about the origin of the debt, ignoring the fact that by agreeing beforehand to a payment of $4.5 million the two parties "forever eliminated those questions from discussion." The Dominican government had kept "a dignified silence" on many questions that could have been "presented in a light far from favorable to the Improvement Company."[25]

The Dominican countercase punctured the lofty, disinterested discourse that Moore fabricated to protect the Improvement Company. But the attorneys for the Dominican Republic failed to unmask the apparent objectivity of the arbitration itself, which was as fictitious as the innocence of the SDIC. Moore held up arbitration as one of the most progressive developments in international law. In practice the Dominican arbitration was vitiated by personal influences of exactly the sort that the great powers condemned in Latin America and sought to avoid through the internationalizing tactic of arbitration.

The tribunal's authority rested in part on the prominence of the two American jurists, Justice George Gray and John G. Carlisle. Both men were well-known and respected public figures. Despite Dominican hopes that the legal system would "stop the damaging intrusions of political influence," however, both American members of the tribunal had strong personal ties to the Improvement Company. Judge Gray had been a personal friend of John Bassett Moore's for decades. John G. Carlisle had served as secretary of the treasury in the second Cleveland administration and, as a member of Grover Cleveland's inner circle, almost certainly knew Smith M. Weed, president of the SDIC.[26] Nor was the Dominican representative on the tribunal necessarily a nationalist. Manuel de Jesus Galván, a noted author and statesman, had favored Spain's reannexation of the Dominican Republic in 1860; later he refused to condemn the Grant administration's plan to absorb the republic. The Morales regime tried without success to rescind Galván's appointment on the ground that he "was not a lover of his country." Galván was known in Washington: it was he who negotiated the reciprocity treaty of 1891. Thus, while presenting itself as an appeal to a higher standard of justice, the arbitration in fact resembled the victory of one set of local interests over another.[27]

When, on July 14, 1904, the arbitration tribunal rendered a unanimous decision favorable to the SDIC, few on the American side could have been surprised. The ruling closely followed Moore's more pragmatic recommendations, setting up a schedule of payments by the Dominican government and a timetable for the surrender of SDIC assets. Most important, the tribunal provided that in the likely event that the Dominican government could not meet the payment schedule, the U.S. government would itself appoint a financial agent to take over up to four Dominican custom houses to collect moneys on the SDIC's behalf, making the Americans the only bloc of creditors with an unshakable guarantee of repayment. The tribunal also doubled the sum that the Dominican government had to pay each month. It did not, however, address the larger issue of reforming the political system to ensure stability, nor did it discuss the claims of European creditors that theoretically would be paid out of the same revenue as the SDIC award.[28]

The Improvement Company had good reason to feel satisfied. Through the award, Moore had succeeded in involving the United States in the collection of the company's debt. In Santo Domingo, however, the SDIC award was greeted as an unalloyed disaster. President Carlos Morales called it "the most serious problem that the Republic has experienced since its foundation." Within weeks of the decision, the Dominican minister of finance asserted the "impossibility economically of the 'Hacienda' of the Dominican Republic at the present time to discharge the obligation."[29] At first, the government refused to recognize the award, contending that the tribunal had gone beyond its legitimate powers to impinge on Dominican sovereignty. "It is a principle universally recognized by statesmen," Morales declared, "that states cannot declare themselves incapable of continuing to exist independently. . . . Yet without economic autonomy, political autonomy is impossible. Without full control of our resources, national independence is fictitious. That is the basis of our protest."

To undergird his protest, Morales looked to the recently formulated doctrine of Luis Drago, the Argentine minister of foreign relations, in defense of the rights of small republics. During the European intervention in Venezuela, Drago had created a stir by declaring the forced collection of public debts illegal. Morales paraphrased Drago to the effect that "the republic cannot accept what amounts to nothing more or less than a disguised intervention."[30]

The resort to Drago did not help the Dominicans. It did no good to argue that the tribunal had trod upon Dominican sovereignty: the whole point of arbitration was to supersede local law. The Dominican protest "presupposes that two enlightened nations agreed upon a measure for the settlement of important differences," the U.S. minister patiently explained, ". . . and at the same time left it in the power of one of the parties to undo all that has been done by a simple claim that the measure is inconsistent with its own laws." To placate the Dominicans, the State Department promised to hear their objections, but only after Morales accepted the tribunal's ruling. The Dominican government did so, then launched its own investigation of the arbitration. By the time that study was concluded, the custom houses had passed under direct U.S. control. Further protest was pointless.[31]

Drago and Theodore Roosevelt might have agreed that European intervention would no longer be tolerated in the Caribbean. Drago took pains to show that outlawing the use of force to collect public debts perfectly complemented the Monroe Doctrine. He explained that his proposal sought "to avoid for the people of this continent the calamities of conquest in the disguise of financial intervention, in the same way in which the traditional policy of the United States . . . condemned the oppression of the nations of this part of the world and the control of their destinies by the Powers of Europe."[32] Yet for the United States, the Drago thesis could not serve as a corollary to the Monroe Doctrine, since it would also forbid U.S. intervention. John Bassett Moore had argued that only American power could rehabilitate the Dominican Republic and, by extension, other abnormal states. From Washington's perspective, the Drago doctrine was a false start on the road to the Roosevelt Corollary, as Morales would shortly learn.[33]

With the United States more involved than ever in protecting the SDIC, the company set about consolidating its victory, sparing no effort to see that the arbitral award was followed to the letter. Its main instrument in Washington continued to be John Bassett Moore. Moore had no official status at Foggy Bottom, yet he regularly made use of his contacts there, from junior officials to the Secretary of State himself. The SDIC was anxious that the American financial agent, whose appointment seemed inevitable given the state of Dominican finances, be friendly to the company. Soon after the award was announced, the company asked Moore to arrange for the appointment of John T. Abbott, an Improvement Company official, as U.S. financial agent. SDIC president Smith M. Weed claimed that Abbott had the company's full confidence and was "persona grata" to all Dominican officials. In fact, Abbott was well known and widely disliked by the Dominicans.[34]

A few days after the tribunal's ruling, Moore made a case for Abbott to Secretary of State Hay. "As the substantial financial interest in the award is held by the American Companies," Moore wrote, "it seems proper that the Financial Agent should be a person who . . . enjoys, as Judge Abbott does, the Companies' entire confidence." Lest Abbott seem entirely a creature of the company, however, Moore added an assurance that he in turn had received from the SDIC: "Should he be appointed Financial Agent, he will, as I am advised, at once resign all connection with them [The SDIC and its sister companies]."[35]

Within a week, Under Secretary of State Loomis told Moore "that the President approves the appointment of the Hon. John T. Abbott as financial agent."[36] Contrary to the assurance Moore had given to Hay, however, Abbott did not give up his work for the SDIC. Throughout his tenure as government-appointed agent, Abbott continued to work for the American company, as Moore knew and the State Department probably did as well.[37] Like Moore, Abbott had taken on a public charge while drawing a salary from the private company most interested in his execution of that office. Abbott's "double dipping" would later lead him into indiscretions that prompted Loomis to comment, "Abbott appears to be a fit subject for the activities of the fool killer."[38]

The merger of United States and SDIC interests continued after the Dominicans failed to make the first payment under the award in September 1904. Through U.S. Minister Thomas C. Dawson, the State Department pressed Morales to accept and enforce the award by allowing John T. Abbott to take charge of the customs house at Puerto Plata. In early October, Dawson wired Washington that the Dominican government would cede Puerto Plata only if the SDIC guaranteed that government a minimum monthly income. The Dominican position violated the terms of the award and threatened to undermine the SDIC's legal victory.

Moore was at the State Department when Dawson's cable was deciphered. With both Loomis and Hay absent, Moore and two minor officials swiftly "agreed on a reply to Dawson and immediately on Mr. Hay's reaching the Department . . . I laid it before him. He signed it without hesitation."[39] The cable read in part: "This Government must insist on recognition of award . . . United States cannot undertake to review and undo arbitrators' unanimous decision."[40] A week later the Dominican government recognized the award, and Abbott's agent took control of the Puerto Plata customs house on October 20, 1904, though not without facing popular opposition.[41] According to the British consul at Puerto Plata, "it required all the tact of the Government at Santo Domingo, and of the Governors of provinces and towns to keep down an armed demonstration of dissatisfaction."[42]

Moore's dispatch, which amounted to an ultimatum, achieved the end sought both by the SDIC and the State Department. After seeing the text of the cable, SDIC vice president Wells praised Moore's timely intervention on behalf of the company. "The cable of Mr. Hay is admirable — terse & exactly what we want — it is your style — Good!"[43] The Improvement Company now spoke in the voice of the Secretary of State.

The SDIC had its agent in place, but the arrangement soon faced attack on a second front. European governments had at first applauded the appointment of an American financial agent, hoping the move signaled active United States support for the claims of all the foreign creditors. The American minister, Dawson, told Washington after meeting with several European consuls in Santo Domingo that "it looks to me as if the representatives of all the foreign creditors, with the possible exception of the Spaniard, are really anxious that the United States shall put the Award in execution."[44] When duties from Puerto Plata began flowing to the SDIC, however, it became clear that the arrangement boded ill for other creditors. The Dominican government had from the first argued that complying with the award would make it impossible to keep the government operating, much less make payments to other foreign creditors. By November, several European foreign ministries were complaining to the United States that the moneys collected for the SDIC made it almost impossible for the Dominicans to pay the other creditors.[45]

Moore had long insisted that the arbitral award would neither bankrupt the Dominicans nor prevent payment of the European claims. He had argued before the tribunal that the country could pay all its obligations if only it had "a well-ordered administration." That the republic was not yet orderly was suggested by Moore's condition-laden note to Secretary Hay on October 1. If the Dominican government's expenditures, Moore insisted, "are to be confined to its legitimate and economical requirements . . . then the revenues, if honestly and efficiently collected, will under the existing tariff be ample for the payment of all just debts of the Republic and especially of those of an international character." Moore added that the Dominican Republic was "perfectly solvent" and that payment of the SDIC award, even in "revolutionary times . . . would not injure the rights of any other creditor."[46] To the tribunal, Moore had said that American intervention to reform the state could make the Dominican Republic "normal." Now, even without those reforms, he contended that disorder did not justify the failure to pay the foreign creditors.

Moore's argument persuaded Hay. In detailed instructions to Dawson regarding the U.S. position toward the award and the European creditors, the Secretary of State essentially restated Moore's arguments.[47] As European protests waxed more insistent after November, Moore continued to assert that the SDIC award did not block the settlement of other claims. Right down to the eve of American intervention in February 1905, Moore assured the State Department that the Dominicans had enough revenue to pay the European bondholders.[48]

The State Department, meanwhile, was getting a different message from the American minister in Santo Domingo. Even as he insisted that the Dominicans comply with the SDIC award, Thomas Dawson admitted that the "practical effect might be to render less probable the resumption of payments on the Belgian-French bonds by reducing the amount which the Dominican government would freely dispose of."[49] The private letters of Morales confirm the desperate condition of Dominican finances. In August 1904 Morales commented on the "disastrous state" of the treasury and took steps to cut government spending. In mid-December, the Dominican leader said the situation remained "desperate."[50]

Dawson's realistic view of the situation convinced the SDIC that he had gone soft on the Dominicans. "The trouble with Dawson is that he is good natured and not sufficiently on his guard against the wiles of the crafty Dominican politicians," SDIC vice president Charles W. Wells wrote Moore in early October. Wells especially objected to the fact that "Dawson has several times, and in this instance emphatically and deliberately, said . . . that he is much opposed to the use of force by the United States to execute the Award." The refusal to threaten the Dominicans with American intervention, Wells believed, created a situation in which "*nothing but force*, and strong force will accomplish results which otherwise might be accomplished by firmness simply."[51] To the company, the threat of U.S. intervention was the only real guarantee that the Dominican government would carry out the award.

Despite Dawson's qualms, the State Department stood by Moore and the SDIC throughout the fall of 1904, insisting that the company's award could and must be paid in full. In light of the developing impasse between American and European creditors, Moore's insistence on the viability of the SDIC award had important consequences. By convincing the State Department not to suspend, revise, or even review the award to the SDIC — indeed by orchestrating State Department support for the award — Moore helped perpetuate the standoff among creditors that would shortly prompt Roosevelt to intervene directly in the Dominican Republic.[52]

The fusion of American and SDIC interests became still more complete when Moore requested U.S. naval support for the company's takeover of three more custom houses. In late October, the Morales administration agreed to allow the American financial agent to begin collecting customs at three additional northern ports.[53] Fearing local resistance when the American agent arrived, Moore wired the State Department about "unsettled conditions" in the northern part of the island. Secretary Hay responded by promptly calling for naval support.[54] The Secretary of the Navy notified Hay that "in reply to your request of the 28th instant for a vessel to be sent to Puerto Plata, pending the existence of unsteady conditions there as reported by Professor John Bassett Moore, I have to inform you that the Commanding Officer of the "BANCROFT" has been ordered to proceed from San Juan to Puerto Plata."[55]

Moore was not satisfied with having a naval vessel dispatched to Dominican waters: he wanted John T. Abbott to arrive in the Dominican Republic aboard a warship. On November 3, Moore took the issue up with President Roosevelt. "I left the White House yesterday too late to call on you again," he explained to Loomis, "but the President desired me to tell you that he considered it proper, when the Dominican Government should proceed to install the United States financial agent in the collection of the duties at the other three ports, to give it the moral support of the presence of an American man of war."[56]

As the Dominican situation became a full-blown crisis at the end of 1904, Moore showed no inclination to cut his ties to the Improvement Company. On the contrary, he signed a new contract with the SDIC in November of that year. The company pledged to compensate Moore "for past services in representing [the SDIC] before the Department of State," while the jurist promised to perform "any such services as may be necessary in the case within three and a half years after the first payment made by the Dominican Government." Moore collected $10,000 at once and was to receive $800 each month from moneys remitted by the Dominican government to the SDIC. In the event of default by the Dominicans, the SDIC promised to pay Moore a minimum of $3,500 a year, while the unpaid portion of his salary would bear 4 percent interest. Moore would remain actively involved in Improvement Company business until 1908.[57]

At the end of 1904, Washington's policy in the Dominican Republic consisted of forcefully backing up the claims of the San Domingo Improvement Company. Moore's confident reliance on the "moral support" of U.S. power was, however, about to be shaken to its foundation. Washington's unflinching support for the SDIC was in fact already in question, and by early 1905 it would be sharply reversed. The new official attitude followed from the realization that blind support for the company was backfiring. In the international arena, favoring American over European investors was stoking tensions with the great powers. At the same time, channeling money to the SDIC seemed likely to doom Morales to early overthrow. As Washington groped toward a more coherent form of Dollar Diplomacy, the commanders of the U.S. Caribbean Squadron on duty in Dominican waters illuminated the way. Those officers looked beyond the SDIC's demands for repayment to address the condition of political anarchy that John Bassett Moore had both described and denied in his argument before the arbitration tribunal in 1904.

8 A World Safe for Capitalism

Stabilizing the Dominican Republic, 1901–1905

I am more convinced each day that we must find a solution that will make us capable of becoming a nation.
—Carlos Morales[1]

The law of the Twelve Tables that authorized the creditors to quarter the debtor and to divide his members among themselves cannot obtain for nations within the pale of contemporary civilization.
—Luis Drago[2]

It is possible that this [Dominican] question may become one of exceptional importance. It has given rise to much discussion regarding the future attitude of the United States in the matter of the Monroe doctrine. . . . But the American public is curiously ignorant of everything connected with the conduct of foreign affairs, and it is by no means certain that the Senate is any better informed.
—British Ambassador H.M. Durand[3]

From 1901 to 1904, the United States had become a forceful champion of the SDIC. With John T. Abbott's takeover of the custom house at Puerto Plata in 1904, seconded by the "moral support" of a navy man-of-war, the conflation of American foreign policy and private profit-seeking seemed complete. Even as Washington's goals merged with those of Wall Street, however, a second tendency developed within U.S. policy toward Santo Domingo. Well before the takeover of Puerto Plata, Washington's frustration with political disorder had led to a new form of intervention in Dominican affairs. This parallel intervention, executed primarily by the U.S. Navy rather than the Department of State, sought to stop the revolving door of revolution in a country where, in the words of one officer, "to take up politics . . . is to take up revolution."[4] By 1904, American naval officers were determining the outcome of internecine conflicts, always seeking to construct a political settlement satisfactory to Washington.

Neither President Roosevelt nor Secretary of State John Hay celebrated the use of naval power in the Dominican Republic. In fact, naval intervention was a clear sign that the policy of supporting the Improvement Company had failed. Ongoing political and economic chaos in the republic suggested the incompetence and greed of the SDIC's stewardship in Santo Domingo. If control of Dominican finances by a private company had led to continuous U.S. naval intervention to keep the peace and guarantee the payment of interest on the foreign debt, then surely there was something wrong with this early version of Dollar Diplomacy. Secretary of State Philander K. Knox would, a few years later, reflect on the causes of instability in the Caribbean from a perspective that was just emerging in 1904. "True stability," Knox would declare in 1910, "is best established not by military but by economic and social forces. . . . the problem of good government is inextricably interwoven with that of economic prosperity and sound finance."[5] The naval officers who reported on volatile conditions in Santo Domingo in 1904, like John Bassett Moore at the arbitration tribunal, were pointing the way toward the more comprehensive intervention that would soon come with the Roosevelt Corollary and the Dominican customs receivership.

Not surprisingly, the mission of bringing stability to the Dominican Republic was problematic from the first. Writing of British policy toward Latin America in the nineteenth century, Charles Lipson has observed that the Foreign Office "understood that diplomatic threats and naval gestures would scarcely touch the causes of . . . instability."[6] Having recently assumed new imperial burdens in Puerto Rico, the Philippines, and to a lesser degree in Cuba and Panama, Washington policymakers were chary of adding the rationalization of the Dominican state to their other tasks. Theodore Roosevelt himself vigorously denied any intention of assuming political control over the Dominican Republic. In fact, he insisted that he had "about the same desire to annex it as a gorged boa constrictor might have to swallow a porcupine wrong-end-to." Despite this famous disclaimer, the United States found itself drawn into a confrontation with the deeper sources of political instability in the Dominican Republic. Privately, Roosevelt admitted that it seemed inevitable that the United States would eventually exercise "protection and regulation" over a number of Caribbean states.[7]

In lieu of the more formidable means of imposing order that the United States would develop under the customs receivership, at this point stabilizing the Dominican Republic came to mean little more than sustaining the precariously seated government of Carlos Morales. Morales had seized the presidency in November 1903 and succeeded in winning premature recognition by the U.S. minister by mid-January 1904. Both diplomatic and naval officials reported that Morales was more sympathetic to U.S. interests than his main rivals. Press coverage in the United States followed the official lead. In a glowing profile, the *New York Times* praised Morales as "a strong man — far more forceful and honest of purpose than any of his ephemeral predecessors since President Ulises Heureaux." The article noted with approval that the leader's "lustrous black hair is slightly curled, without, however, showing any traces of kink."[8]

By January 1904, the U.S. Caribbean squadron had taken up position in Dominican waters, where it effectively hampered opposition to Morales.[9] The squadron was omnipresent as events unfolded throughout 1904 and 1905, and naval officers regularly advised Washington how to restore order.[10] "The only way of stopping these revolutions, is to have possession of the custom houses," Commander Albert Dillingham advised his superiors in Janaury 1904. Although taking control of the custom houses was well beyond Washington's goals at that point, Dillingham, Admiral Charles Sigsbee, and other naval officers became major players in the power struggle underway in the Caribbean republic.[11] They met regularly with President Morales as well as with Juan Isidro Jimenes, Horacio Vásquez, and other pretenders to the presidency, as well as with troublesome local leaders such as Desiderio Arias in the border town of Monte Christy. Dillingham, who spent months trying to negotiate an end to the fighting among rival caudillos, reported to Washington that "this vessel is a factor in all that transpires."[12]

The naval officers made no secret of their efforts to stabilize the Morales regime. "The provisional government [of Morales] has been gaining ground steadily," Dillingham reassured his superiors in May 1904, "and with the presence of our vessels in the ports, I think the ports will remain in the possession of the Government." Aware that American policy in Santo Domingo was leading toward commitments that might give rise to debate in Congress, Dillingham added in June that "the Morales Government can be kept in power until after the United States Congress meets in December."[13]

The naval officers understood that by choosing sides among the Dominican belligerents, they were violating international standards of neutrality.

"Of course," Dillingham told his superiors, "we appreciate the rights of neutrals as guaranteed by International Law, but . . . the principles of International Law can hardly be applied, if it is desired to stop this insufferable nuisance of perpetual revolution; International Law can be applied here only so far as it suits the convenience of the United States Government." Like John Bassett Moore, the officers found themselves in the contradictory position of negating the rights of the state they had ostensibly come to rebuild. Dillingham and Sigsbee called attention to the country's inability to sustain the reality or even the pretense of sovereignty. "The great difficulty that we experienced," Sigsbee complained after meeting with a group of Dominican politicians, "was to convince these people as completely as possible that the creditor nations had reached the point at which they cared nothing for the workings of the Dominican constitution or of Dominican law."[14]

No doubt American warships arrived in Dominican waters laden with the prejudices of the powerful toward the weak. Yet the U.S. naval intervention was far from unilateral. If the United States saw in Morales the linchpin of a new stability, Morales looked on Washington as the guarantor not only of his regime but of the Dominican state itself. Both Dominican and American documents suggest that it was not just U.S. concern about European encroachment in the Caribbean, but also the initiative of the Dominican political elite itself, that brought on American intervention.[15] Months before the emergence of a supposed threat to the Monroe Doctrine, Morales besieged Washington with requests for help. Roosevelt later insisted that he established the customs receivership in response to those pleas. That explanation should be taken seriously, not to vindicate Roosevelt but to understand the logic of Dominican leaders as the state dissolved around them.

Even before winning formal recognition by Washington, Morales had begun to seek some form of U.S. protectorate over the republic. In early January 1904, Morales asked Roosevelt to authorize a treaty that would provide "the assistance necessary for the maintenance of internal order." The Dominican minister in Washington followed up a few weeks later by requesting an arrangement "which would establish, in a practical manner a proceeding that would realize the pacification of my country." Morales sweetened the offer by proposing that the United States lease Samaná Bay for 50 years, with the proceeds of the lease to be dedicated to paying the foreign debt.[16]

In February 1904 Roosevelt complained that the Dominican government "has been bedeviling us to establish some kind of protectorate over the islands, and take charge of their finances." Roosevelt still refused to commit himself.[17] In the spring of 1904 the United States-Dominican arbitration was underway, with the return of some custom houses to the SDIC a likely outcome. Roosevelt was almost certainly aware of the arbitration; he may also have been unconvinced that European powers posed an immediate threat either to Dominican sovereignty or the SDIC's claims. He took the situation seriously enough, however, to send Admiral George Dewey and Assistant Secretary of State Francis B. Loomis to the Dominican Republic to investigate conditions in early 1904. Loomis recommended that the United States take over the custom houses to "put an end to the fight for control by the natives." He also suggested elevating the diplomatic post in Santo Domingo. Soon after, Thomas Dawson became the first U.S. minister resident in Santo Domingo.[18]

Roosevelt and Hay were still not ready to intervene officially, but their response to Loomis's recommendation underscores that the withering away of the Dominican state, not European meddling, was the main issue. Hay told Loomis in late March that the President believed that "in the present state of affairs, he sees no way in which the United States could take part in the pacification of the Republic."[19] Still, the Dominican minister in Washington insisted that the solution to the internal crisis his government faced, "painful as it becomes to confess it — cannot be found by the Dominican Government with the strength of the country itself" and called for U.S. support "to consolidate the interior peace of the country."[20]

Despite Roosevelt's refusal to launch a pacification campaign, American naval officers were in fact still playing a decisive role in Dominican political life. Although the interests of the SDIC had spurred Washington's involvement in Dominican affairs, the magnitude of the intervention was beginning to overwhelm the financial interests at stake.[21] American naval officers noted the disproportion between the expense of intervention and the value of the U.S. interests they were protecting. Admiral Charles D. Sigsbee lectured a meeting of Dominican politicians "that it cost the United States at least one million five-hundred thousand dollars per annum to maintain the Caribbean Squadron in Caribbean waters merely for the protection of the interests of American citizens, and that it would probably be cheaper for the United States to pay the claims of its own citizens . . . than to maintain the squadron."[22]

The point is not that deployment of the Caribbean Squadron in Santo Domingo was a strategic error, a miscalculated quid pro quo between the

American state and American capitalists. Instead, the ongoing presence of U.S. warships in Dominican waters, and of American intervention in Dominican politics, had acquired a rationale beyond the protection of specific American interests. By assuming the role of peacekeeper, the United States was doing more than ensuring the repayment of an American company — it was taking over key functions of the Dominican state itself.

Archival evidence shows that both Dominicans and Americans acted on this assumption. The Dominican government viewed the U.S. navy as an auxiliary to the state, while U.S. naval officers subordinated themselves to the goal of sustaining the Morales regime. "Would it not be well," Admiral Sigsbee asked the Secretary of Navy, "as a general rule, to allow the government of Santo Domingo to take the initiative, the United States, as represented by myself . . . to act as the supporter of the immediate measures of the government of Santo Domingo . . rather than that my force shall seem to take the initiative."[23] The relationship became more explicit after the customs receivership, created in April 1905, clinched the bond between the two nations. In June the Dominican minister of foreign relations told the U.S. consul that "a revolutionary movement has broken out in Barahona," adding that "since the town of Barahona is a seaport with a custom house under the control of the United States, I point this out so that if you feel it necessary you will send the cruiser "Des Moines" to that port."[24]

The American policy was not disinterested. By loaning its coercive power to the Dominican state, the United States allowed Dominicans to direct their resources to building infrastructure and, naturally, paying the foreign debt. Washington had long been aware that the Dominican Republic "cannot pay one cent on its foreign debt for all its revenue is needed to suffocate the constant revolutions."[25] The Dominican minister of foreign affairs made the same point in January 1906. Emiliano Tejera reported to the U.S. minister an attack on Puerto Plata by rebel forces, an outbreak which "a mere gesture by one of the American warships . . . would have been enough to avoid." Tejera reminded the minister that "the brake on revolution" was "that the United States would show its hostility to those who tried to overthrow the seated government" and warned of the consequences if the United States remained passive in the face of civil unrest. "Once this brake is removed, the country will return to its previous anarchic condition, and the government will find itself obliged to employ all its resources to rescue the nation from those who see it as no more than a treasury to be sacked."[26]

The Dominican government was using the U.S. Navy for its own ends, repressing local *caudillos* and rebel movements. As leverage, the government threatened to redirect its spending toward the military, with predictable consequences for the country's creditors.[27] Once again, Dominican leaders were supplying the missing elements of "stateness" by looking abroad. Heureaux had sustained his government through foreign loans, in effect supplementing domestic sources of wealth and internal mechanisms of extraction by sending revenue-raising functions abroad. In 1904–5, the Morales regime resurrected a shattered state by importing the coercive power of the United States.[28] Morales acted on premises not far different from those of John Bassett Moore: the Dominican Republic was structurally unsound and needed fortification that only American intervention could provide.[29] In effect, well before the customs receivership formalized American intervention, U.S. military assistance had become a vital prop of the Dominican state.

By the spring of 1904, Washington and Santo Domingo had formed a close if informal military and political alliance to maintain peace and keep Morales in power. That hard-won stability would face a trial by fire after the decision of the arbitral tribunal in the SDIC case on July 14, 1904. With that verdict, U.S. policy strained under the dual mission of sustaining Morales and extracting revenue on behalf of the Improvement Company. The tension between those two policies would lead Theodore Roosevelt to rethink the larger purpose of U.S. policy in the Dominican Republic.

With John T. Abbott's takeover of the custom house at Puerto Plata in October 1904, the Dominican government lost desperately needed revenue, dashing the hopes of European creditors for equal treatment under the United States-sponsored arrangement. By December, the foreign creditors had at last reached their limit. Moore and the State Department might argue that the SDIC award in no way prejudiced European interests, but the fact remained that no creditors but the Americans and their British allies were getting paid. The Italian ambassador at Washington put the issue clearly: the United States must either let other nations do as it was doing in the Dominican Republic, or it must do for their citizens what it was doing for the SDIC.[30]

The French ambassador met with Secretary Hay twice in mid-December and urged him to accept international control of Dominican finances. Hay demurred, preferring the option of unilateral action.[31] Dawson reported that several European consuls in Santo Domingo were openly discussing the seizure of southern ports. Although the likelihood of intervention is not certain, pressure from the Europeans reinforced the slowly dawning realization that, far from solving the Dominican crisis, Washington's unconditional support for the SDIC only made it worse. The forcible repayment of the American firm was strangling Morales and angering the European powers.

Meanwhile, the Dominicans found their finances further undermined by a different problem, this one internal. As has been noted, nearly all state revenue came from import and export taxes. Yet the largest group of exporters, the sugar estates, had taken advantage of the country's political turmoil to free themselves from all taxation. In 1903, the fledgling Morales government, desperate for cash, had offered sugar planters a 20-year exemption from export taxes in return for an immediate payment of $40,000.[32] The government later regretted the arrangement and tried to impose a "production tax" virtually identical to the export tax. Since many of the sugar planters were Americans, they called on the U.S. consul to intervene to prevent collection of the tax. Underlying the planter's request was a basic contradiction between the two blocs of American capitalists on the island, the SDIC and the sugar planters. To increase its own revenues and those of the government, the SDIC wanted to maintain or increase export and import taxes. The sugar planters, who exported thousands of tons of raw sugar and imported the machinery, food, and other supplies they used, preferred low imposts or none at all.

In their protests, the American planters put the underlying conflict in bold relief, taking direct aim at the SDIC and the other creditors who were to benefit from the tax on sugar. "I cannot get myself to understand," the treasurer of two of the largest American-owned estates complained,

> why the sugar estates . . . should be held up to pay tribute to satisfy any set of Bondholders or raise a fund for the payment of any claim, such as for instance the San Domingo Improvement Company, concerns who have come to this country with no enterprise . . . but simply to finance for profit and increase the National debt . . . while the sugar interests have come with large capital in permanent investment . . . employing many thousands of laborers, thus increasing the purchasing power of all laboring classes.

The complaint concluded that SDIC officials did no more than "scheme and finance" and then, because of their incompetence, "fall back on their Government to compel a weak and small Republic, by force of arms, to pay most unjust . . . claims."[33]

The U.S. government found itself caught between clashing American

interests. American minister W. F. Powell explained the predicament —
whether or not to tax one group of Americans to pay another — to the State
Department. "The travesty of the affair is this," he complained. "With one
hand I demand of them [the Dominican government] the payment of American Claims, while with the other hand present them with a protest from
Americans calling upon this Government to allow this particular interest to
transact business free of all tax."[34]

The complaints of the sugar planters gave the U.S. government another
reason to look unfavorably on the SDIC's handling of Dominican finances.
Nevertheless, the State Department continued to back the company in spite
of the planters' claim to represent productive capital as against the SDIC's
financial scheming. The new U.S. minister, Thomas Dawson, assured the
planters that "it is my earnest desire to be of service to the large investments
of American capital which you represent," but concluded, "I see no way for
you to avoid payment." The United States could do nothing since the planters' "redress lies by way of an appeal to the Executive or Legislative authority," a very different stance from the State Department's vigorous defense
of the SDIC's claims.[35] Washington tried to appease all parties to the conflict
by directing Dawson to champion the interests of both the sugar planters
and the SDIC, to the obvious prejudice of the Dominican government. In
April 1905, after the creation of the customs receivership made the U.S.
government itself responsible for raising revenue, Dawson was told to cease
defending the sugar interests.[36]

By the time President Theodore Roosevelt delivered his annual message
to Congress on December 5, 1904, the Dominican situation was critical.
The Morales regime's payments to the SDIC made it impossible to satisfy
European creditors. Sugar planters fought taxation, threatening a further
reduction in revenue. And European governments threatened to seize Dominican custom houses if their citizens did not get equal treatment. A few
months earlier, Roosevelt had refused to intervene formally in the Dominican Republic. By December he had changed his mind. His message to
Congress described the Dominican situation and outlined the extension of
the Monroe Doctrine that would shortly bear his name. Roosevelt stressed
the disintegration of the Dominican state:

> Chronic wrongdoing, or an impotence which results in a general loos-
> ening of the ties of civilized society, may in America, as elsewhere,
> ultimately require intervention by some civilized nation, and in the

Western Hemisphere the adherence of the United States to the Monroe Doctrine may force the United States, however reluctantly, in flagrant cases of such wrongdoing or impotence, to the exercise of an international police power.[37]

Roosevelt followed this apologia for intervention with decisive action. In late December, he instructed Dawson to seek Dominican approval of an American customs receivership and sent Commander Albert Dillingham, who had done so much to keep Morales in power, to Santo Domingo to help with the negotiations.[38]

As the only creditors actually receiving money from the Dominicans, the directors of the Improvement Company watched the unfolding intervention with intense interest. Moore still saw the company's interests as identical to those of the government, and he urged the SDIC to cooperate with Roosevelt's plan. On January 20, Moore suggested that the company cable John T. Abbott and instruct him that "Dillingham's mission apparently not adverse to our interests. Would avoid suggesting any conflict."[39] The following day, the American and Dominican negotiators signed a draft protocol calling for U.S. officials to take over the collection of customs revenue throughout the Dominican Republic.[40]

Meanwhile, Santo Domingo buzzed with rumors of an imminent American annexation. Morales now reaped the political consequences of his willingness to invite American pacification and financial control. Facing opposition within his cabinet and the threat of rebellion, he launched a letter-writing campaign to convince prominent Dominicans that a customs receivership was both desirable and inevitable. "We have saved the republic from anarchy, in every realm of national life," he declared, "both the political and economic." While admitting that it was "better for a people to raise themselves through their own efforts," Morales claimed the arrangement was the "best solution, and the only one possible, to allow the ship of state to navigate the bottomless ocean of Dominican politics." The accord was "almost paternal" and the advantages "are ours, all ours, since they [the Americans] will be forced by the duty and moral obligation which they have assumed before the whole world to help us with the project of political and social regeneration, which must be founded on the realization that we can no longer live lives of disorder, that we have no right to set ourselves against the march of civilization."[41] Morales was broadcasting the self-serving arguments of a *vendepatria*. But the letters also reiterated time-honored ideas about progress, order, and civilization that must have resonated with the president's elite correspondents.

Officials of the SDIC still believed that Roosevelt's proposed customs receivership would safeguard their interests. After a conversation with Smith M. Weed, Wells reported on January 26 that "like myself he is much pleased with the situation." Two weeks later Wells told Moore "evidently what the State Department is doing is all right . . . and I 'guess' it's coming out to our interests."[42] Moore had enough confidence in the SDIC's standing with Roosevelt and the State Department to believe that they would do nothing to infringe upon the company's rights. This hope was reinforced in late January when Roosevelt invited Moore to Washington to discuss the Dominican situation. By that time, the proposed intervention had become a heated partisan issue and front-page news across the country. Opponents of the treaty attacked both the extension of U.S. power in the Caribbean and Roosevelt's evident attempt to sidestep the Senate's treaty-making power in order to put his plan into effect. The ensuing conflict over the Dominican receivership was "among the most significant in the long contest between President and Senate," according to one expert.[43] It was thus in an atmosphere of controversy and pressing need that Moore met with Roosevelt on January 24 and again on January 26.

Assistant Secretary of State Loomis took Moore to see the President, mentioning to Roosevelt

> that I was specially familiar with Dominican finances and intimated that I might outline a plan of adjustment. I remarked that I ought to call the President's attention to the fact that I represented the United States before the arbitrators last summer in the settlement of the claims of the American companies, and that previously I had acted as counsel to the American companies. The President and Loomis both remarked that this would make no difference, as the matter was settled and was not to be disturbed.

Since Moore had just signed an agreement to represent the SDIC for the next three and half years, his statement to Roosevelt and Loomis that he "previously" had been SDIC counsel was disingenuous.[44] It is not clear if Loomis and Roosevelt knew that Moore still had formal business ties to the SDIC. Two months later, however, both the *New York Times* and *Sun* would identify Moore as attorney for the SDIC.[45]

At a second meeting, Loomis broached a topic that stunned Moore. "To my great surprise," Moore confided in his memorandum of the meeting, "[Loomis] . . . intimated that all claims and debts would have to be revised. I wondered whether he precisely understood the bearing of what he said, and after some conversation I came to the conclusion that he was speaking at random." Loomis had hinted at precisely what Moore and the Improvement Company feared most: a general review of claims against the Dominican Republic. Such a revision would endanger the SDIC's interests in several ways. First, it threatened to end the priority that the SDIC enjoyed by placing all creditors on the same footing. Further, given the state of the Dominican treasury, it was likely that a revision would scale down all claims. Finally, the company had reason to worry about close scrutiny of its business practices during the Heureaux years. All the ground Moore had won in the arbitration was suddenly contested once more.

Loomis's remark was the first hint of a shadow falling between the State Department and the SDIC. Moore was heartened later the same day, however, when he asked State Department counsel W. L. Penfield "whether Loomis had discussed with him the question of ripping up international settlements [the SDIC's arbitration award]. Penfield declared he had not and said it could not be done, that it would be a matter of too great delicacy; and that, as to international awards, they could not be set aside save on the ground of fraud." For the time being, Moore was reassured that the SDIC's pride of place among Dominican creditors would not be challenged.

Moore soon had the chance to press the company's view of the Dominican crisis on Roosevelt himself as the President forged a new policy. Penfield read Moore and Loomis "a draft of an outline of a message which the President had dictated two or three days before." Roosevelt would send the message to Congress on February 15, along with the protocol setting up the customs receivership. The message would be widely taken as an important statement of the new policy known as the Roosevelt Corollary to the Monroe Doctrine.[46]

Although the Dominican protocol concerned only the United States and the Dominican Republic, Roosevelt framed the corollary in multinational rather than bilateral terms. The root problem was the debt that the Dominican government owed to private creditors throughout Europe. The legitimate grievances of these creditors could not be redressed through "a blockade, or bombardment, or the seizure of the custom houses" because the Monroe Doctrine as Roosevelt now construed it forbade Europeans to resort

to those normal steps in the collection of international debts.[47] By keeping
the Europeans at arm's length the United States was refusing to "allow other
powers to take the only means at their disposal" to satisfy their citizens, thus
prolonging the standoff. This policy was "incompatible with international
equity" since American creditors, sheltering under the protection of the
Monroe Doctrine, were the only investors receiving any payments at all from
the Dominicans, a fact that increased the discontent of the Europeans.[48] It
seemed clear that Roosevelt was leaning toward an approach to the Dominican crisis that would satisfy all the country's creditors and stabilize the republic's finances and government.

Moore's reaction to the draft showed the differences crystallizing between
Roosevelt and the SDIC. "The whole thing," Moore wrote of Roosevelt's
framing of the corollary,

> was very unconsidered, as it seemed to me, containing no exposition
> of Dominican conditions, but expatiating on the development of a
> new policy . . . I told Loomis and Penfield that, in my opinion, it was
> inadvisable to thrust to the front a "new policy" and leave in the back-
> ground or altogether omit the exceptional conditions which rendered
> it necessary to do something in Santo Domingo without regard to any
> new policy.

By focusing on the "exceptional conditions" rather than a "new policy,"
Moore evidently hoped to keep the SDIC's claims foremost in the President's
mind. The same day Moore candidly presented his view of the important
message to the President himself. Roosevelt, he reported, was willing to
accept some of the criticisms he offered.

> I told the President that I had read . . . what he had dictated, and
> that it seemed to me that it was important that the actual conditions
> existing in Santo Domingo rather than the question of policy should
> be placed in the forefront. He seemed to agree with this, saying that
> what he had dictated was rough and hastily done, and asked me
> whether I had written anything. I told him that I had dictated a brief
> memorandum . . . but that it was susceptible of much elaboration. I
> then handed him the paper hereto annexed. He read it and expressed
> his approval of it. I observed that in it the phrase ought to be employed
> that the custom houses had become "the nuclei of revolutions." He
> said that was "good" and took a pen and wrote it in.[49]

The memorandum that Moore passed to Roosevelt concentrated in law-
yerly fashion on the republic's failure to honor its contracts with the SDIC
and favored a far more limited declaration than what the President had
written.[50] After briefly rehearsing the various European claims, the note
warmed to a familiar theme, declaring that "the state of things in Santo
Domingo has become hopeless, unless the United States or some other
strong Government shall interpose to bring order out of the chaos." The
custom houses "have become unproductive for the discharge of indebtedness," and the chronic disorders "have become exceedingly dangerous to
the interests of Americans holding property in that country." Moore empha-
sized the conflict between the creditors and the debtor, not disagreements
among the different creditor nations. He also objected to the unrestricted
nature of what was to become the Roosevelt Corollary. The new policy risked
making the United States the debt-collector for the Western Hemisphere.
Moore may have realized that the open-ended commitment Roosevelt envisioned would mean ongoing intervention necessarily entailing a reassess-
ment of the Dominican Republic's foreign and internal debts.

Ironically, Moore's collaboration on the message was the last time he and
Roosevelt stood shoulder to shoulder. Roosevelt's message declared that it
was "impossible under existing conditions . . . to defray the ordinary expenses
of the [Dominican] Government and to meet its obligations," contradicting
Moore's conviction that the Dominican Republic was able to repay all its
creditors.[51] The hybrid origin of the document explains why it included the
specific grievances of American investors against the Dominican government, yet announced a policy ultimately at odds with the special interests
of the Improvement Company. It is a further irony that Moore, champion
of a global approach to U.S. foreign policy, found himself arguing against
Roosevelt's broad policy in favor of a restrictive interpretation better suited
to the SDIC's narrow interests.

The final version of Roosevelt's message was largely the broad policy
statement Moore objected to combined with Moore's enumeration of the
difficulties faced by investors in the Dominican Republic.[52] Although
Roosevelt discussed the role of the SDIC in some detail, he did not use
violations of the company's rights as grounds for intervention, except in the
passage he took from Moore's memorandum. On the contrary, Roosevelt
declared that the intervention was disinterested and would not serve the ends
of any nation's investors. "It is in the highest degree necessary," the President
vowed, "that we should prove by our action that the world may trust in our
good faith and may understand that this international duty will be performed

by us within our own sphere, in the interests not merely of ourselves but of all other nations, and with strict justice toward all."[53] At the same time, Roosevelt clearly declared the right of the United States to intervene in the internal affairs of Latin American nations in order to prevent the spread of disorder that might invite powerful, opportunistic rivals from getting a foothold in the region. In this sense, the Roosevelt Corollary was a step in the direction of National Security Council–68, the interventionist blueprint for the early years of the Cold War, which extended the corollary's concern with hemispheric disorder to the entire planet. The later document warned that "in a shrinking world the absence of order among nations is becoming less and less tolerable" and called for a new policy that "rejects the concept of isolation and affirms the necessity of our positive participation in the world community."[54]

The corollary message was immediately recognized as a watershed in U.S. foreign policy. The New York Times, Sun, and Tribune, as well as the Washington Post, reprinted it in full. "While interest in the terms of the new protocol was extremely great, the President's message overshadowed it in the attention it attracted among Senators on account of its many important statements concerning the Monroe Doctrine," reported the Sun. The French ambassador at Washington wrote a detailed analysis of Roosevelt's "tres long message" and noted that Monroe "certainly would no longer recognize" the policy that bore his name.[55]

The corollary would be the "basic idea that inspired the Caribbean policy of the United States in the first two decades of the twentieth century," according to Dana C. Munro.[56] As the Dominican intervention unfolded from 1905 to 1907, it became the prototype for a new strategy in which Washington officials helped arrange loans for unstable countries that agreed to some form of financial supervision. "The Dominican model," Emily Rosenberg argues, "became the first major effort to forge the kind of partnership that would continue to be at the heart of dollar diplomacy: a triangular relationship among financial advisers wishing to practice their new profession of fiscal rehabilitation of foreign countries; investment bankers seeking higher interest rates in foreign markets; and activist government officials eager to assert international influence." The "practice of linking loans to financial advice" would in the post-World War II period become "enshrined in the International Monetary Fund."[57]

The importance of the Roosevelt Corollary was evident to contemporaries as well as to generations of historians of U.S. foreign relations. The role of the San Domingo Improvement Company in spurring the creation of the new policy, however, has been largely ignored. The SDIC helped create both the chaotic political and economic conditions in the Dominican Republic and the confrontation between American and European creditors that triggered Roosevelt's intervention. Moreover, the company's behind-the-scenes maneuvering to protect its interests at all costs clearly influenced Roosevelt's thinking about the most effective way to settle the Dominican crisis. Restoring the role of the SDIC to the historical record places the Roosevelt Corollary in a new light. The Corollary can be seen for what it was: a calculated step away from an earlier policy of unexamined support for private interests in the Caribbean. The parallel between Roosevelt's handling of the SDIC and his support of federal regulation of trusts to protect the public good also becomes more evident. The Roosevelt Corollary did seek to keep European warships out of Dominican ports and prevent revolutions in Santo Domingo, but it also ended the delegation of U.S. foreign policy to a company that had operated with Washington's support, but without its supervision, for more than a decade.

Naturally, other factors influenced Roosevelt's decision to make the Dominican crisis the occasion for declaring a major new foreign policy. A conjunction of world events in early 1905 no doubt encouraged Roosevelt to calm "a situation fraught with grave danger to the cause of international peace," as he put it.[58] The new policy in Latin America would help step down tensions among the great powers that were being stoked elsewhere in the world. In Britain, anti-German feeling peaked at the end of 1904 as a result of Kaiser Wilhelm II's attempts to construct an anti-British league. Tension between Germany and France increased even before the Moroccan crisis of March 1905. The fall of Port Arthur in January 1905 foreshadowed Japanese victory over Russia and raised the specter of further great power contention in the Far East. Roosevelt's personal efforts to settle the Russo-Japanese conflict and defuse the German-French confrontation indicate that the danger presented by great power friction was not far from his mind. Finally, in January 1905 Britain's new First Sea Lord announced a redeployment of British ships away from Latin American waters. This succession of events may have prompted Roosevelt to act decisively to reduce friction among the European states and to assume new responsibilities and assert new powers in the Americas.[59]

While many European newspapers criticized Roosevelt for staking out a U.S. sphere of influence in Latin America, European foreign ministries generally saw the corollary as an effort to create stability. In Britain, even the press for the most part reported favorably on the corollary. The *Outlook*, of London, observed that "Europe is not likely to complain of a policy that relieves her from an infinity of petty vexations, that preserves order and makes for that social and political stability which is the foundation of commerce, and that ranges the United States at last and definitely on the side of civilization."[60]

By creating the Dominican customs receivership and announcing the corollary to the Monroe Doctrine as a major new policy, Theodore Roosevelt moved American policy to a new plane of activism and commitment toward Latin America in general. The San Domingo Improvement Company had triggered this transformation, intentionally through John Bassett Moore's lobbying of the President and the Secretary of State, but also inadvertently by exacting payments from the Dominican Republic that meant, in practical terms, a default on the claims of any creditors not represented by the company. The SDIC's greed created a standoff with European creditors that presented Roosevelt with the choice of standing aside while European powers used intimidation, if not force, to get their slice of the Dominican pie, or to take on the task of settling that nation's financial crisis by intervening. Roosevelt chose intervention. The exact meaning of that intervention for the interests of the SDIC would become clear only over time.

9 From the Gilded Age to Dollar Diplomacy

The SDIC and the Roosevelt Corollary, 1904–1907

The San Domingo Improvement Company. . . . administered our Custom Houses, but never rendered an account of its financial stewardship. At last, without presenting its accounts it caused to be recognized (in its favor a debt of) $4,500,000, thanks to the complacency of the Washington Government and to the notorious weakness of the Dominican Government. . . .

The Dominican Congress and people . . . wish the Republic to re-establish its credit and good name by religiously paying its legitimate creditors, but they cannot consent to have the Nation despoiled of four millions in order to satiate the appetite of unscrupulous adventurers.
— Carlos Morales[1]

The delay . . . in the Dominican matter is annoying and exasperating; but in this respect it is on a par with Latin-American affairs generally, and there is need for the same patience and forbearance which every dealing with these childlike peoples requires.
— Jacob H. Hollander[2]

I hope the creditors will not be too greedy and kill the goose that is laying and will keep on laying — if kindly treated — the golden eggs.
— Thomas Dawson[3]

Theodore Roosevelt's response to the 1905 Dominican crisis went beyond what John Bassett Moore and the Improvement Company had hoped for. It was not immediately clear, however, in what way the intervention would affect the American company's interests. The SDIC, accustomed to stalwart support from Washington, was slow to realize the implications of the Roosevelt Corollary as it took practical shape in the form of U.S. officials collecting customs revenue in half a dozen Dominican ports. True, Roosevelt's February 15 message to the Senate declared that some of the claims against the Dominican Republic were inflated or even fraudulent — certainly a worrisome idea for the SDIC. Despite this warning sign, John Bassett Moore threw himself into the campaign to win Senate approval for the Dominican treaty.[4] It would take months for Moore to see that Roosevelt's strategic goals in the Dominican Republic had become distinct from those of the Improvement Company.

Moore's hope that the special status of the SDIC claims would be preserved under the receivership was bolstered on February 10, 1905, when the customs house of a second Dominican port was taken over by a U.S. naval officer on behalf of the SDIC, not as part of the newly proclaimed customs receivership.[5] On the ground in the Dominican Republic, the meaning of this second takeover was not so clear. An exasperated Admiral Sigsbee explained to Desiderio Arias, rebel leader of the remote city of Monte Christy, that he was under orders to take "charge of the custom house at Monte Christy, under the Arbitral Award in the case of the San Domingo Improvement Company." Sigsbee was at pains to clarify whose interests he was serving. "This incident has nothing to do with the terms of the recent convention, which also related to the custom-houses."[6]

The confusion in Santo Domingo was understandable, but in New York the blinders soon fell from Moore's eyes. The U.S. Senate, angered by Roosevelt's high-handed actions in the Caribbean, refused to approve the receivership. The President then implemented his plan by executive fiat, hoping that the Senate would be forced to approve the receivership later, when it had proven itself workable. The modus vivendi, as the arrangement was called, permitted American receivers to collect customs at all Dominican ports. The receivers would hold 55 percent of the revenues in escrow while the claims of creditors were reviewed. In the weeks following Roosevelt's announcement, the U.S. receiver took over the ports previously dedicated to the SDIC's claim, reducing the company to the status of the rest of the creditors of the Dominican Republic. The SDIC protested, but to no avail.[7] The company had lost control of the custom houses that at once symbolized the priority of its claims and guaranteed their regular payment.

Even as the United States undermined the company's special rights, Moore and Wells still fretted that the Dominican government might turn the intervention to its own advantage. Wells, as always thinking narrowly of the SDIC's interests, expected the worst from the Dominicans. "The whole scheme is intended by Morales largely as an attack on the Award," he wrote, ". . . . and we think it would be very wrong, if the plan [affirmed] by Prest. Roosevelt should be allowed to work out in favor of domestic creditors . . . to the great detriment of American creditors under a solemn Protocol and Award." Noting that the financial agent had stopped collecting customs for the company, Wells added that the SDIC should continue "protesting as we do against the violation by the United States Government of its own Protocol and Award."[8]

In late March, Roosevelt also announced that Jacob Hollander, a professor of economics at Johns Hopkins who had earlier set up Puerto Rico's financial system, would undertake a thorough investigation of the Dominican debt as a special agent for the United States. Roosevelt was, of course, aware of John Bassett Moore's qualifications and familiarity with Dominican finances. In fact, the President had asked Moore to prepare a brief history of Dominican finances that was sent to the Senate along with the Dominican protocol and Roosevelt's message of February 15. The President's choice of Hollander to study the Dominican debt suggests that he preferred to rely on the findings of a disinterested newcomer rather than a well-informed but compromised expert such as Moore.[9]

Meanwhile, months of public debate about the Dominican Republic had focused unwonted attention on the SDIC. Muckraking newspapers found in the Improvement Company a convenient, if elusive, villain. "The modus vivendi," reported the *Chicago Tribune*, reflecting the opprobrium that had begun to gather around the company, "shall displace and obliterate the most sinister feature of the whole [Dominican] affair — the special precedence given to the $4,500,000 claim of the ever mysterious 'Santo Domingo Improvement Company of New York.' "[10] British ambassador Hugh O'Beirne confided to the Marquis of Lansdowne that the rough handling of the SDIC "is not entirely the result of a lack of sufficient information on the part of the President and the Secretary of War. There exists a certain amount of hostility to the Companies in the Senate, and the President appears to have been unfavourably influenced by adverse reports, which Mr. Moore assures me are quite unfounded, regarding their dealings with the Santo Domingo Government."[11]

Moore expressed alarm about attacks on the SDIC in the American press and the President's apparent embrace of them. "I was astonished," Moore wrote privately, when I saw the President's statement, which implied that charges had been made against the Improvement Company. When I . . . inquired whether any charges had been made against the American Companies, he replied, "Well, yes; I believe a number of them." I then asked what they were, and the only thing he could specify was that Senator Burrows had repeated in the Senate a statement made to him by somebody to the effect that the Companies had put only $1,500 into the country.

Moore explained to the President that this was an old charge based on the fact that a company incorporated in New Jersey was required to have an initial capital stock of $1,500. That the President could repeat such a charge was, for Moore, frightening proof that the SDIC's influence was ebbing. "The President's statement must have been prepared in consultation with persons who were not familiar with the facts, since anyone in the Department of State could have told him no actual charges had ever been made against the American Companies."[12]

By the spring of 1905, Moore and the Improvement Company realized that their claims were being overwhelmed by Roosevelt's commitment to harmony among the great powers, fair play for international capital, and stability in the Dominican Republic. The president had moved the game to a new, international terrain, and they scrambled to follow. If Roosevelt wanted to play the great power card, the SDIC would seek to trump him with Britain, the greatest power of all.

The officers of the SDIC had a long and close relationship with the Council of Foreign Bondholders in London. In April, Moore sent a draft memo to the CFB outlining the grievances of the American and British creditors and calling on the State Department to uphold their rights.[13] In May, the British ambassador to the United States, Hugh J. O'Beirne, sent the State Department a letter based on Moore's memorandum. He noted that "some anxiety has been aroused in the minds of the British shareholders" because Roosevelt's executive order "does not contain any explicit recognition of the special rights" of the SDIC. In a personal meeting with Secretary of War William Howard Taft, a disappointed O'Beirne learned that "the United States Government might properly re-open the question of the capital amount which the Improvement Company were entitled to receive from Santo Domingo." In other words, the SDIC's demand for $4.5 million was suddenly in doubt. The blow was hardly softened when the

State Department later advised O'Beirne that "the President is unable to recognize any special rights and privileges of the said companies over any other creditors, American or foreign."[14] For the first time a high American official stated outright that the SDIC's award might legitimately be revised if found to be excessive.

Moore hoped that Taft's position did not represent that of the President. "Judge Taft no doubt was brought into the case without any prior acquaintance with its details," he wrote optimistically, "though he may have seen what was published in the Washington *Post*, which as I am advised, contained several absurd attacks upon the Improvement Company."[15] But Moore would not be able to close his eyes much longer to the fact that U.S. policy, not just the attitudes of a few officials, had shifted against the SDIC.

In the meantime, the Dominican Congress had declared that the protocol and award under which the SDIC had been collecting customs were of no effect because, among other reasons, the American companies had never submitted a general rendition of their accounts. In a long letter to John Hay, Moore denied the charges of the Dominican Congress and warned that the Dominican Congress "seeks to take advantage" of the receivership by negating the SDIC's award. The arbitral award was "a definitive settlement," Moore said, adding that all the SDIC requested was that the Dominican Government "be informed that the protocol and the award cannot be invalidated by the act of that Government."[16]

The State Department's reply was discouraging. W. L. Penfield, the department's legal counsel who was well known to Moore, replied that "it will not be possible for Judge Taft to consider your personal letter drafted to the Secretary of State" since Taft was preparing to leave for the Philippines. "I do not think that I ought to discuss the matter with Secretary Hay or to ask him to give it consideration on account of the state of his health."[17] (Hay died on July 1, 1905). Moore wrote an exasperated reply to Penfield. The SDIC's request "is simple, and so carefully guarded, so as not to commit the Department to any ulterior question." If the State Department deferred its response until the fall, as Penfield suggested, "the Dominican Government would infer, and naturally so, that the Department had accepted the resolution." Moore ended on a note of injury: "It seems to me that it would be only a matter of simple justice to the American Companies, who, in the recent transactions, have never had a hearing or any opportunity to be heard in regard to their rights, that this much should be done."[18]

In his confidential reply, Penfield informed Moore that his letter to the secretary could not be located, but that when it was found, he would lay it before Taft or Roosevelt himself, if Moore so desired.[19] A few days later, Moore received a boilerplate answer from Acting Secretary of State Herbert H. D. Peirce advising him that his (now recovered) letter had been given to the President, "who has directed the Department to say that the matter will be given due consideration."[20]

Moore's long history as successful mediator between the SDIC and the State Department was coming to an end. Company officials now learned that they had misunderstood the mission of Jacob Hollander, the special agent investigating the Dominican debt. After a three-hour meeting at the SDIC's offices in New York, Moore reported that Hollander "almost wholly confined the discussion . . . to an effort to induce the companies to commit themselves to the surrender and abandonment of all their legal rights, . . . and to come in on the same basis with other creditors."[21] The government, through Hollander, intended not simply to study the debt but actually to seek a settlement among the bondholders, a duty that became official some months later.[22] To the SDIC, that could only signal official hostility to their claims.

Hollander's suspicions about the SDIC had been fed by Roosevelt himself. In a private letter to the economist the President warned that if the statements of George R. Colton, director of the new customs receivership, "about this Improvement Company are true we must take sharp measures to disassociate the Government from all responsibility for the debt." Roosevelt added that he was "always afraid of seeming to back any big company which has financial interests in one of these South American states."[23] Hollander's doubts about the SDIC took the form of dozens of queries about the company's past, which the economist submitted to John T. Abbott. The questions plumbed the depths of the SDIC's business in the Dominican Republic, asking about the origin of the Dominican debt and the destination of hundreds of thousands of dollars in loans raised by the SDIC. Hollander often followed up by asking for clarification of Abbott's replies.

The directors of the SDIC betrayed anxiety as Hollander completed his investigation. On September 20, 1905, Abbott asked Moore to write Hollander "in your capacity as legal Counsel for the Companies, calling his attention to the fact that we have now endeavored to fully comply with all his desires." If Hollander had "encountered testimony which seriously conflicts with that which we have presented," Abbott said, "it would seem just and fair" that the company get a chance to respond.[24] Moore wrote Hollander along the lines Abbott suggested, concluding his letter with a collegial reference to the rigors of the recently begun academic term. Hollander replied that Abbott had responded "with the utmost courtesy and promptness," adding that whenever the SDIC's explanations were "at variance" with other evidence, Hollander "put the apparent contradiction" before Abbott "with the result that it has been either adequately explained or the sources of misapprehension ascertained."[25]

Reassured by the friendly tone, neither Abbott nor Moore anticipated problems from the Hollander report. "There seems to be nothing unfavorable in the air just now," Abbott concluded in late September.[26] In early October, SDIC president Smith M. Weed alerted Moore that Hollander's report had reached the Secretary of State. Weed believed the company still wielded enough influence to demand special consideration from the President. "I think it is due from the President to you," Weed told Moore,

> that even if he is not going to give out the report, which we hope he will not do, that he should in confidence permit you to see it. I trust that if he has not received it the Secretary of State will let you see it. . . .
>
> The making of this report, it seems to us, furnishes you with a good excuse for going down there and finding out what the report does say and what our status is at present with Mr. Root and the President.[27]

Weed had misjudged the company's standing with the President and Elihu Root, the new Secretary of State. Hollander's report, which reached Roosevelt in October 1905, went far toward completing the destruction of the SDIC's image. In one section, Hollander summarized the Dominican government's charges against the company: "looseness and fraud" in the administration of customs; "wastes and irregularities" in bond issues; "incompetency and extravagance" in railroad construction; dereliction of duties as trustee of the bondholders; and an "unsatisfactory" rendering of accounts. The SDIC's "presence and activity in Santo Domingo have been a continuous embarrassment and impediment to the course of orderly and economical government."[28]

Hollander declined to pass judgment on the charges against the SDIC on the grounds that doing so lay beyond the scope of his inquiry. Yet he offered his "very decided personal conviction" that the SDIC claims "should be subject to as careful and rigid investigation" as the rest of the debt. He asserted that "there are many episodes in the history of the Improvement

Company which would be looked at askance by conservative American financiers," softening the comment by adding that "Santo Domingo in the past thirty-five years has not been a place where conservative financiers have flourished."[29]

In arguing against special treatment for the SDIC, Hollander showed that he fully understood the tendency of Roosevelt's new Latin American policy. "The United States proposes to assume before the eyes of the whole world the rôle of disinterested receiver and trustee" for the Dominican Republic. It would be "to the last degree unfortunate" if the "principal American creditor," the SDIC, were "uniquely exempt from . . . scrutiny." In a confidential attachment to the report, Hollander criticized the longstanding official support for the SDIC. "The subordinate role of backing up or tacitly supporting the contracts of a financial corporation is, in the light of past events, neither a dignified nor a promising one for the United States to assume in Dominican affairs," he chided.[30] The key word was "subordinate." Under the customs receivership, the U.S. government would assume direct responsibility for collecting the republic's revenue, orchestrating future Dominican loans, and supervising the American companies that refinanced the debt.

In keeping with the high-minded tone of his report, Hollander began to construct a refunding plan that would raise Dominican finance to a new plane. His negotiations involved some of the leading investment banks of the time, including National City Bank, Kuhn, Loeb & Co., William Salomon & Co., and Morton Trust. Hollander worked with Jacob Schiff, Charles Conant, and William Salomon, among the most imposing figures of American finance, men who had little in common with Smith M. Weed. The companies were eager to take part in the Dominican refinancing.[31]

"It would be a splendid thing," Hollander told Charles Allen of Morton Trust, "for the Dominican Government to have its financiering placed on the high level which connection with the Morton Trust would mean." The effect of a "high class financial institution" assuming such a role would go well beyond the Dominican case. "Why should not the Morton Trust Company," Hollander proposed,

> under your guidance become the instrument for the fiscal reorganization first of San Domingo, and thereafter for other Latin-American governments that — if we should only turn the trick well — will surely have recourse to the United States to have done for them what we have already done for Cuba and are now asked to do for San Domingo.

You know Latin-American conditions and temperaments, and Mr. Root is sponsor for the policy.[32]

Allen heartily agreed. If "some well-established financial institution" handled the Dominican refinancing, "it would establish a prestige for a broad way of doing things." The question of reputation was especially important for "a loan of that magnitude, embracing as it would a question of policy, perhaps more important than the loan itself."[33]

The new Dominican loan would avoid all the pitfalls that had spelled disaster for the Improvement Company. Instead of the sporadic, informal support Washington had given the SDIC, the success of the new arrangement would "rest entirely upon the fact that the United States is to administer the customs of the country," as Hollander advised Roosevelt.[34] Furthermore, the New York banks wanted assurances that the Dominican tariff would not be altered in a way that would reduce the revenue dedicated to paying a new loan. "With the experience of investors in San Dominican bonds," wrote Jacob H. Schiff of the investment banking house Kuhn, Loeb, "no one, I believe, will touch the proposed new Bonds unless the United States will undertake to look to the sufficiency of the customs tariff, to its proper collection and application to the service of the debt, and unless the Bondholders can look to the United States for this, no bankers, who value their reputation should undertake to sell the Proposed bonds to the public."[35] Finally, any new financial arrangement was contingent upon Senate approval of the Dominican treaty. The modus vivendi was a stopgap measure that collected and escrowed Dominican customs. The new Dominican loan, however, needed the rock-solid foundation of long-term U.S. government commitment to the adjustment which only a treaty could give.

Hollander and Allen shared a broad vision of the role of finance in the ambitious geopolitical project of the United States at the beginning of the twentieth century. SDIC officials were clearly outclassed. The company knew that opposing a government-sponsored arrangement put them in an awkward position, yet they steadfastly refused to give up their claim to priority. With the modus vivendi still in effect, and 55 percent of Dominican customs revenue accumulating in National City Bank in New York, Moore took a long vacation from the SDIC. In August 1906, he received a detailed letter from John T. Abbott about Washington's efforts to devise a plan that would satisfy all the creditors. Elihu Root, Jacob Hollander, William Cohen of the Corporation of Foreign Bondholders, and Dominican Minister of

Finance Federico Velasquez had met in Washington, but could not reach agreement. Officials of the SDIC were notably absent from the meeting. Hollander objected to a plan suggested by the British bondholders "because he said it was simply a scheme to keep the Award at par" — that is, to reinstate the SDIC's special rights to Dominican revenue. "At any rate there does not seem to be anything for the American Companies to do," Abbott concluded fatalistically, "as our participation in any scheme or our fathering any scheme would be the easiest way to prevent its being adopted by Mr. Hollender [sic]."[36] The SDIC and their British allies remained the main obstacles to reaching an agreement.

By September 1906, Hollander had the elements of a refunding plan in place. Kuhn, Loeb & Company would float a new loan for $20 million to be applied to both the internal and external Dominican debt, after reduction and consolidation, and contingent upon Senate approval of the customs receivership. On paper, the plan looked favorable to the SDIC, which was promised 90 percent of the value of its claims, while other foreign creditors got only 50 percent. In a crude reflection of the relative power of the different lenders, much of the debt held by Dominicans themselves was to be paid at only 10 percent. The SDIC directors insisted, however, that they had already radically scaled down their claims when, in 1903, they accepted a valuation of only $4.5 million for their assets. After studying Hollander's plan in detail, John T. Abbott noted with disgust that "Americans are 16 percent worse off than if they were Belgians."[37] The company refused to accept the additional 10 percent reduction.

Hollander was irritated by the SDIC's intransigence and the overvaluation of its assets, especially the Central Dominican Railroad and the national bank. At one point Hollander "spoke of the Railway as '40 miles of old junk' and the Bank as 'one that practically never opened its doors.' "[38] Meanwhile, he obtained the agreement of the European bondholders, with the exception of the British, who continued to work in tandem with the SDIC.[39]

As Hollander's plan was worked into a treaty between the United States and the Dominican Republic, the SDIC came under intense pressure to go along with the other creditors. The American company was the sole stumbling block to an accord that would once and for all settle a long-festering international problem.[40] Moore understood the implications of continuing to thwart a financial rescue organized by the U.S. government, and in January 1907, the company finally acquiesced. Moore painted the event as the surrender of private interest to a greater good: "The American Companies, recognizing the high purposes of the Government of the United States and the importance of rehabilitating the finances of San Domingo . . . deem it to be their duty to make the sacrifice requested of them."[41]

In a plaintive telegram to London, however, the Americans made clear that they had little choice in the matter, and called on their allies in the CFB to accept the settlement.

> Everything has been exhausted. . . . If the offer is not accepted will destroy not only financial arrangement but it is most probable also plans of Government which likely to involve high interests foreign policy. There is reason to fear Government would be unfriendly and no support can be expected from. In which case it will result in disaster.[42]

The British bondholders reluctantly accepted Hollander's plan. In February 1907, the U.S. Senate ratified the treaty that embodied the refunding scheme, and in May the Dominican congress followed suit.

Although Roosevelt strongly backed the arrangement, Kuhn, Loeb & Co. were not satisfied with the President's personal commitment and sought reassurances from John Bassett Moore. "Some of our European friends," the financiers explained, wondered "how far the present Convention would be binding on any future Government of the United States." What would happen if a new president were to "shirk the duty of collecting the revenues" or "decline to enforce the rights of bondholders"? Moore replied that the $20 million loan would be secured "in the amplest manner" and that "the duty and obligation of the United States . . . could not be affected . . . by any change of Government either in the United States or in Santo Domingo."[43] The new scheme would not rest on the personalist arrangements that had characterized the SDIC's operations.

Before the loan plan took final shape, a financial panic struck New York, and Kuhn, Loeb withdrew from the field. Hollander dutifully assembled a new package through the Morton Trust Company, which finally became effective in 1908. The refinancing plan ended the SDIC's business in the Dominican Republic, and the company passed out of existence shortly thereafter.

The SDIC had survived through its political influence both in Washington and Santo Domingo. When that influence withered, first in the Dominican Republic and later in the United States, the SDIC was doomed.

In spite of the Improvement Company's name and its genuine if short-lived attempt to modernize the Dominican Republic, it had neither the resources nor the vision to reshape Dominican society. That project began haltingly with the customs receivership of 1905 and in earnest with the U.S. marine occupation that began in 1916 and implemented many of the reforms that John Bassett Moore had outlined more than a decade earlier.[44]

Although his unique species of politician-capitalist may have been destined for the trash bin of history, Smith M. Weed, the individual, lived on. It is impossible to calculate the ultimate profit or loss of the SDIC. At the time of the 1908 refunding, however, local papers in upstate New York reported that the president of the SDIC had reaped a bonanza. The settlement "will net him half a million," the *Plattsburgh Sentinel* reported bluntly, a "fact that will be learned with pleasure by every one of Mr. Weed's numerous friends."[45] At least temporarily, the windfall had restored Weed's position as *caudillo* of the Adirondacks.

The transition from old-fashioned cronyism to Progressive rationalism was not instantaneous. Not even the enlightened Jacob H. Hollander emerged unsullied from the Santo Domingo affair. In 1908, while he was still acting as financial agent for the United States, Hollander collected a $100,000 fee from the Dominican government. Secretary of State Elihu Root was furious. Hollander vigorously defended his action to Root and to a congressional inquiry, but his dignity and reputation remained tarnished.[46]

For John Bassett Moore, the Dominican affair was a minor episode in a long and distinguished career. By seeking to square the SDIC's profit motive with an increasingly global U.S. foreign policy, Moore had tried to serve two masters, and failed. When Roosevelt moved Dominican policy to a new plane, he left behind the small-minded program of the SDIC. Unlike Smith M. Weed, however, Moore could make the transition to the new world order. For the rest of his long life, Moore remained a prolific legal scholar, indefatigable advocate of international arbitration, and counsel to major international corporations such as Standard Oil. In 1921 he reaped the ultimate reward for his high-mindedness when he was chosen first American judge to the World Court at the Hague.[47]

Conclusion

The dozen years from the Improvement Company's arrival in Santo Domingo in 1893 to the creation of the American customs receivership in 1905 traced the waning of the solvency and sovereignty of the Dominican Republic. The period also witnessed a fundamental shift in the way Washington handled the role of private business interests in furthering U.S. foreign policy, abandoning an earlier, ineffective form of Dollar Diplomacy and inventing a new, progressive strategy as a way to remake chaotic and apparently ungovernable tropical societies. That shift was proclaimed publicly in the Roosevelt Corollary, which committed the United States to intervene in Latin America when necessary to protect "civilization," implicitly defined as the payment of international loans. On a practical level, the new policy took shape in the customs receivership and the close collaboration among U.S. government officials, financial experts, and New York bankers that made the plan work, at least at first.[1]

Historians have long ignored the role of the San Domingo Improvement Company in creating the economic and political conditions that prompted U.S. government intervention in the Dominican Republic in 1905, just as they have ignored the powerful influence the company exerted in Washington in pursuit of its special interests. The Improvement Company's network of businessmen, diplomats, politicians, and lawyers, including Frederick William Holls, Smith M. Weed, John T. Abbott, and most emphatically John Bassett Moore, bridged the lofty world of diplomacy and the sordid world of Latin American finance. Lacking the resources commanded by the large multinational firms emerging at the time, the company served Washington's strategic interests by privately expanding U.S. influence in the Caribbean. By 1905, however, the SDIC had proven to be both an obsolete business organization and a retrograde influence on the foreign policy establishment. As the United States emerged as a genuine superpower, American policy evolved from unthinking support of private interests to a critical, global vision that freed policymakers from the thrall of the SDIC.[2]

Although this underlying shift provides the political and economic context in which U.S.-Dominican relations gain meaning, the episode examined here is not simply a case study that reflects a broad change in policy. The SDIC itself propelled Washington's reconsideration of its earlier policy. The company's egregious conduct in Santo Domingo forced Washington to confront the drawbacks of delegating foreign policy to a private firm. And precisely because the Improvement Company had so much influence in Washington, it forced Theodore Roosevelt to rethink the effects of private influence. The conferences between John Bassett Moore and the president over the meaning of the Roosevelt Corollary are the most concrete expression of the way that the Improvement Company influenced Roosevelt's new departure — negatively, as an example of how *not* to make foreign policy.

The Dominican customs receivership that Roosevelt imposed in 1905 replaced the unstable and destructive policy of support for the SDIC with a revamped and thoroughly progressive version of Dollar Diplomacy. For the meager assets of the Improvement Company, Roosevelt substituted the deep pockets of major New York investment banks. To prevent the fast-and-loose financial transactions that had characterized the Improvement Company's bond flotations, Roosevelt imposed government supervision on the lending institutions that took charge of Dominican finances. In fact, the President had financial expert Jacob Hollander study the Dominican debt and reduce the inflated sums demanded by the country's numerous creditors — including the Improvement Company — before negotiating a new, $20 million loan. That loan had a favorable rate of interest because of the security provided by U.S. government control of Dominican finances.

The SDIC disaster also demonstrated to Roosevelt that a private company did not have sufficient coercive power to enforce its nominal control of Dominican finances, even with regular visits by U.S. warships. To correct that weakness, Roosevelt stationed American officials in Dominican custom houses and posted U.S. naval vessels in Dominican ports. In the years after

1905, the American intervention was irresistibly drawn into supplying the elements of "stateness" that the Dominican Republic so notably lacked. The receivership's use of U.S. naval vessels and its creation of a Frontier Guard on the Haitian border, both originally intended to be used to interdict smuggling, quickly became important props of the Dominican state. The Dominican government "soon came to depend on the [revenue] cutters to quickly combat distant revolutionary outbreaks," while the Frontier Guard "began to serve the dual purpose of a quasi-police force for the central government."[3]

The American side of the SDIC's Dominican venture is only one part of the story told here. The company arrived in the Caribbean proclaiming its mission of modernizing the Dominican economy and state. Both Heureaux and the SDIC wanted progress, if progress means commercializing agriculture, reducing peasant self-sufficiency, boosting imports and exports, and increasing government revenue. The company and the dictator failed to transform Dominican social life, however, and the limits on the exercise of even overwhelming power is a theme that unites different aspects of this study. To read its contracts, the SDIC enjoyed effective control over the Dominican treasury. In practice, Heureaux largely evaded the American company's supervision by creating a network of local and European creditors that lay beyond the reach of the SDIC. Yet in spite of his remarkable success in turning the tables on the Americans, Heureaux was far from omnipotent. The dictator's attempts to force march a wary peasantry from subsistence to commercial agriculture faced such stubborn resistance that, in the end, he looked elsewhere for the resources needed to hold together his regime. The SDIC's losing struggle to control Dominican finances and Heureaux's frustrated campaign to fortify the state and put the masses on the road to progress reflect the debility of formal structures of power.

Formal claims to power frequently met informal obstacles at the level of state-to-state relations as well. The asymmetries of wealth and power between two nations could hardly be greater than they were, and are, between the Dominican Republic and the United States.[4] This vast disparity of power enabled Americans to define the economic and political arena in which the Caribbean's destiny was determined in the late 1800s — by granting or denying loans, by opening metropolitan markets to goods from some nations but not others, by annexing, establishing protectorates over, or simply ignoring different states in the region. Against the flow of power outward from the center, however, ran a countercurrent that kept metropolitan elites from simply imposing predetermined outcomes on Caribbean states and populations. While the great powers enframed small, poor, and weak nations like the Dominican Republic within the global capitalist and interstate systems, they had more difficulty determining what happened inside that frame. Not even the brazen use of force necessarily brought results. Louis Pérez, Jr., notes the failure of U.S. designs in Cuba after 1898 even though "the island was occupied militarily and governed by the United States."[5] The same would prove true in the Dominican Republic.

The second half of this study analyzes how the U.S. government was drawn into the vacuum created by the withering away of the Dominican state under the impositions of the SDIC. Washington was far from eager to assume new commitments in Santo Domingo, preferring to achieve its goals indirectly and on the cheap through the SDIC. While the United States almost always sought to evade the cost, responsibility, and political controversy that came with outright territorial control, this evasion need not be attributed to benign commitment to self-rule, as some diplomatic historians have assumed.[6] "Refusals to annex are no proof of reluctance to control," John Gallagher and Ronald Robinson pointed out long ago in the British context. If the United States sought to avoid formal colonialism, the reason, Emily and Norman Rosenberg suggest, "lies less in some anticolonial commitment or exceptional past history than in the availability of neocolonial substitutes."[7] Although it ultimately proved unsatisfactory, for more than a decade the SDIC served precisely as such a neocolonial substitute. The failure of the SDIC's neocolonial option led to the creation of a more effective, state-directed mechanism after 1905, yet one that remained shy of outright annexation or military occupation, at least until 1916.

Despite the increasing involvement of the U.S. government in Dominican affairs after 1901, the process was not simply the unilateral imposition of imperial control. After Heureaux's assassination in 1899, Dominican leaders struggled to assemble the elements of "stateness" from whatever internal and external resources they could tap. They saw direct U.S. intervention as an alternative to exploitation by the SDIC and used U.S. naval forces as a supplement to the feeble state power at their command. Naturally, the interests of American policymakers and Dominican politicians did not fully converge. At first, American diplomatic and military intervention supported the SDIC; the goal of stabilizing the Dominican Republic was subordinate to seeing that the American creditors were repaid. Slowly, Washington realized that backing up the SDIC contradicted the goal of imposing order.

As the United States committed itself to propping up the Morales regime and lending its coercive power to the Dominican state, the disordering political and economic effects of enforcing the Improvement Company's claims became clearer.

The crystallization of differences between U.S. policy and the goals of the New York company by the end of 1904 did not mean that the Washington had become hostile to capitalism, however, but rather that both American capitalism and the American state had changed. The Dominican intervention is thus a significant episode in the American state's assertion of supremacy over private corporations in the name of a greater good, both for the state and for American capitalism in general. Just as some corporations trampled the public good at home, Theodore Roosevelt believed that the Improvement Company had failed to operate its Caribbean business responsibly. The evolution of Washington's position from defender of the SDIC to opponent of its policies paralleled a larger change as the Gilded Age gave way to the Progressive Era.

When Roosevelt made the SDIC a pariah, he turned his back on earlier State Department practices and took a step toward the rationalization of foreign policy that would proceed during Elihu Root's tenure at the State Department.[8] The new structure of financial oversight defused a simmering international crisis by guaranteeing a level playing field for all the creditors of the Dominican government. By implementing the *modus vivendi* without Senate approval and by abrogating the Improvement Company's arbitral award, Roosevelt took strong, controversial, even doubtfully constitutional action. In one stroke he asserted the primacy of the executive over Congress in foreign policy and the authority of the federal government over private corporations in defense of the public good. The presidential victories were not final, of course, and struggles over the same ground would continue, but they signaled the direction in which the American state would develop.

Roosevelt's handling of the Dominican crisis demonstrates that foreign policy and domestic economic developments moved in stride, raising the country's "ideological horizon from that of the short-term, the single-interest, and the provincial to the long-term, the multi-interest, the national, and the international," in the words of Martin Sklar.[9] At home and abroad, Roosevelt was moving toward what Sklar calls a "statist" approach to corporate power. Roosevelt's new policy meant that "the substitute for the dispersed power of the past was to be a vigorous national democracy that subordinated economic power to public policy . . . implemented by an executive acting as the steward of the public welfare."[10] The subordination of private interest to public policy is precisely what Roosevelt achieved when he replaced the crude venality of the Improvement Company with a government-sponsored and government-supervised receivership that promised to stabilize the Dominican Republic and defuse conflicts among the great powers. Yet the new version of Dollar Diplomacy Roosevelt invented was based not on the expulsion of U.S. business interests from the republic, but on an even more formidable intrusion of U.S. capitalism in the Dominican Republic.

As an episode in the history of imperialism, the case of the SDIC in Santo Domingo is *sui generis*. Since it commanded modest financial resources, the SDIC did not embody surplus American capital going abroad. On close examination, the SDIC did not even represent the penetration of capitalist market forces that John Gallagher and Ronald Robinson, Eric Hobsbawm, and Walter LaFeber, among others, have identified as a disruptive force in many parts of the nonindustrial world, although the company clearly favored the commercialization of Dominican agriculture. The operation of the SDIC was indeed destructive, but not for its direct effect on Dominican markets and social structures. The company did not infiltrate the economy so much as the state, which was a willing accomplice in bankrupting the treasury and eventually the economy at large.[11]

The San Domingo Improvement Company possessed some of the traits of "modern capitalist-investment imperialism," which Martin Sklar has contrasted with settler or territorial imperialism. The more modern form of imperialism encompassed a project that went to the heart of the host society's internal affairs to transform class relations, social structures, and political and financial institutions.[12] The SDIC sought just such a transformation but fell far short of its ambitions. The customs receivership, combining private investment with U.S. intervention, moved the Dominican Republic further along the road to "progress," and for a few years was held up as a model for making over a tropical society. But by 1911 the weaknesses of the customs receivership had begun to show, as the assassination of President Ramón Cáceres opened the door to another series of revolutions, once thought to have been rendered impossible by U.S. control of the Dominican treasury. The search for stability would lead to a U.S. marine occupation that lasted from 1916 to 1924, bringing an even more heavy-handed reform of Dominican society. One legacy of the centralization of power achieved by the marines was the rise of Rafael Trujillo to power in 1930, creating a brutal dictatorship that would last 31 years. The American campaign to bring stability, prosperity, and democracy to the Dominican people, erratically begun by the SDIC, reinvented by Theodore Roosevelt's customs receivership, and then imposed by direct military rule, never worked. Only at the end of the twentieth century, after the receiverships, occupations, and dictatorships were over, did Dominicans themselves begin to make progress toward those goals.

Notes

Introduction

1. *NYT*, 22 Jan. 1905, 1.
2. On U.S. economic growth, see David Pletcher, *The Diplomacy of Trade and Investment* (Columbia: University of Missouri Press, 1998), 9fn; on the U.S. Navy, see George W. Baer, *One Hundred Years of Sea Power* (Stanford: Stanford University Press, 1994), 40.
3. William T. Stead, *The Americanisation of the World, or the Trend of the Twentieth Century* (London: Review of Reviews, 1902), X.
4. Pletcher, *Diplomacy of Trade*, 148–79.
5. The amendment limited Cuba's power to contract loans or sign treaties and allowed U.S. intervention to ensure "a government adequate for the protection of life, property, and individual liberty." Robert Holden and Eric Zolov, eds., *Latin America and the United States: A Documentary History* (New York: Oxford University Press, 2000), 82.
6. *Collier's* vol. 34, no. 19 (4 Feb. 1905), 12, and *Harper's* vol. 49, no. 2511 (4 Feb. 1905), 148.
7. Emily S. Rosenberg, *Financial Missionaries to the World: The Politics and Culture of Dollar Diplomacy, 1900–1930* (Cambridge: Harvard University Press, 1999), 60.
8. *NYT*, 20 Feb. 1893, 6.
9. "The revenue of the whole Republic may be said to be not only mortgaged to this Company, but under their immediate control," according to the British vice consul in Santo Domingo. Printed pamphlet,"Diplomatic and Consular

Reports on Trade and Finance, Dominican Republic, Report for the Year 1893, Trade of Santo Domingo, No. 1373," May 1894, FO 23/93.

10. In Roosevelt's annual message to congress in December 1904, he declared, "Chronic wrongdoing, or an impotence which results in a general loosening of the ties of civilized society, may in America, as elsewhere, ultimately require intervention by some civilized nation, and in the Western Hemisphere the adherence of the United States to the Monroe Doctrine may force the United States, however reluctantly, in flagrant cases of such wrongdoing or impotence, to the exercise of an international police power." *Presidential Addresses and State Papers of Theodore Roosevelt, Part Three* (New York: Kraus Reprint Co., 1970), 175–77.

11. One part of that transition was Secretary of State John Hay's formulation of the Open Door Policy. See William Appleman Williams, *The Tragedy of American Diplomacy* (New York: Dell, 1962), 16–50, and Walter LaFeber, *Cambridge History of American Foreign Relations*, vol. 2 (New York: Cambridge, 1993), 169–77.

12. *Presidential Addresses*, 260.

13. Rosenberg, *Financial Missionaries*, especially 56–60.

14. Richard H. Collin, *Theodore Roosevelt's Caribbean* (Baton Rouge: Louisiana State Univ., 1990), 11.

15. J.A. Hobson, *Imperialism* (London: J. Nisbet, 1902), 48–49, 79.

16. S. Nelson Drew, *NSC — 68: Forging the Strategy of Containment* (Washington: National Defense University, 1994), 54.

17. James L. Huskey describes a group of expatriates characterized by cultural openness and alienation from their national communities in "The Cosmopolitan Connection: Americans and Chinese in Shanghai during the Interwar Years," *Diplomatic History* 11 (Summer 1987), 227–32.

18. See William Becker, *The Dynamics of Business-Government Relations* (Chicago: University of Chicago Press, 1982).

19. The relationship is similar in many ways to the bond between French bankers and the viceroy of Egypt described by David S. Landes in *Bankers and Pashas: International Finance and Economic Imperialism in Egypt* (New York: Harper & Row, 1969).

1. The Gilded Age Goes Abroad

1. Bureau of the American Republics, *Handbook of Santo Domingo* (Washington: Government Printing Office, 1894), 43.

2. Heureaux to I. Mendel, 14 Feb. and 15 May 1898, tomos 65 and 66, UH.

3. *NYT*, 11 Feb. 1893, 6.

4. At the time of the SDIC's takeover of the Dominican debt, the United States was again trying to negotiate the lease of Samaná Bay, as discussed in the next chapter. For the near-cession of the bay in 1869–70, see William Javier Nelson, *Almost a Territory: America's Attempt to Annex the Dominican Republic* (Newark: University of Delaware Press, 1990), W. Stull Holt, *Treaties Defeated by the Senate* (Gloucester, MA: Peter Smith, 1964), and Charles Callan Tansill, *The United States an Santo Domingo, 1798–1873* (Gloucester, MA: Peter Smith, 1967).

5. For the growing importance of American capital in the Dominican Republic's fastest growing export sector, see Michel Baud, "The Origins of Capitalist Agriculture in the Dominican Republic," *Latin American Research Review* 22, no. 2 (1987), 143. Frederick William Holls to Andrew Dickson White, 27 Feb. 1893, Box 20, Letterbook v. 19, FWH.

6. See Julio G. Campillo Pérez, *Historia Electoral Dominicana, 1848–1986* (Santo Domingo: Editora Corripio, 1986), 538–42.

7. The *Gaceta Oficial*, official voice of the government, reprinted verbatim the SDIC's 2 Aug. 1892 letter to the Dominican government, as well as the reply of Sánchez rejecting the transfer. Ministro de Hacienda y Comercio to Smith W. Weed [sic] and George S. Bixby, 18 Aug. 1892, and to Westendorp & Ca., 18 Aug. 1892, legajo 35, MHC.

8. [Charles W. Wells?] to J. F. Sánchez and T. Cordero y Bido, 16 Aug. 1892, legajo 35, MHC.

9. According to Jacob Hollander, Charles W. Wells visited the Dominican Republic early in 1892, even before the SDIC was formed to buy out Westendorp & Co. Hollander, manuscript of Report, Jacob Hollander Papers, National Archives, Box 3, 10.

10. "President Heureaux's needs were getting too heavy for Westendorp, particularly after the Barings of London failed, and he was anxious to be relieved of his job. A friend of Mr. Wells abroad knew of Westendorp's desire and communicated with the New York lawyer," the *New York Tribune* later reported. *NYTr*, 17 Jan. 1901.

11. *NYT*, 18 Dec. 1892, 16.

12. Holls to Andrew Dickson White, 27 Feb. 1893, FWH.

13. See Jacob Hollander, "Report on the Debt of Santo Domingo," 6; William H. Wynne, *State Insolvency and Foreign Bondholders* (New Haven: Yale University Press, 1951), 2: 212–17; John Bassett Moore, "Outline History: San Domingo Improvement Co. and Allied Companies," JBM; and César Herrera, *Finanzas*, 1: 204–23. The contracts are reprinted in *Colección de Leyes, Decretos y Resoluciones Emanados de los Poderes Legislativos y Ejecutivos de la República Dominicana*, Tomo 13 (Santo Domingo: Imprenta del Listin Diario, 1929); Holls to White, 27 Feb. 1893, FWH.

14. The *New York Times* reported that the "the rebels style themselves anti-annexationists, meaning that they are opposed to the annexation of San Domingo to the United States, which they charge President Heureaux with attempting to bring about." *NYT*, 8 April 1893, 8.

15. *NYT*, 18 Dec. 1892, 16.

16. See, for example, David Healy, *Drive to Hegemony* (Madison: University of Wisconsin Press, 1988); Robert Beisner, *From the Old Diplomacy to the New, 1865–1900* (Arlington Heights, Il.: Harlan Davidson, 1986); and Walter LaFeber, *The New Empire* (Ithaca: Cornell University Press, 1963).

17. None of the standard studies of United States-Dominican relations, the Roosevelt corollary, and the customs receivership seriously attempt to investigate the role of the San Domingo Improvement Company. See Sumner Wells, *Naboth's Vineyard* (New York: Payson & Clarke, 1928); Dana C. Munro, *Intervention and Dollar Diplomacy in the Caribbean, 1900–1921* (Princeton: Princeton University Press, 1964); Lester Langley, *Struggle for the American Mediterranean* (Athens: University of Georgia Press, 1976); David Healy, *Drive to Hegemony* (Madison: University of Wisconsin Press, 1988); and Richard H. Collin, *Theodore Roosevelt's Caribbean* (Baton Rouge: Louisiana State University Press, 1990).

18. In recent years, the formulation of public policy in an age of unbridled capitalism has been the subject of innovative study by Martin Sklar, Stephen Skowronek, L. Ray Gunn, Richard L. McCormick and other scholars. Martin Sklar, *The Corporate Reconstruction of American Capitalism, 1890–1916* (New York: Cambridge University Press, 1988) and *The United States as a Developing Country* (New York: Cambridge University Press, 1992); Stephen Skowronek, *Building a New American State* (New York: Cambridge University Press, 1982); L. Ray Gunn, *The Decline of Authority* (Ithaca: Cornell University Press, 1988); Richard L. McCormick, *The Party Period and Public Policy* (New York: Oxford University Press, 1986).

19. New York State pioneered new legal mechanisms, particularly general incorporation and free banking and train laws, that opened the market to all comers, making "benefits available to everyone who met certain requirements rather than to favored recipients only." L. Ray Gunn, *Decline*, 208; Lee Benson, *Merchants, Farmers and Railroads* (Cambridge: Harvard University Press, 1955), vii–viii, 1–6.

20. By the 1890s, the destructive effects of ungoverned capitalism had become so destabilizing that new, anticompetitive ideas began to take root among forward-looking bankers, corporate officers, labor leaders, and economists. Corporate leaders and Progressive reformers succeeded in taming the worst effects of competition, ushering in a new "corporate-administered" economy through what

Sklar calls the "corporate reconstruction of American capitalism." Sklar, *Corporate Reconstruction*, 52, 25.

21. James C. Scott, in a comparative study of corruption, argues that societies unable to guarantee property and contract rights (seventeenth-century England, modern Thailand) produce politicians "able to manipulate . . . power in a way that maximizes their own wealth." Scott calls this variant of corruption "politically oriented capitalism," which involves "the granting by the state of privileged opportunities for profit." Scott, *Comparative Political Corruption* (Englewood Cliffs, NJ: Prentice-Hall, 1972), 69, 50, 52.

22. Morton Keller notes that Gilded Age scandals "touched on activities . . . that were part of the postwar expansion of national government" and Eric McKitrick, following Robert K. Merton, mentions that one function of corrupt political machines was to resolve problems faced by business, "such problems as the need of smaller business men for protection against each other." Neither looks at corruption as a way to re-create the conditions of limited competition that existed under the mercantilist system of legislative charters and monopolies. Keller, *Affairs of State* (Cambridge: Harvard University Press, 1977), 245; McKitrick, "The Study of Corruption," *Political Science Quarterly* 72 (Dec. 1957), 506.

23. Cited in *NYT*, 12 April 1871, 1.

24. Altina L. Waller, "The Political Economy of the New York State Prison System," unpublished paper, Special Collections, Feinberg Library, SUNY Plattsburg, 19–20; James K. McGuire, ed., *The Democratic Party of the State of New York* (New York: United States History Company, 1905), 2: 266.

25. The fight for the electoral vote of South Carolina is described in some detail by Eric Foner in *Reconstruction* (New York: Harper & Row, 1988), 573–82.

26. In one message to Henry Havemeyer, Weed wrote "majority of board have been secured. Cost is 80,000. . . . all to be five hundred or one thousand bills; notes to be deposited as parties accept." *NYT*, 17 Oct. 1878, 1–2.

27. The Democratic Party in South Carolina had used a "reign of terror" to keep blacks from casting votes for the Hayes. See Foner, *Reconstruction*, 574–75. Weed's testimony to the congressional subcommittee that investigated the election appears in the *NYT*, 6 Feb. 1879, 1–2.

28. *NYT*, 28 March 1879, 1; 14 Nov. 1877, 1.

29. *NYTr*, 30 July 1888, 1.

30. See F. W. Taussig, *The Tariff History of the United States* (New York: Capricorn, 1964), 254–55.

31. *NYTr*, 30 July 1888, 1.

32. "Important leaders in the Democratic party had also warned against sweeping tariff reduction," according to Tom Terrill. "Democratic protectionists, including Smith M. Weed, New York industrialist and adviser to Cleveland . . .

warned against making tariff reduction a major Democratic policy." Terrill, *The Tariff, Politics, and American Foreign Policy,* 109–10.

33. "The brutal treatment and treachery [Weed] received at the hands of Gov. Hill," the *Times* commented, "have never been surpassed in the history of the State." *NYT,* 9 April 1891, 7.

34. Weed obituary in *NYTr,* 8 June 1920, 8.

35. Waller sees Weed losing out to the corporations and fading from public view by the 1890s. In fact, Weed had moved his game to a new ground, by interesting himself in what might be called state-supported foreign investment. Waller, "New York State Prison System," 24.

36. See, for example, Weed to Cleveland, 9, 17, 25 May and 17 Nov. 1893, Grover Cleveland Papers. Weed was very much an expression of the "American party state" described by Stephen Skowronek in *Building a New American State,* 39–46.

37. The Nicaragua Canal was "one of the great American dreams in the nineteenth century." See Lawrence A. Clayton, "The Nicaragua Canal in the Nineteenth Century: Prelude to American Empire in the Caribbean," *Journal of Latin American Studies* 19: 2 (Nov. 1987), 323, 328–32, and Dwight Miner, *Fight for the Panama Route* (New York: Columbia University Press, 1940), 25–32.

38. Ironically, this came to be precisely the predicament of the San Domingo Improvement Company, which Smith M. Weed became president of in 1892. John Sherman's speech, reprinted in *The Inter-Oceanic Canal of Nicaragua* (New York: Nicaragua Canal Construction Company, 1891), Appendix VI, 45.

39. The *Sun* and *Herald,* 8 June 1920, 11.

40. Smith M. Weed to Grover Cleveland, 12 Sept. 1892, Grover Cleveland Papers. Weed refers to Cleveland's approval of the congressional bill granting a charter to the Maritime Canal Company in early 1889.

41. Smith M. Weed to Grover Cleveland, Nov. 1893 [n.d.], Grover Cleveland Papers.

42. Walter Q. Gresham to Smith M. Weed, 18 June 1894, Walter Q. Gresham Papers, Library of Congress Manuscript Division.

43. "Mr. Weed was the first man in the Civil War to pay bounties for enlistment," reported Weed's obituary in the *New York Tribune,* 8 June 1920, 8. No biography of Weed exists; this sketch of Weed's life is based on newspaper accounts, correspondence in presidential and other papers, and a brief biographical note in McGuire, *Democratic Party.* Weed's papers, at SUNY/Plattsburg, end in 1892, the year the SDIC was organized.

44. An interesting but unanswerable question is the extent to which monopolistic terms of trade in Latin America attracted investors. Latin American governments offered exclusive rights to railroads, shipping companies, bridge and harbor builders, and even plantation owners. Some concessions fixed a rate of

return; if income fell below a stipulated amount, the government was obliged to make up the difference. The lure of monopoly concessions in the periphery, and its relation to anticompetitive tendencies in the United States, deserves investigation. *NYT*, 1 June 1894, 8.

45. Figures for British investment are from J. Fred Rippy, *British Investments in Latin America, 1822–1949* (Minneapolis: University of Minnesota Press, 1959), 36. See also David Felix, "Alternative Outcomes of the Latin American Debt Crisis," *Latin American Research Review* 22: 2 (1987), and Carlos Marichal, *A Century of Debt Crises in Latin America* (Princeton, NJ: Princeton University Press, 1989).

46. *Bradstreet's*, 23 Jan. 1892, 52. "Effects of the panic were soon felt in other nations of Latin America," Carlos Marichal writes of the Argentine collapse, "because the panic provoked a marked reduction in the flow of foreign capital. During the 1890s, European bankers were reluctant to extend more new loans for the governments of the region." Marichal, *Century of Debt Crises*, 151.

47. Marichal, *Century of Debt Crises*, 172. See also Paul Philip Abrahams, *The Foreign Expansion of American Finance and its Relationship to the Foreign Economic Policies of the United States, 1907–1921* (New York: Arno Press, 1976), chapter 1.

48. Carlos Marichal, *A Century of Debt Crisis*, 81.

49. *Bradstreet's*, 23 April 1892, 259. Although New York was a significant capital market by 1890, nearly all its loans went to domestic projects. London was the preeminent source of capital for peripheral states. See Albert Fishlow, "Lessons from the Past: Capital Markets During the 19th Century and the Interwar Period," *International Organization* 39: 3 (Summer 1985).

50. See Charles A. Conant, "The Economic Basis of Imperialism," in *The United States in the Orient* (Boston: Houghton Mifflin, 1900) and J. A. Hobson, *Imperialism* (London: Allen & Unwin, 1902).

51. *Bradstreet's*, 4 June 1892, 354.

52. In the passage Sklar is discussing loans to China during the Taft administration. See also Emily S. and Norman L. Rosenberg, "From Colonialism to Professionalism: The Public-Private Dynamic in United States Foreign Financial Advising, 1898–1929," *Journal of American History* 74 (June 1987), especially 65–74; Sklar, "Dollar Diplomacy According to Dollar Diplomats: American Development and World Development," in *The United States as a Developing Country* (New York: Cambridge University Press, 1992), 89.

53. Reply to Question 20, JHH.

54. John T. Abbott to Jacob Hollander, 20 Sept. 1905, box 1, JHH.

55. David McLean, "Finance and 'Informal Empire' Before the First World War," *Economic History Review* 29: 2 (May 1976), 292.

56. *New York Sun*, 17 Jan. 1901.

57. See *In Memoriam: Frederick William Holls* (privately printed, 1904), especially 5–10, as well as correspondence in FWH.

58. Frederick William Holls to Stephen B. Elkins, 12 Feb. 1892, Box 14, Letterbook v. 10, FWH.

59. Frederick William Holls to Messrs. Brown and Wells, 18 Feb. 1892, Business Letterbook V.5–8, FWH.

60. Frederick William Holls to Stephen B. Elkins, 10 March 1892, Box 14, Letterbook v. 10, FWH; on Tracy's important role, see Walter LaFeber, *The New Empire* (Ithaca: Cornell University Press, 1963), 122–27; and Benjamin Franklin Cooling, *Gray Steel and Blue Water Navy* (Hamden, CT: Archon Books, 1979), 85–109.

61. Frederick William Holls to Stephen B. Elkins, 26 Feb. 1892, Box 14, letterbook vol. 10, and to S.D. Horton, 26 Sept. 1892, Business Letterbook V. 5–8, FWH.

62. *Times* (London) 29 April 1892, 5; *NYT*, 18 Dec. 1892, 16.

63. Negotiations for the American lease of Samaná are discussed in the next chapter.

64. Heureaux promised "that he would guarantee to the United States both Samana Bay and Mole St. Nicholas" in return for "the help of the United States at least to the extent of preventing the Haytians from bombarding the seaport towns of San Domingo" during the projected conquest of Haiti. The plan was more than a pipe dream. According to Holls, "it appears that he sent a confidential messenger with this proposition to Washington so long ago as the summer of 1890 but Mr. Blaine . . . declined the offer without even communicating it to the other members of the cabinet. I met Secretary Tracy on the street yesterday and told him about it, and he at once said that he had heard nothing of it and regretted very much as he would have taken the responsibility himself at the time and helped San Domingo." Holls to Andrew Dickson White, 23 Feb. 1893, FWH.

65. Frederick William Holls to Andrew Dickson White, 27 Feb. 1893, FWH.

66. The SDIC did not invoke the international commission during Heureaux's reign because "it believed that that great remedy should not be applied except in extreme cases, and preferred negotiation and arrangement," according to SDIC attorney John Bassett Moore. After Heureaux's death, the company demurred because Europeans were "distinctly hostile to American interests" and it felt that "the United States might look with displeasure on the establishment of a Commission . . . controlling the financial interests of a Republic so near a neighbor to herself." John Bassett Moore, "Counter-Case of the United States Before the Commission of Arbitration," United States [vs.] Dominican Republic, [n.p.], 12 April 1904, 97, 106–7.

67. *NYT*, 20 Feb. 1893, 6.

68. Thomas J. McCormick has called on diplomatic historians to "articulate how the interstate and world-economy systems intersect to reinforce or constrain each other." McCormick, "Something Old, Something New: John Lewis Gaddis's 'New Conceptual Approaches,'" *Diplomatic History* 14 (Summer 1990), 431.

69. *NYT*, 20 Feb. 1893, 6.

2. Remapping the Caribbean

1. *El Republicano* (Santo Domingo), 16 March 1901.

2. Unnamed Dominican minister at cabinet meeting, 7 June 1892, reported in John Durham to James G. Blaine, 14 June 1892, vol. 2, USM.

3. Akira Iriye, "Culture and Power: International Relations as Intercultural Relations," *Diplomatic History* 3 (Spring 1979), 120.

4. Tom E. Terrill notes that Benjamin Harrison and Blaine created "a tightly integrated plan and moved with vigor and skill to implement that plan." Even David M. Pletcher, who argues that historians have exaggerated policymakers' commitment to expansion, agrees that after 1889 Blaine pursued "consistent policies of trade expansionism" that were cut short by failing health. Terrill, *The Tariff, Politics, and American Foreign Policy, 1874–1901* (Westport, CT: Greenwood, 1973), 141; Pletcher, "Rhetoric and Results: A Pragmatic View of American Economic Expansionism, 1865–98," *Diplomatic History* 5 (Spring 1981), 97.

5. The goal of supplanting Britain as the leading commercial power in the hemisphere was overt. Under Blaine, "the State Department had begun to evolve a vigorous policy aimed at displacing European and especially British influence in Latin America." Joseph Smith, *Illusions of Conflict* (Pittsburgh: University of Pittsburgh Press, 1979), 46, 117; see also Homer E. Socolofsky and Allan B. Spetter, *The Presidency of Benjamin Harrison* (Lawrence, Kansas: University Press of Kansas, 1987), 117.

6. By the end of the century "friendship with the United States became one of the major goals of British diplomacy," according to Warren G. Kneer. Kenneth Bourne notes that "by the end of 1901 the government was willing to express its approval of the Monroe Doctrine openly before the House of Commons." As early as 1871 Bismarck declared "we frankly recognize the paramount influence of the United States on the entire continent as both natural and supportive or our best interests." Kneer, *Great Britain and the Caribbean, 1901–1913* (East Lansing: Michigan State University Press, 1975), ix; Kenneth Bourne, *Britain and the Balance of Power in North America, 1815–1908* (London: Longmans, 1967), 350; Manfred Jonas, *The United States and Germany* (Ithaca: Cornell University Press, 1984), 32.

7. British officials felt the United States had become second in the world by 1906; the U.S. Congress acknowledged that the American navy was second to Britain in first-class capital ships two years later. George W. Baer, *One Hundred Years of Sea Power* (Stanford: Stanford University Press, 1994), 40. See also Bourne, *Balance of Power*, 338, and Richard H. Collin, "The Caribbean Theater Transformed: Britain, France, Germany, and the U.S., 1900–1906," *The American Neptune* 52 (Spring 1992), 102–12.

8. "American expansion seemed to the Admiralty, as to Salisbury, inevitable but unwelcome," notes Kenneth Bourne, while Warren G. Kneer finds that "Britain had to sacrifice little strategic or political interests [sic] in the Caribbean" since "British influence there had been declining for decades." Joseph Smith argues that "the implications of American political preeminence in the Western Hemisphere were not disturbing or threatening to European nations, who attached, after all, marginal strategic significance to this area." Bourne, *Balance of Power*, 344; Kneer, *Great Britain and the Caribbean*, ix; Smith, *Illusions*, 46.

9. By the end of the century, Washington could not doubt that "a nation as patently ambitious as Germany would sooner or later seek some territory, at least for a naval base, in the Western Hemisphere." Jonas, *United States and Germany*, 52.

10. On German commercial expansion in Latin America, see Ian L. D. Forbes, "German Informal Imperialism in South America before 1914," *Economic History Review* 31: 3 (Aug. 1978).

11. Noting that "Europe and the United States were therefore economic rather than political rivals in Latin America," Lester Langley maintains that "the policy of American expansionism in Latin America did not seriously undermine European economic interests." In the case of Germany and the United States, "even in Latin America, where both countries made substantial efforts to expand their trade, the problems each encountered had little to do with the competition provided by the other." Lester D. Langley, *Struggle for the American Mediterranean* (Athens: University of Georgia Press, 1976), 31; Jonas, *United States and Germany*, 41.

12. *Presidential Addresses and State Papers of Theodore Roosevelt, Part Three* (New York: Kraus Reprint Co., 1970), 175–77.

13. Blaine's foreign policy is discussed at length in Alice Felt Tyler, *The Foreign Policy of James G. Blaine* (Hamden, CT: Archon Books, 1965) and Walter LaFeber, *The New Empire* (Ithaca: Cornell University Press, 1963).

14. Every Latin American nation except the Dominican Republic attended the conference, which met in Washington, D.C., from October 1889 until April 1890. Dominican president Ulises Heureaux refused Washington's invitation on the grounds that the United States had slighted his country in 1884 by negotiating a reciprocity treaty and then failing to ratify it. The expatriate Cu-

ban intellectual José Martí, a close observer of American foreign policy in general and the Pan-American Conference in particular, wrote that through the conference the United States was seeking "the frank and forthright achievement of an era of U.S. dominion over the nations of America." See Felt Tyler, *Foreign Policy of Blaine*, 175–81; Socolofsky and Spetter, *Benjamin Harrison*, 117–18; Terrill, *Tariff*, 155; and José Martí, *Inside the Monster*, ed. Philip S. Foner (New York: Monthly Review, 1975), 351.

15. The reciprocity treaty with Hawaii, which went into effect in 1875, led to a boom in Hawaiian sugar production, a sharp loss in United States customs revenue, and little savings to American consumers. "The Reciprocity Treaty of 1875 was a perfect example of a commercial and economic negotiation dictated by political motives. It was designed primarily to extend American influence over the Islands." Merze Tate, *Hawaii: Reciprocity or Annexation* (East Lansing: Michigan State University Press, 1968), 117.

16. Cited in Terril, *Tariff*, 160.

17. "The results of the reciprocal trade arrangements between Cuba and the United States were as dramatic as they were instant," according to Louis Pérez, Jr. in *Cuba: Between Reform and Revolution* (New York: Oxford, 1988), 149; Luis E. Aguilar, "Cuba, c. 1860–c. 1930," in *Cuba: A Short History*, ed. Leslie Bethell (New York: Cambridge, 1993), 28.

18. Percentages calculated from data in Bureau of the American Republics, *Handbook of Santo Domingo* (Washington: Government Printing Office, 1894), 30–32, 42, and Luis Gómez, *Relaciones de Producción Dominantes en la Sociedad Dominicana, 1875–1975* (Santo Domingo: Alfa y Omega, 1984), 64.

19. The Dominicans reduced or eliminated tariffs on American corn, oats, barley, coal, tallow, most meats, iron, steel, and machines "for agriculture, mining, manufacturing, industrial, and scientific purposes" as well as "telegraphic, telephonic, electrical apparatus of all kinds." Bureau of the American Republics, *Handbook of Santo Domingo*, 45–48.

20. "Resumen de los derechos que dejó de cobrar el Gobierno, por motivo del contrato de reciprocidad con los Estados Unidos de América, durante el ano de Marzo de 1893 á Febrero de 1894," in report from Tomás D. Morales to Ulises Heureaux, 28 Feb. 1894, library collection, AGN.

21. According to Richard Collin, when the United States refused to provide guarantees to Heureaux against European trade reprisals, "Heureaux backed down and the reciprocity agreement died." In fact, the treaty went into effect and had significant economic and political consequences. Collin, *Theodore Roosevelt's Caribbean* (Baton Rouge: Louisiana State University Press, 1990), 360. Dominican government receipts detailed in "Case of the United States before the Commission of Arbitration," United States [vs.] the Dominican Republic, [n.p.], 12 Feb. 1904, 56–57.

22. British officials saw reciprocity as the opening shot of a tariff war. Smith, *Illusions*, 147.

23. Howard Owen & Co. to Lord Kimberly, 5 March 1894, in Vice Consul at San Domingo, 1894, FO 23/90. Imports of British goods into Haiti and the Dominican Republic reportedly declined from a value of over £500,000 in 1890 to under £250,000 in 1892. Bureau of American Republics, *Handbook of Santo Domingo*, 40–41.

24. The comments refer to negotiations between the United States and Dominican Republic to restore reciprocity in 1897, but presumably reflected British policy based on the experience from 1891 to 1894. Note to A. Cohen, initialed "S" [Marquis of Salisbury?], 29 July 1897, FO 23/101.

25. "Germany's insistence that her products shall have the same advantages" as those of the United States and "the combination of European powers to press this matter at Santo Domingo" were reported to Washington by the American minister to the Dominican Republic. John Durham to James G. Blaine, 13 Feb. 1892, vol. 2, USM.

26. The American position, described by Acting Secretary of State William F. Wharton in 1891, was that "the clause of treaties which guarantees the *treatment of the most-favored nation* relates only to gratuitous concessions, and does not embrace privileges granted for a consideration or by means of a reciprocity arrangement." 11 Sept. 1891, vol. 3, DI. Controversy over how bilateral reciprocity treaties affected most-favored-nation agreements with other countries predated the treaties negotiated by Blaine. See Tate, *Hawaii*, 36–37 and 209.

27. [British Ambassador] to Marquis of Salisbury, 29 April 1892, FO 140/6.

28. "I am requested by President Heureaux to say to you that he is in a very difficult position and that he begs you to use your good offices to secure the settlement of this reciprocity trouble," the U.S. minister wrote to Secretary of State John W. Foster on 22 May 1892, adding "Poor man, he reproached me so this morning privately! He says that but for our assurances, he would not have made the Reciprocity arrangement." John S. Durham to John W. Foster, 23 May 1892, vol. 2, USM.

29. John S. Durham to James G. Blaine, 14 June 1892, vol. 2, USM.

30. William F. Wharton to John S. Durham, 11 March 1892, DI.

31. Heureaux recognized that, in theory, every nation enjoyed sovereign equality, regardless of its size or wealth. "We, the weak states, are equal to the strong states, and in no case should we find ourselves prevented from acting according to our national interests, as long as we respect the legitimate rights of other nations." Heureaux to W. Powell, 23 June 1898, tomo 67, UH.

32. John S. Durham to James G. Blaine, 14 June 1892, vol. 2, USM.

33. "I telegraphed to President Heureaux early this morning," the American minister reported in July 1892, "stating to him that if he will take a firm stand, he

will be sustained." In October Durham informed Washington that "the present Government will do nothing further in considering the protests of the European nations." John S. Durham to William F. Wharton, 2 July 1892 and 29 Oct. 1892, vol. 2, USM.

34. J. Pauncefote to Lord Salisbury, 13 March 1893, FO 140/6. Two studies of United States-Dominican relations that do not take take account of the SDIC's advent are puzzled about the cessation of European protests. See William Raymond Tansill, "Diplomatic Relations Between the United States and the Dominican Republic, 1874–1899" (Ph.D. diss., Georgetown University, 1951), 167–68; and David Charles MacMichael, "The United States and the Dominican Republic, 1871–1940" (unpublished Ph.D. diss., University of Oregon, 1964), 47.

35. The incidents are recounted in detail in Charles Callan Tansill, *The United States and Santo Domingo, 1798–1873* (Gloucester, MA: Peter Smith, 1967).

36. William S. McFeely, *Frederick Douglass* (New York: W. W. Norton, 1991), 346–58.

37. Although the don of American naval policy, Alfred Mahan, believed that only Cuba, Puerto Rico, and Hawaii were vital to U.S. interests, Harrison's Secretary of the Navy, Benjamin Tracy, favored the acquisition of bases throughout the Caribbean. See David Healy, *Drive to Hegemony* (Madison: University of Wisconsin Press, 1988), 29–31.

38. Durham took credit for suggesting the lease of Samaná in October 1890, recalling later that "I spoke privately with President Heureaux on the matter; and he expressed his willingness to negotiate." In March 1891 Durham traveled to the United States, "with the understanding that Señor Galvan would follow in April as the Reciprocity Envoy." John S. Durham to James G. Blaine, 16 Jan. 1892, vol. 2, USM.

39. "The first advance on that subject, as now considered, was made to this government in May last by Senor Galvan, the Minister of the Dominican Republic, during the negotiation in this city of the reciprocity arrangement; and it was at his request, as representing the views of the President of San Domingo, that a basis for the lease of a coaling station in Samana Bay was drawn up and approved by him. The negotiations were purely of an informal character." James G. Blaine to John S. Durham, 28 Jan. 1892, vol. 3, DI.

40. Durham added that "the more President Heureaux reflects upon the proposition, the more is he disposed to magnify its importance to the United States and to increase his terms." In another dispatch he commented that "General Heureaux wants money for his Government; but he also has his ideas as to the value of Samaná as a naval station." John S. Durham to James G. Blaine, 16 Jan. and 27 March, 1892, vol. 2, USM.

41. John S. Durham to James G. Blaine, 25 April 1892, vol. 2, USM.

42. John S. Durham to [John W.] Foster, 27 August and 9 Sept. 1892, vol. 2, USM.

43. John S. Durham to [John W.] Foster, 27 Aug. and 9 Sept. 1892, vol. 2, USM.

44. "Germany's threatened action assumes a political aspect of the gravest character for the Heureaux administration," reported Durham. "The Cibao district has been nearly a unit in opposing the Heureaux policy toward the United States." John S. Durham to William F. Wharton, 16 April 1892, vol. 2, USM.

45. John W. Foster to John S. Durham, 6 Aug. 1892, vol. 3, DI.

46. John S. Durham to Alvey A. Adee, 7 Sept. 1892, vol. 2, USM; John W. Foster to John S. Durham, 28 Sept. 1892 [appears out of sequence on 721–23], vol. 3, DI.

47. John S. Durham to John W. Foster, 6 Oct. 1892, vol. 2, USM.

48. "Express deep dissatisfaction with failure of the President of San Domingo to comply with assurances voluntarily given." [John W.] Foster to [John S.] Durham, 17 and 29 Jan. 1893, vol. 3, DI.

49. A. S. Crowninshield to Secretary of the Navy, 13 March 1893, AF.

50. *New York Sun*, 17 Jan. 1901, 10.

51. J. Pauncefote to Marquis of Salisbury, 13 March 1893, FO 140/6.

52. Langley, *American Mediterranean* (Athens: University of Georgia, 1976), 152–63. Richard E. Welch, Jr., concludes that both Cleveland and Olney "wished to promote United States diplomatic hegemony in the New World" but that "neither thought in geopolitical terms or ever devised a hemispheric strategy." Welch, *The Presidencies of Grover Cleveland* (Lawrence: University Press of Kansas, 1988), 180–94; at 189. On Cleveland and the navy, see Benjamin Franklin Cooling, *Gray Steel and Blue Water Navy* (Hampden, CT: Archon Books, 1979), 57, 71, 113.

53. Richard Collin claims that Blaine "briefly considered acquiring Samaná" and that, although lower-echelon officials and consuls urged the project, "leading American diplomats and naval intellectuals such as Blaine and Mahan seldom wavered in regarding Cuba and Puerto Rico as the only serious American strategic objectives in the Caribbean." Collin, *Roosevelt's Caribbean*, 358–59; see also MacMichael, "United States and Dominican Republic," 56.

54. Collin's study, which uses no Dominican archival sources, recapitulates this error.

55. Crowninshield to Secretary of the Navy, 13 March 1893, vol. 218, AF.

56. See also Sumner Wells, *Naboth's Vineyard* (New York: Payson & Clarke, 1928), I, 468–69, 479–81, 486–93, and II, 528–34, and Tansill, *Diplomatic Relations*, 172–202.

57. The position, which might be called *patria dependiente o morir*, was scarcely unique to Heureaux among "progressive" Caribbean leaders. The annexationist impulses of various elites are well known. In Cuba, for example, "the propertied, the educated, the white . . . wanted close and permanent ties with the

United States." Louis A. Pérez, Jr., *Cuba: Between Reform and Revolution* (New York: Oxford University Press, 1988), 181.

58. "The Dominican Government desires to lean on the United States under this urgent pressure from Germany," John S. Durham informed Secretary of State Blaine in 1892. John S. Durham to James G. Blaine, 14 June 1892, vol. 2, USM.

59. A. Crowninshield to Secretary of the Navy, 14 March 1893, vol. 219, AF.

60. Heureaux comments on the contest between McKinley and Bryan in a letter to Alejandro Wos y Gil, 1 Aug. 1896, tomo 53, UH. Only Spain and France competed with the United States as objects of interest and concern to Heureaux.

61. "There are those who believe," Heureaux continued, "that the French have not forgiven my government for signing the reciprocity treaty . . . nor for the concessions we made to the 'San Domingo Improvement Company' for the conversion of the loan of 1890 and completion of the central railroad; for all those reasons we find an active interest . . . in disturbing our commercial relations and friendship with the United States, whose influence in the Antilles is apparently seen negatively." Heureaux to Charles W. Wells, 14 Nov. 1896, tomo 55, and 8 Feb. 1895, tomo 44, UH.

62. Crowninshield to Secretary of the Navy, 18 March 1893, vol. 218, AF.

63. Diplomatic dispatches seemed to confirm Heureaux's point of view. Germany in particular had increased its diplomatic activity in Hispaniola, John S. Durham warned, and "Germany's course at both of these capitals can reasonably be interpreted as indicating the purpose of that Government to combat any growth of American influence on this island." John S. Durham to James G. Blaine, 14 June 1892, vol. 2, USM.

64. Ulises Heureaux to Grover Cleveland, 27 March 1894, tomo 39; Heureaux to C. W. Wells, 10 May 1894, tomo 40; Heureaux to Smith M. Weed, 10 July 1894, tomo 41, UH.

65. See Smith M. Weed to Grover Cleveland, 22 Dec. 1892, 18 March, 13 May and 17 May 1893, 17 Nov. 1893, 11 Jan. and 14 April 1894, 15 March 1895, Grover Cleveland Papers. According to Allan Nevins, Weed became "a constant correspondent of Cleveland." Nevins, *Grover Cleveland: A Study in Courage* (New York: Dodd, Mead, 1932), 152. Weed also had contact with the Republican administration that succeeded Cleveland; see correspondence from William McKinley's secretary to Weed for 18 Sept. 1899, 15 March, 11 June and 3 Dec. 1900 and 30 Jan. 1901, the latter arranging a meeting between Weed and McKinley, William McKinley Papers.

66. The State Department's inattention to Dominican affairs is not surprising. In his study of U.S. military rule over that country from 1916 to 1924, Bruce Calder notes that even after American officials "assumed dictatorial powers . . .

2. Remapping the Caribbean

there were no clearly stated goals." The State Department, "though theoretically maintaining its control of policy, tended to leave Dominican matters to
the Navy Department, which in turn granted the military government considerable freedom." Bruce Calder, *The Impact of Intervention* (Austin: University
of Texas, 1984), 23–24.

67. For example, the *Kearsarge* visited Santo Domingo in December 1893 after
reports of a plot to assassinate Heureaux. *NYT*, 21 Dec. 1893, 8.

68. Immanuel Wallerstein has noted that the interstate system attributes to all
nations "sovereign equality, but the states are in fact neither sovereign nor
equal." Weak states in the periphery have "participated in the interstate system
as formally sovereign entities" even though their sovereignty was "of course
encroached upon by arrangements such as the 'concessions' in China." "States
in the institutional vortex," 33; "The world-economy and the state-structures in
peripheral and dependent countries (the so-called Third World)," 81; both in
The Politics of the World-Economy (New York: Cambridge University Press,
1984).

69. Heureaux to José Ladislao de Escoriaza, 14 May 1898, tomo 66, UH; a translation of Heureaux's speech was reprinted in its entirety in *NYTr*, 5 May 1992, 3.

70. Heureaux to Alejandro Wos y Gil, 18 Jan. 1896, tomo 49, and 3 Dec. 1896,
tomo 56, UH.

3. Peasants in the World Economy

1. D. Coen to Marquis of Salisbury, 2 March 1891, FO 23/87.
2. *NYT*, 20 April 1894, 2.
3. It is reasonable to suppose that the SDIC knew little about the Dominican
Republic before beginning its operations, although the Bureau of the American
Republics, created after the first Pan-American Conference of 1889–90, published the *Handbook of Santo Domingo* in 1892, which provided a detailed
economic and geographical profile of the country — another sign of increasing
United States interest in the nation.
4. In 1905 a leading newspaper decried the lack of reliable census data: "We still
don't know, because we have never bothered to find out, the exact population
of the republic. Some put the number at 600,000; others at four or five hundred
thousand; still others at about 300,000. No one, however, can speak with precision or offer statistics other than incomplete local surveys, which officials
have gathered when they feel like it." *Listin Diario* (Santo Domingo), 9 March
1905.
5. The ecclesiastical survey of 1887 was carried out nationally. A census of the
city and province of Santo Domingo was conducted in 1908, and again by the
U.S. military occupiers in 1919. *Censo de Población y Otros Datos Estadísticos*

(Santo Domingo: J.R. Vda. Garcia, 1909); *Censo y Catastro de la Comun de Santo Domingo, Año 1919* (Santo Domingo: El Progreso, 1919). The figures are from Frank Moya Pons, "Nuevas Consideraciones sobre la Historia de la Poblacion Dominicana," *Eme Eme*, 3: 15 (Nov.–Dic. 1974), 13–16.

6. Assuming a population of about half a million in the mid-1890s, the population density of the Dominican Republic was roughly 27 persons per square mile. This compares with an estimated density of 110 in Haiti, 277 in Puerto Rico, and 36 in Cuba at approximately the same time. According to a survey by the U.S. War Department, the population of Puerto Rico in October 1899 was 953,243; San Juan had 32,048 inhabitants. Cited in *Nuevo Régimen* (Santo Domingo), 2 Sept. 1900. Cuba's population in 1899 was 1,572,800, according to Heinrich Friedlaender, *Historia Económica de Cuba* (Havana: Editorial de Ciencias Sociales, 1978), 2: 523; Haiti's population in 1880 was estimated to be 1.2 million by Johanna von Grafenstein, *Haití 2* (Mexico City: Instituto de Investigaciones, 1989), 110.

7. *NYT*, 20 April 1894, 2.

8. *Censo y Catastro de la Común de Santo Domingo* (Santo Domingo: El Progreso, 1919), 6–10, 51.

9. Hostos quoted in Juan Bosch, *Capitalismo Tardío en la República Dominicana* (Santo Domingo: Alfa y Omega, 1990), 14; *Censo de Población*, 73; Franciso Alvarez Léal, *La Republique Dominicaine* (Paris: Lucien Beillet, 1888), 37–41. According to Roberto Cassá, "the cities were extremely small, little more than commercial and administrative centers." Cassá, *Historia Social y Económica de la República Dominicana*, vol. 2 (Santo Domingo: Alfa y Omega, 1992), 149.

10. For trades and professions in the towns of Baní and San Cristobal, see *Censo de Población*, 100–101, 113.

11. Pedro San Miguel notes that while merchants sought to control peasant production, they "were not particularly interested in forcing the expropriation of the peasantry" or creating latifundia; "they continued depending on the peasantry to satisfy their demand for cash-crops." San Miguel, "The Dominican Peasantry and the Market Economy: The Peasants of the Cibao, 1880–1960" (unpublished Ph.D. diss., Columbia University, 1987), 122–123, 150.

12. Roberto Cassá describes the merchant class as "a bourgeoisie made up largely of foreigners, who had however become dominicanized." Cassá, *Historia Social y Económica 2*, 162.

13. Dominican social classes are described in Paul Mutto, "The Illusory Promise: The Dominican Republic and the Process of Economic Development, 1900–1930 (unpublished Ph.D. dissertation, University of Washington, 1976), 136–74. The business dealings of Juan B. Vicini, the country's wealthiest resident foreigner, are explored in detail in Alfonso Huet, "Juan B. Vicini y la Acu-

mulación Originaria, 1870—1900 (master's essay, Universidad Autónoma de Santo Domingo, 1980).

14. Holls to Andrew Dickson White, 27 Feb. 1893, FWH.

15. According to Michiel Baud, in the Cibao "the infrastructure of the region hadn't changed substantially since the colonial era," with the result that "the cost of transportation within the country was higher than transatlantic shipping." *NYT*, 20 April 1894, 2; Michiel Baud, *Historia de un Sueño: Los Ferrocarriles Públicos en la República Dominicana, 1880–1930* (Santo Domingo: Fundación Cultural Dominicana, 1993), 9, 10.

16. "The La Vega-Sánchez railroad has contributed significantly to an increase in the production of cacao and coffee," wrote *El Eco del Pueblo* in 1891. Quoted in Patrick E. Bryan, "La Producción Campesina en la República Dominicana a Principio del Siglo XX," *Eme Eme*, 7: 42 (Mayo–Junio 1979), 35.

17. A carriage road through the *cordillera* that separated the Cibao valley from Santo Domingo city was not built until the early 1920s, during the first U.S. military occupation of the island. Roberto Cassá, *Historia Social y Economica* 2, 150.

18. The editorial appeared in *Oiga*, a daily edited by the prominent intellectual José Ramón López. It continued: "The person who brings it does more good than the one who puts it to use. We shouldn't, therefore, put too many conditions on the person who brings us the chickens. When the henhouse is well stocked, we can be more scrupulous and demanding. Meanwhile, let the promoters of growth keep coming!" *Oiga*, 14 July 1904.

19. Helen Ortiz identifies the practice of granting concessions with earlier governments, especially that of Fernando A. de Meriño (1880–82). Helen Ortiz, "The Era of Lilís: Political Stability and Economic Change in the Dominican Republic" (unpublished Ph.D. diss., 1975, Georgetown University), 118.

20. In 1878 Clyde obtained a ten-year concession granting an exemption for port duties and promising him 3.5 percent of the import and export duties levied on the cargoes his ships carried. The concession was renewed with modifications several times, Clyde complaining that the government consistently failed to live up to its obligations. See [Edward C.] Reed, general agent of Clyde, to Jacob Hollander, 9 May 1905, JHH.

21. La Société Française des Télégraphes Sous-marines and La Société Télégraphique des Antilles, respectively. Alvarez Léal, *Republique Dominicaine*, 21.

22. The Banco Nacional de Santo Domingo, as it was known in the republic, had its main office in Paris and was created through a 50-year concession to the French banking house of Credit Mobilier. César A. Herrera, *Las Finanzas de la República Dominicana* (Santo Domingo: Impresora Dominicana, 1955), 2: 124–27.

23. Three years after the Central Dominican Railroad opened, for example, a Santiago newspaper complained that "instead of helping our commerce, the Central railroad damages it, and hurts the people generally" because of its high rates. *El Constitucional* 19 Sept. 1900.
24. The diplomatic correspondence of the Dominican Republic is filled with records of complaints from companies, seconded by their respective governments, that sometimes resulted in the promise of indemnization by the Dominican government. See chapter 4 of David Charles MacMichael, "The United States and the Dominican Republic, 1871–1940: A Cycle in Caribbean Diplomacy" (unpublished Ph.D. diss., University of Oregon, 1964), 72–98.
25. "The products of this island," an official of the Clyde steamship line reported, "75% of which went to Europe in 1878, has [sic] been diverted out of that channel until to-day nearly 75% goes to the United States." In the seven Dominican ports where Clyde steamships called, "every respectable native provision and dry goods house . . . imports his goods direct from New York to-day, saving the expense of the middle-man." [Edward C.] Reed to Jacob Hollander, 9 May 1905, Box 2, JHH.
26. By 1893, trade between the two nations had increased notably in real terms, although the relative position of the United States declined somewhat. In that year, the United States provided 40 percent of the republic's imports and took 42 percent of its exports. This may be explained in part by the tremendous surge in exports during these years, from $2,926,039 in 1891 to $5,658,276 in 1893. Percentages calculated from data in Bureau of the American Republics, *Santo Domingo* (Washington: Government Printing Office, 1894), 30–32, 42, and Luis Gómez, *Relaciones de Producción Dominantes en la Sociedad Dominicana, 1875–1975* (Santo Domingo: Alfa y Omega, 1984), 64.
27. Pedro San Miguel, "Dominican Peasantry," 356. Even in the province of Santo Domingo "wide open spaces lie completely cleared in some parts and covered with trees and underbrush in others, through most of this central province." *El Eco de la Opinión* (Santo Domingo), 4 Nov. 1893.
28. Frank Moya Pons, "Datos Sobre la Economía Dominicana durante la Primera República," *Eme Eme* 4: 24 (Mayo–Junio 1976), 28–29.
29. Michiel Baud, "The Origins of Capitalist Agriculture in the Dominican Republic," *Latin America Research Review* 22: 2 (1987), 139.
30. Frank Moya Pons, *Manual de Historia Dominicana* (Santo Domingo: Editora Corripio, 1984), 404–5. By the mid-1850s, "the deficit in Santo Domingo's balance of trade was covered by the constant surplus in the Cibao's tabacco trade." Moya Pons, "Datos sobre la Economía Dominicana," 42.
31. Cassá, *Historia Social y Económica* 2, 136. Dominican production was still only a tiny fraction of the vast Cuban harvest. In 1895, Cuba produced just

over a million long tons of sugar, of which 824,000 tons were shipped to the United States. Friedlander, *Historia Económica de Cuba*, 2: 534.

32. Eugenio María de Hostos, quoted in Franc Báez Evertsz, *Azúcar y Dependencia en la República Dominicana* (Santo Domingo: Universidad Autonoma de Santo Domingo, 1978), 23.

33. Pedro Francisco Bonó cited in Ramonina Brea, *La Formación del Estado Capitalista en Haiti y Santo Domingo* (Santo Domingo: Editora Taller, 1982), 139–40.

34. By 1884 sugar was selling at its lowest price in 40 years, reaching 3.5 cents in the New York market. Martin F. Murphy, *Dominican Sugar Plantations* (New York: Praeger, 1991), 15.

35. A *central* was a large sugar mill with steam-powered equipment that processed cane from its own lands and from those of sharecroppers and small farmers in the area.

36. Roberto Cassá, *Historia Social y Economica*, 2: 132; Paul Mutto, "La economía de exportación de la República Dominicana, 1900–1930," *Eme Eme* 3: 15 (Nov.–Dic. 1974), 74.

37. William Bass to Ulysses Heureaux [sic], 7 April 1897, leg. 13, CE.

38. The source of the imported workforce changed in the 1920s, during the U.S. military occupations of the Dominican Republic and Haiti. The dual occupation made it easy to arrange the annual importation of Haitian laborers to the Dominican sugar *bateys*, a practice that has continued until today and has contributed to the conflictive relations between the two nations. The development of the modern sugar industry in the Dominican Republic is discussed in Patrick E. Bryan, "La cuestión obrera en la industria azucarera de la República Dominicana a finales del siglo [XIX] y principios del XX," *Eme Eme* 7: 41 (mayo–abril 1979), 57–77; José del Castillo, "Azucar & braceros: Historia de un Problema," *Eme Eme* 10: 58 (Enero-Febrero 1982), 3–19; Michiel Baud, "Sugar and Unfree Labour: Reflections on Labour Control in the Dominican Republic, 1870–1935," *Journal of Peasant Studies* 19: 2 (Jan. 1992), 301–325; and Michiel Baud, "Capitalist Agriculture," 135–153.

39. Eric Foner discusses the mechanisms Caribbean and East African planters used to control land, credit and marketing after emancipation in *Nothing but Freedom* (Baton Rouge: Louisiana State University Press, 1983), 8–38.

40. Although Santiago province had a higher-than-average population density and a long history of cash-crop production, San Miguel's study allows glimpses of incomplete and episodic participation in the market. As late as 1940, peasants in the commercialized area around Santiago dedicated only 23 percent of their lands to cash crops, while using 72 percent for traditional food crops. The 1918 census showed that only "a handful of rural sections (19 out of 112) accounted for over 76 percent of the land tilled in cacao in the municipality of Santiago,

while in almost 44 percent of the wards no cacao was cultivated at all. Something similar happened with coffee." To the extent that peasants sold foodstuffs in towns, of course, a strict distinction between food and cash crops is untenable. Even so, despite San Miguel's argument that "as new economic opportunities came at hand, peasants rushed to sow cash-crops," his own evidence suggests that not all peasants wanted or were able to move into cash-crop production. Roberto Cassá, personal interview; San Miguel, "Dominican Peasantry," 98, 104, 108.

41. Quoted in Jaime de Jesús Domínguez, *La Dictadura de Heureaux* (Santo Domingo: Editora Universitaria, 1986), 66–67, 207. See also Raymundo González, "Ideología de progreso y campesinado en el siglo XIX," *Ecos* 2 (1993), 25–43.

42. Like all bureaucrats, these officials no doubt preferred to report good news, and few could have doubted that the Heureaux government favored increased commercialization of agriculture. Even so, the evidence of a growing market in cash-crops is overwhelming. GO, 20 Nov. 1897; GO, 27 May 1899; *Las Noticias* (Santo Domingo), 31 May 1894. Many other reports of growing cash-crop production can be found in newspapers of the 1890s.

43. There are 6.45 *tareas* in an acre. GO, 13 Junio 1892; 22 Julio 1893; 21 Mayo 1898. While the evidence is not conclusive, since enforcement may have been lax, these reports suggest that San Miguel may not be correct when he asserts that unlike Puerto Rican peasants, Dominican campesinos were not subject to vagrancy laws. "Dominican Peasantry," 270–71.

44. It is useful to recall that the ongoing articulation of a market for cash crops did not necessarily undermine the peasants' desire for self-sufficiency. In the Peruvian highlands, penetrated by commercial agriculture, wage labor, indebtedness, and commodification of land long before the Dominican hinterland, Florencia E. Mallon has shown that "commercial capital did not destroy the basic core of self-sufficiency." Mallon, *The Defense of Community in Peru's Central Highlands* (Princeton: Princeton University Press, 1983), 33.

45. Harry Hoetink notes that "since independence the internal frontiers of the Cibao have slowly disappeared." Hoetink, "El Cibao 1844–1900: Su Aportación a la Formación Social de la República," in *Santo Domingo y El Caribe* (Santo Domingo: Fundación Cultural Dominicana, 1994), 56.

46. One Dominican historian has noted an increase not only in the importation of machinery and capital goods by businesses, "but also in individual consumption. Population growth, the assimilation of capitalist habits, the expansion of bourgeois institutions and ideas, the increase in disposable income as production, credit, and banking expanded, all spurred personal consumption." Luis Gómez, *Relaciones de Producción*, 68.

47. "In a certain sense, cacao monoculture in the north complemented sugar monoculture in the south." Bryan, "La producción campesina," 47.
48. Michiel Baud, "Capitalist Agriculture," 144, 146.
49. In 1900, food, beverages, and medicines accounted for 42 percent, and cloth and clothing made up more than a third, of customs revenue. "These indirect taxes were largely paid by the poor, that is, the majority of the country's population." Jaime de Jesús Domínguez, *La Sociedad Dominicana a Principios del Siglo XX* (Santo Domingo: Colección Sesquicentenaria, 1994), 184–85.
50. In recent years, Caribbean historians have been concerned with the ways that peasants in postemancipation societies related to the market. Detailed studies of Cuba and Jamaica caution against assuming that former slaves retreated into subsistence or fled "into a vacant hinterland, like air into a vacuum." Rebecca Scott and Thomas Holt, among others, find that "reconstituted" peasantries had a more complex articulation with the market in which they sought autonomy from a coercive plantation system but nevertheless had "a commitment to the market as well as to subsistence." Rebecca J. Scott, *Slave Emancipation in Cuba* (Princeton: Princeton University Press, 1985), 247; Thomas C. Holt, *The Problem of Freedom* (Baltimore: Johns Hopkins University Press, 1992), 160. In East Africa, "whether the peasant household embraced or resisted the world market and whether it was helped or hurt by the expansion of cash crop production depended very much on exactly how the penetration of commercial capital took place," according to Frederick Cooper, *From Slaves to Squatters* (New Haven: Yale University Press, 1980), 13. See also Michel-Rolph Trouillot, "Discourses of rule and the acknowledgment of the peasantry in Dominica, W.I., 1838–1928," *American Ethnologist* 16: 4 (Nov. 1989), 704–18. In some ways the Dominican case is closer to that of Central and South America, where relatively autonomous peasant communities saw communal landholding threatened by the encroachment of coffee and sugar plantations. On Venezuela and Guatemala, see William Roseberry, *Coffee and Capitalism in the Venezuelan Andes* (Austin: University of Texas Press, 1983), especially 82–116, and J.C. Cambranes, *Coffee and Peasants* (Stockholm: Institute of Latin American Studies, 1985), 67–84.
51. Between 1884 and 1899, import and export taxes collected by customs officials never accounted for less than 95 percent of government revenue, with internal taxes making up the difference. Gómez, *Relaciones de Producción*, 69. In 1887, total revenue from import duties was 1,195,531 Mexican pesos and from export taxes 289,645, or 80 and 20 percent, respectively. Léal, *Republique Dominicaine*, 10.
52. The figures, especially for imports, are not wholly reliable because merchants typically undervalued imported goods to avoid paying customs duty. As a result,

actual figures for imports were almost certainly higher. See Roberto Cassá, *Historia Social y Económica* 2, 99.

53. According to Roberto Cassá "the aspects of the state that were strengthened were essentially those tied to repression." *Historia Social y Económica* 2, 181.

54. Loans proliferated during times of disorder, when both the government and rebels needed money to pay soldiers and buy arms. Merchants often hedged their bets by lending to both sides, at rates of 2 percent a month or more. In the early 1880s this system of short-term borrowing was to some extent rationalized by the creation of *Compañías de Crédito* made up of leading merchants in the main towns. The companies shared out participation in state loans according to each lender's resources. The first *Compañía de Crédito* was created by a decree of President Buenaventura Báez in 1877; a few years later Gregorio Luperón authorized new Juntas de Crédito that charged the government monthly interest of only 10 percent as against 28 percent by the original company. Herrera, *Finanzas* 1: 157–158; Frank Moya Pons, *Manual de Historia Dominicana*, 392–93.

55. The loan, which was officially earmarked for the development of "the public works, the trade and the manufactures" of the country, is described in Herrera, *Finanzas*, 1: 129–143; Charles Callan Tansill, *The United States and Santo Domingo, 1798–1873* (Gloucester, MA: Peter Smith, 1967), 347–51, 379–80; and William H. Wynne, *State Insolvency and Foreign Bondholders* (New Haven: Yale University Press, 1951), 2: 199–206. The House of Commons report and transcripts of testimony appear in *Parliamentary Papers* (1875), vol. XI, Reports from Committees, at pp. xxvii–xxx; lxxxi–lxxxiii; 125–142 (queries 3126–3495); and 230–233 (queries 5114–5173). A useful overview of the London exchange is "The Victorian Capital Market," in A. K. Cairncross, *Home and Foreign Investment, 1870–1913* (Cambridge: Cambridge University Press, 1953), 84–102.

56. Hartmont added that "by granting me a concession, the Dominican Government did not part with anything of value to them. It would have been of value to them if it had been worked." *Parliamentary Papers*, queries 3178, 3415.

57. *Parliamentary Papers*, query 3444.

58. The treaty eventually failed to win U.S. Senate approval: the vote was 28 in favor and 28 against, but a two-thirds majority was needed for passage. Ortiz, "Era of Lilis," 67–74; W. Stull Holt, *Treaties Defeated by the Senate* (Gloucester, MA: Peter Smith, 1964), 123–29.

59. Tansill, *United States and Dominican Republic*, 379–380.

60. Although Hartmont testified that the bonds were resold at about 50 percent of par, investigators found that the bonds had been quoted on the London exchange at between 64 and 71 percent. See *Parliamentary Papers*, xxx and query 3272.

61. The Dominican government denied that Hartmont ever offered to pay the balance of the loan, insisting that beyond the initial payment in May 1869, Hartmont had shipped only some £10,000 to Santo Domingo, which the government had refused to accept and returned. *Parliamentary Papers*, queries 3307, 3309, 3319, 5124, 5125.

62. The committee concluded that these contentions were not supported by the original contract and subsequent actions of the Dominican government. *Parliamentary Papers*, xxix.

63. Hartmont had evidently been notified of the repudiation in August 1870 by Colonel Joseph Fabens, an American scheming to achieve annexation of the republic. Tansill, *United States and Santo Domingo*, 349.

64. The remainder of the money, some £93,000, was neither paid to the Dominicans nor returned to the "innocent bondholders." Instead, Hartmont frankly told the investigators, it was invested "in my business; partly good investments and partly bad investments." *Parliamentary Papers*, queries 3436, 3360.

65. *Parliamentary Papers*, queries 3348, 3418, 3329, 3415–16.

66. "European bankers," Carlos Marichal observes, "adopted a substantially different behavior when dealing with the larger and more dynamic nations of Latin American than when arranging business deals with the smaller, poorer republics," which were "fair game for all kinds of speculators." Marichal, *Century of Debt Crises*, 119.

67. Domínguez, *Dictadura*, 69.

68. Had the Hartmont loan been fulfilled according to its prospectus, the Dominican government would have received 55.48 percent of the nominal value; in the case of the Westendorp loan the percent was to have been 57.48. As noted above, the annuity for the earlier loan was set at £58,900, and the total amount to be repaid over 25 years was £1,472,500.

69. The Hartmont notes were refunded at a ratio of 5 to 1, for a total of £142,860 ($714,300).

70. "The Westendorp loan momentarily relieved the tense economic, political, and social situation in 1888." Domínguez, *Dictadura*, 52–54, 74.

71. To further enhance the security of the loan, the government agreed to consult the director of the Regie when appointing new customs officials, and also promised to end the practice of giving reductions and exemptions in customs duties to merchants who had loaned money to the government. Employees of the Regie "went beyond their legal duties, maintaining constant quarrels with the Dominican civil servants." Hererra, *Finanzas*, 184–85, 193; Wynne, *State Insolvency*, 207–8.

72. The actual quantity of bonds sold in Europe from this second loan is not known. Hererra, *Finanzas*, 193–202.

73. The director of customs reported to President Heureaux that in the year from March 1893 to February 1894, the government had forfeited 103,787.37 pesos in customs revenue as a result of the reciprocity treaty with the United States. Undated pamphlet, biblioteca, AGN.
74. Domínguez, *Dictadura*, 143.
75. Jaime Domínguez observes that the crisis was rooted in the paradoxical position of the Dominican Republic, indebted to Europe but bound to the United States by trade patterns. "Between the loans of 1888 and 1890," Domínguez explains, "and the free exchange treaty there was a grave contradiction, given that it had been expected that the loans would be amortized with customs receipts, and these would be seriously reduced by the free entry of some United States goods and a 25 percent reduction on others." Domínguez, *Dictadura*, 145.
76. *NYTr*, 21 June 1891, 18.
77. Westendorp to Ministro de Hacienda y Comercio, 21 Enero 1892, leg. 32, MHC.

4. Dictating Development

1. *NYT*, 1 June 1894, 8.
2. Eugenio María de Hostos, "Civilización o Muerte," in *Páginas Dominicanas*, ed. E. Rodríguez Demorizi (Santo Domingo: Editora Taller, 1979), 174.
3. At least initially, the company seemed committed to the rationalizing goals of "capitalist-investment imperialism," in the words of Martin Sklar. In contrast to earlier forms of commercial and territorial imperialism, investment imperialism "went to the very heart of the host societies' internal affairs" to modernize "fiscal, budgetary, and tax systems" and "laws of property and contract" as well as to tie banking and monetary systems to international structures of exchange. In other words, investment imperialists sought to restructure nonindustrial societies along lines similar to those favored by Heureaux and the SDIC. Sklar, *Corporate Reconstruction of American Capitalism* (New York: Cambridge University Press, 1988), 81–83.
4. Heureaux is the subject of a popular folkloric tradition that no other leader before the age of Trujillo has inspired. See, for example, Demorizi, *Cancionero de Lilís* (Santo Domingo: Editora del Caribe, 1962); Virgil Díaz, *Lilís* (Santo Domingo, n.p., n.d.), a collection of incidents from Heureaux's life; Victor M. de Castro, *Cosas de Lilís* (Santo Domingo: Editora Taller, 1986), a similar collection of apocryphal stories; Tulio M. Cestero, *La Sangre* (Santo Domingo: n.p., n.d.), subtitled "Life Under the Heureaux Dictatorship" and originally published in 1914; as well as the many poems about Heureaux by the popular poet Juan Antonio Alix in *Décimas Políticas* (Santo Domingo: Editora de Santo Domingo, 1977).

5. Alix, *Décimas Políticas*, 105.
6. *Las Noticias* (Santiago), 29 Aug. 1894.
7. Frame, Alston & Co., a mercantile company with offices in London and New York, congratulated Heureaux after the 1896 elections in terms that suggest the attitude of the foreign business community: "We have always admired your untiring energy to advance your Government, the protection you give to foreigners and the progress you have installed in your Country. . . . As lovers of peace which is the road to success for all nations we were much delighted to hear of your re-election." Geo. R. Alston to Ulysis [sic] Heureaux, 15 Feb. 1897, CE.
8. *Las Noticias*, 1 Sept. 1894.
9. Congress gave Heureaux the title in perpetuity, perhaps recognizing that the task of pacification would never end. Frank Moya Pons, *Manual de Historia Dominicana* (Santo Domingo: Editora Corripio, 1984), 414. Heureaux's annual message to congress appears in GO, 4 March 1899.
10. Heureaux's vice president declared in 1892, "What is the meaning of those telegraph wires that put us in communication with the rest of the world, with the number of presses and libraries, and the locomotive that gives life to the deserted countryside . . . what are these but the fruits of peace!" GO, 20 Aug. 1892. In his annual address to congress in 1897, Heureaux frankly referred to his mandate as "the age of pacification," rather than an era of peace, and added that "the productive forces of the nation develop and are encouraged, due most of all to our condition of peace." GO, 6 March 1897.
11. Heureaux's brutality was selective. He preferred to intimidate or bribe opponents than to murder them outright. "As for your enemies," Heureaux advised one political ally, ". . .treat them kindly and attract them with your friendship, making them understand the need to live in peace. . . . you may note that most of those who wished to assassinate me, now . . . are at my side, protecting me from the few enemies I still have." Heureaux to Manuel Polanco, 3 Jan. 1895, tomo 49, UH.
12. By the late 1800s, the failures of republican and liberal governments led elites in much of Latin America to espouse authoritarian rule. Claiming that liberty had been achieved and that order and progress were the tasks of the day, the advocates of "responsible authoritarianism" took Bismarck as a political model. See Charles A. Hale, "Political and social ideas," in *Latin America: Economy and Society, 1870–1930*, ed. Leslie Bethell (New York: Cambridge University Press, 1989), 245–47.
13. Dominican civic pageantry served the pragmatic ends of the dictatorship, and so had much in common with the didactic ceremonies elaborated by European monarchs from the time of the Renaissance, including the use of symbolic arches and the personification of virtues. The escorted entry into a provincial

city was itself a time-honored convention that sought to honor the sovereign and to entertain and instruct the people. See David M. Bergeron, *English Civic Pageantry 1558–1642* (London: Edward Arnold, 1971), 1–10.

14. Philip Corrigan and Derek Sayer, *The Great Arch: English State Formation as Cultural Revolution* (New York: Blackwell, 1985), 3. William Roseberry points out that the process Corrigan and Sayer describe required "an extremely dense, centralized, and effective state" that was absent in Mexico and to an even greater degree lacking in the Dominican Republic. Roseberry, "Hegemony and the Language of Contention," in Gilbert M. Joseph and Daniel Nugent, eds., *Everyday Forms of State Formation* (Durham: Duke University Press, 1994), 364.

15. Heureaux directed one governor to hold meetings with ranchers and farmers "to explain to them the advantages that the new [agrarian] law will have for both interests." When the devaluation of the country's paper money spurred a popular outcry, Heureaux instructed another governor to explain the government's policy to ordinary people "in plain and simple language." Heureaux to Miguel A. Pichardo, 30 Aug. 1895, tomo 47, and to Manuel M. Castillo, 9 July 1897, tomo 60, UH.

16. Paul J. Vanderwood, *Disorder and Progress: Bandits, Police, and Mexican Development* (Wilmington: Scholarly Resources, 1992), 80.

17. Heureaux to C. W. Wells, 1 Oct. 1894, tomo 41, UH.

18. "I am convinced that the entire country has embarked on the road of order, fully and resolutely, and for that reason we will more easily achieve the establishment of positive progress," the dictator commented in a letter to the SDIC. Heureaux to Y. Mendel, 27 Sept. 1894, and to C. W. Wells, 1 Oct. 1894, tomo 41, UH.

19. Holls to White, 27 Feb. 1893, FWH.

20. *La Prensa* (Santiago), 20 May 1895.

21. Although Heureaux is typically described as a modernizer, Dominican historians have concentrated on the political structure of the regime. No careful study of the relation between his policies and the transformation of Dominican society has been made, although Jaime Domínguez lists the positive and negative effects of foreign investment in the country. Domínguez, *La Dictadura de Heureaux* (Santo Domingo: UASD, 1986), 69–76.

22. The literature on progress and economic liberalism in nineteenth-century Latin America is vast. Sharply contrasting interpretations of the topic are given by E. Bradford Burns, *The Poverty of Progress* (Berkeley: University of California Press, 1980) and Joseph L. Love and Nils Jacobsen, *Guiding the Invisible Hand* (New York: Praeger, 1988), especially Florencia A. Mallon, "Economic Liberalism: Where We Are and Where We Need to Go." See also Peter F. Klarén and Thomas J. Bossert, *Promise of Development* (Boulder, CO: Westview, 1986)

Cristóbal Kay, *Latin American Theories of Development and Underdevelopment* (New York: Routledge, 1989). Works on the idea of progress in the Dominican Republic include Raymundo González, *Bonó, Un Intelectual de los Pobres* (Santo Domingo: Centro de Estudios Sociales, 1994) and "Ideología del progreso y campesinado en el siglo XIX," *Ecos* 2 (1993); and by Michiel Baud, "Ideología y Campesinado: El Pensamiento de José Ramón López," *Estudios Sociales* 64 (April–May 1986) and *Historia de un Sueño* (Santo Domingo: Fundación Cultural Dominicana, 1993).

23. "At the end of the nineteenth century everybody talked about economic growth and the sacred idea of progress." Michiel Baud, "Ideología y Campesinado," 64.

24. "The way of life in the countryside," notes Raymundo González, ". . .was subsumed by the dominant ideology of the period under the category of barbarism, in contrast to the city, which fostered civilization." González, "Ideología del progreso," 32.

25. Thomas C. Holt describes the Jamaican stereotype of the "Quashee — lazy, morally degenerate, licentious, and heedless of the future." In British East Africa, according to Frederick Cooper, colonial officials looked on peasants who "preferred to work for themselves instead of for others" as "lazy and intractable." Holt, *Problem of Freedom*, 167; Frederick Cooper, *From Slaves to Squatters* (New Haven: Yale University Press, 1980), 216.

26. Pedro San Miguel describes *terrenos comuneros* as "large plots of land owned in common by a number of proprietors in a sort of corporate system. The *accionistas* of a common land had the right to use any quantity of land provided that they did not interfere with the . . . other partners." San Miguel, "The Dominican Peasantry and the Market Economy: The Peasants of the Cibao, 1880–1960" (unpublished Ph.D. diss., Columbia Univ., 1987), 44. See also Julie Franks, "The *Gavilleros* of the East: Social Banditry as Political Practice in the Dominican Sugar Region, 1900–1924," *Journal of Historical Sociology* 8: 2 (June 1995), especially 160–64.

27. The United States commission of investigation of 1871 reported that "most of the Cibao, from Santiago to Samaná, belongs to multiple owners under the communal system." Cited in Guillermo Moreno, "De la Propiedad Comunera a la Propiedad Privada Moderna, 1844–1924," *Eme Eme* 9: 51 (Nov.–Dic., 1980), 53–54.

28. For a general discussion of grazing laws, see Domínguez, *Dictadura*, 207–9.

29. *La Prensa* (Santiago), 3 April 1895.

30. González, "Ideología del progreso," 35.

31. According to Roberto Cassá, "the Heureaux regime promoted legislation to provide incentives to both local and foreign capital, offering favorable rates of return and every other type of advantage that the state could offer." Cassá, *Historia Social y Económica*, 2: 171. On immigration, see Francisco José

Peynado, "Por la inmigración," first published in 1909, in *Papeles y Escritos de Francisco José Peynado*, ed. Juan Daniel Balcácer (Santo Domingo: Fundación Peynado Alvarez, 1994).

32. Recent scholarship shows that economic liberalism was not adopted uncritically by Latin American elites. Paul Gootenberg's study of Peruvian elites argues that liberal ideas were "poorly received, ill adaptive, and half-heartedly implemented." Gootenberg, "Beleaguered Liberals: The Failed First Generation of Free Traders in Peru," in Love and Jacobsen, *Guiding the Invisible Hand.*

33. The Dominican leader had had, after all, a lifetime's experience of the prejudice of white Dominicans. "Among the traditional white elites, though they might be forced for economic or political reasons to tolerate him, Heureaux would never be accepted." Ortiz, "Era of Lilis," 144.

34. Holls to White, 27 Feb. 1893, FWH.

35. The conventional images of Haitian barbarism and Dominican civilization noted here were potent enough to override inconvenient details, such as the fact that Haiti was both richer and more powerful militarily than the Dominican Republic. The SDIC's attorney, Frederick William Holls, touched on the issue without any evident sense of contradiction, noting for example that Heureaux needed money to buy new warships because "unfortunately Haiti being richer has bought 3 warships, whereas Santo Domingo can only afford one." Holls to White, 27 Feb. 1893, FWH.

36. The *New York Times* gave an American naval officer's description of the two republics in 1893: "In Haiti . . . black blood predominates . . . and the white intermixture is becoming less and less every year, as the people are slowly, but surely, breeding back to the negro. The result is manifest in the Government, which is one of the worst on earth. In San Domingo the reverse is true. White blood preponderates, and there exists a class which is white, or nearly so, and which is an element of order and peace." NYT, 20 Feb. 1893, 6. In 1902 Octavio A. Acevedo published a pamphlet "to let the people of North America know . . . that the Republic of Santo Domingo and that of Haiti are two different countries." Despite the two nations' proximity, "in every other respect there are billions and billions of leagues of separation between them; *different origin, different languages, different customs, different grades of civilization.* Octavio A. Acevedo, "Dominican Republic or Republic of Santo Domingo" (Washington, D.C.: [no publisher], 1902), 2.

37. Rafael Abreu Licairac, "Contabamos con la Réplica" and "Dominicanos y Haitianos," *Eco de la Opinion*, 27 Aug. 1892 and 12 Nov. 1892.

38. Weed quoted in NYT, 1 June 1894, 8; J. Laurence Laughlin, "Gold and Silver in Santo Domingo," *Journal of Political Economy* 2 (Dec. 1893-Sept. 1894), 537; Douglass to Blaine, 11 Feb. 1890, vol. 1, USM. In fact, the proscriptions on foreign investment and landholding were often evaded in Haiti. See Brenda

Gayle Plummer, *Haiti and the great powers* (Baton Rouge: Louisiana State University Press, 1988), 49, 53.

39. Heureaux to Charles W. Wells, 25 May 1894, tomo 40, UH.

40. Heureaux to Charles W. Wells, 20 April 1894, tomo 40, UH.

41. "Discurso del Presidente de la República en la Inauguración del Ferrocarril Central," GO, 28 August 1897.

42. Despite new access to the interior, few large-scale plantations developed in the Cibao. "The railroads contributed to enhance peasant production for the market rather than to the breaking down of the peasant economy." San Miguel, "Dominican Peasantry," 72.

43. Frederick Cooper, noting a similar phenomenon in British East Africa, comments that "the peasant's partial incorporation into markets . . . [was] a form of subordination which extended to the appropriation of the surplus but not the manner in which labor was performed." Frederick Cooper, *From Slaves to Squatters*, 13.

44. Walter LaFeber describes Dominican society "being thrown into turmoil by the emergence of two agrarian systems" in the north and south, "the first by the replacement of tobacco culture by cocoa, the second by a large influx of U.S. and Cuban capital." But as suggested here, the Dominican peasantry proved remarkably resistant to "economic development and its attendant dislocations." The crisis that brought about Washington's intervention after 1904 was financial, not agrarian. LaFeber, *Cambridge History of American Foreign Relations*, vol. 2 (New York: Cambridge University Press, 1993), 197.

45. Emilio Tejera to Tomás D. Morales, 11 Nov. 1894, reproduced in *Clio* 49 and 50 (Santo Domingo, 1941), 192–93.

46. Petition of Juan Batista Casado, 1 Feb. 1895, leg. 154, MIP.

47. For landowners, the law fixed a maximum number of animals permitted per hectare of land, and also set a minimum number of shares in unfenced and unmeasured *terrenos comuneros* in order to raise livestock. Survey of lands in leg. 156, MIP; GO, 1 June 1895.

48. The conflict corresponds to the clash between modernizing elites and folk cultures described by E. Bradford Burns. Burns overstates the "nonmaterialist" orientation of folk society and its dedication to "interdependence, cooperation, solidarity, and . . . harmony," yet the conflict of cultures he describes was clearly in play in the debate over *crianza libre*. Burns, *Poverty of Progress*, 11.

49. A transcript of the congressional debate appears in GO, 3 Aug. 1895.

50. Ulises Heureaux to Miguel A. Pichardo, 30 Aug. 1895, tomo 47, UH. On *terrenos comuneros* and *crianza libre*, see Richard Turits, "The Foundations of Despotism: Peasants, Property, and the Trujillo Regime in the Dominican Republic, 1930–1961" (unpublished Ph.D. dissertation, University of Chicago, 1997).

51. "The law encountered opposition from ordinary pastoralists and influential landowners in that government, and this opposition was seized upon by political agitators," according to a footnote to Emilio Tejera's letter to Ulises Heureaux about the suspension of enforcement of the new law. *Clio*, 194.

52. Benito R. Pinas to the Minister of the Interior and Police, 26 Aug. 1895, leg. 155, exp. 16, MIP.

53. Emiliano Tejera, prime mover of the reform, wrote to Heureaux in October 1895 that despite the suspension of enforcement "the country will progress, although slowly, and one day will arrive at the point where it will see as beneficial that which it condemns as a terrible evil today." *Clio*, 194–95.

54. *La Prensa* (Santiago) 23 Sept. 1895.

55. As export crop production expanded rapidly in the 1890s and farmers planted new land, conflicts between farmers and herders increased. As late as 1907, more than half of all lawsuits recorded in the country involved disputes between *agricultores* and *criadores*. Bryan, "La Producción Campesina," 53–54. Bruce Calder discusses the attempts of Dominican governments and the U.S. military occupation to deal with the land question in *The Impact of Intervention* (Austin: University of Texas Press, 1984), 102–14.

56. The failed assault on *crianza libre* raises another issue. Steven Hahn has demonstrated that legal restrictions on open-range grazing in the postbellum U.S. south sought to limit the autosufficiency of freedmen in order to expand the plantation labor force. "The 'labor question,' therefore, became linked inextricably with the 'land question,' " as Hahn puts it. Although sugar planters in the Dominican Republic complained about labor costs in the 1890s, the goal of the livestock reform law was apparently not to detach peasants from the soil in order to create an agricultural proletariat. The conflict over *crianza libre* needs further investigation, but it appears that the new law sought to commodify the land, not the peasant. Steven Hahn, "Hunting, Fishing, and Foraging: Common Rights and Class Relations in the Postbellum South," *Radical History Review* 26 (1982), 44.

57. See comments on Bass's proposal in *El Eco de la Opinión*, 11, 18, 25 Oct. and 11 Nov. 189[3?], AGN.

58. Emily S. Rosenberg, *Financial Missionaries to the World: The Politics and Culture of Dollar Diplomacy, 1900–1930* (Cambridge: Harvard University Press, 1999).

59. Charles W. Wells, reply to query 9 of Jacob Hollander, dated September 25, 1905, in box 1, JHH.

60. In the early 1890s, many nations adopted the gold standard to defend their currencies against the sharp worldwide devaluation of silver. Marcello de Cecco describes the process in *Money and Empire* (London: Blackwell, 1974), 39–62.

61. Rosenberg, *Financial Missionaries*, 24.
62. The SDIC stood to benefit for the reason de Cecco notes for Latin America in general: "Those who had made hard currency loans to central or local Latin American governments [favored monetary reform] . . . because inflationary governments usually had difficulty in paying interest on, and repaying the principal of, hard-currency debts." *Money and Empire*, 59. Although inflation of the national currency helped planters already established in the country, as noted below, a stable monetary system was attractive to new investors. See Rosenberg, "Foundations," 172. J. Laurence Laughlin, "Monetary Reform in Santo Domingo," *Atlantic Monthly* 74: 441 (July 1894), 107.
63. Laughlin had visited the Dominican Republic in 1888, while recovering from a nervous breakdown suffered in his last year of teaching at Harvard. Alfred Bornemann, *J. Laurence Laughlin: Chapters in the Career of an Economist* (Washington, D.C.: American Council on Public Affairs, 1940), 1–5, 15; John T. Abbott, reply to query of September 24, 1905, JHH.
64. J. Laurence Laughlin, "Gold and Silver in Santo Domingo," *Journal of Political Economy* 2 (Dec. 1893–Sept. 1894), 547.
65. Laughlin, "Gold and Silver," 555. Laughlin's plan was in essence the gold-exchange standard advocated by Charles Conant as an alternative for peripheral nations to the strict gold standard. Emily Rosenberg describes Conant's theories in "Foundations," 196–98.
66. *NYT*, 11 April 1894.
67. Laughlin, "Monetary Reform," 109. According to Emily Rosenberg, Puerto Rican sugar planters faced the same problem when the United States introduced American currency after 1898. Employers cut wages drastically, while retailers switched from pesos to dollars without reducing prices. In Cuba, planter opposition to paying higher wages kept American officials from imposing the gold-exchange standard. "U.S. gold-standard reformers thus believed their work simultaneously promoted social uplift abroad and stimulated new trade and investment opportunities." See Rosenberg, "United States International Financial Power," 173–76, and *Financial Missionaries*, 14, 20–21.
68. Abbott reply to query 4, JHH.
69. The underlying conflict between sugar planters on the one hand and the Dominican government and the SDIC on the other came to a head in 1903–5 with a public dispute over taxing the production and export of sugar in order to pay foreign bondholders. See chapter 9.
70. Rosenberg, *Financial Missionaries*, 26, 27; Laughlin, "Monetary Reform," 112.
71. *La Prensa* (Santiago) 2 Sept. 1895.
72. "Not being able to remain any longer in this ruinous condition, we are going to proclaim a change in the system. The gold standard will come into effect,

and customs duties will be lowered to 45%." Heureaux to Y. Mendel, 15 March 1894, tomo 39, UH; see also Abbott reply to query, JHH.

73. Abbott reply to query, JHH. De Cecco notes that "in Latin American countries, attempts to introduce the gold standard were doomed." *Money and Empire*, 59.

74. Lowell Gudmundson and Hector Lindo-Fuentes have reached similar conclusions about the nations of Central America in the nineteenth century, arguing that "control of the state through political means alone" was not enough to "ensure the achievement of radical economic ends involving the restructuring of society." Lowell Gudmundson and Hector Lindo-Fuentes, *Central America, 1821–1871: Liberalism before Liberal Reform* (Tuscaloosa: University of Alabama, 1995), 7.

75. Rosenberg, *Financial Missionaries*, 30.

76. *NYT*, 1 June 1894, 8.

77. Arnold J. Bauer, "Rural Workers in Spanish America: Problems of Peonage and Oppression," *Hispanic American Historical Review*, 59: 1 (1979), 53.

78. Both men went to the Dominican Republic on special, short-term assignments for the company. Holls, at least, was remarkably naive in his judgments about the economy of the Caribbean nation. For example, in its contracts with the SDIC the Dominican government pledged to pay all the costs of building the Central Dominican Railroad from Puerto Plata to Santiago and even guaranteed its running expenses for 50 years. Holls deemed these clauses unnecessary since the company had "guarantees of sufficient business from the merchants of Santiago and Porto Plata to make the line one of the most profitable in the world." Holls to White, 27 Feb. 1893, FWH.

79. *NYTr* 17 Jan. 1901.

80. The goal of bankers and brokers in London and other European centers, according to Carlos Marichal, "invariably was to collect commissions from client governments as well as to turn a profit on the 'spread' between the price they paid for the bonds and the price at which they were able to sell them." *Century of Debt Crises*, 113.

5. The Cash Nexus

1. Subtitled "Una vida bajo la tiranía de Lilís," *La Sangre*, published in 1914, is considered to be one of the seminal novels of Dominican literature.

2. Heureaux to I. Mendel, 14 Feb. 1898, tomo 66, UH.

3. Heureaux to William L. Bass, [January 1898?], tomo 64, UH.

4. Until 1897, the Council of Foreign Bondholders kept Dominican loans off the London exchange because of protests by unhappy British holders of Hartmont notes from 1869.

5. The comment is from David S. Landes's study of European bankers involved in Egyptian state finance in the 1860s and 1870s. Similarly, Carlos Marichal reports that "the issue of external bonds was as easy as printing money." David Landes, *Bankers and Pashas* (New York: Harper & Row, 1958), 106; Carlos Marichal, *A Century of Debt Crises in Latin America* (Princeton: Princeton University Press, 1989), 81.

6. The bulk of large loans to Cuba in 1886 and to both Brazil and Mexico in 1889 was to convert securities from earlier flotations into new bonds. Marichal, *Century of Debt Crises*, 129.

7. William H. Wynne, *State Insolvency and Foreign Bondholders* (New Haven: Yale University Press, 1951), 2: 212–217; Jacob Hollander, "Report on the Debt of Santo Domingo," 59th Congress, 1st Session, Executive Document No. 1.4, 6–7.

8. Wynne, *State Insolvency*, 213–17; Hollander, "Debt," 6–7.

9. See Wynne, *State Insolvency*, 219; Hollander, "Report," 13.

10. "Case of the United States before the Commission of Arbitration," United States [vs.] the Dominican Republic, [n.p.], 12 Feb. 1904, 9.

11. Heureaux to Isidor Mendel, 13 Nov. 1896, tomo 32, UH.

12. The company and Heureaux had finally come to terms with holders of Hartmont paper, dating to 1869, and as a result the Council of Foreign Bondholders at last lifted its objection to a London listing. "The Council of Foreign Bondholders has up to the present time felt itself compelled to offer a decided opposition to any attempt to obtain a quotation for any Dominican Loan on the London Stock Exchange," the Council's secretary informed the brokerage house of Brown Janson & Co. in 1896, adding that the council was now "prepared to withdraw their opposition." James P. Cooper to Brown Janson & Co., 11 Aug. 1896, Guildhall ms. 15,802/4, San Domingo Press copy, Vol. IV, CFB.

13. A group of English capitalists had agreed to underwrite the loan by purchasing a large number of bonds. When they realized that the government had failed to buy back from Dominican lenders special fees and charges that had been promised as guarantees on the new loan, they withdrew from the venture. Heureaux refers to "the collapse of the operation undertaken in the British market." "Case of the United States," 13; Heureaux to Charles W. Wells, 15 March 1898, tomo 65, UH.

14. "Large amounts of the Bonds had . . . passed into the hands of Companies and private firms who had made advances against them to the Improvement Company," the secretary of the Corporation of Foreign Bondholders reported, mentioning among other firms the Pelican and British Empire Life Office, London City & Midland Bank, Price, Waterhouse & Company, and Brown, Janson & Company. James P. Cooper to Jacob H. Hollander, 28 June 1905, St. Domingo Press Copy, vol. VI, Guildhall ms. 15,802.

15. Heureaux to Isidor Mendel, 13 Nov. 1896, tomo 32, UH.

16. The contracts permitted the creation of an international financial commission in the event of default. The 1893 contract stated that "The company will have full rights to collect all of the ordinary and extraordinary receipts of the Dominican Republic, resulting from current laws and any future laws enacted, and it will have the right to use these receipts to pay the debts of the Government." The contract also stipulated that the government undertake "a radical reform of the customs service" and stipulated that "all of the officials and employees of the customs service will be named jointly by the Minister of Finance and the Director General of the Caja de Recaudación," who was an employee of the SDIC. It guaranteed that "no merchandise will be imported or exported without control and verification" by the Regie, and specifically mentioned that "no IOU's will be valid" if not approved by the Regie. If the terms of the contact were not fulfilled, "the monthly payments to cover the government budget will stop." *Colección de Leyes, Decretos y Resoluciones* (Santo Domingo: Listin Diario, 1929), 13: 22–23.

17. In one typical letter, Heureaux complained to Wells of "the intrigues against you and against the credit of this country and our mutual interests." Heureaux to C. W. Wells, 26 Oct. 1896, tomo 55, original in English, UH.

18. "The only taxation in the Republic is that upon imports and exports. . . . The cities collect small municipal imposts, but even for the[se] the principal revenue is derived from the National Treasury." "Case of the United States," 17.

19. Recent studies have given new emphasis to the role of local capital. "State and local private capital played a more prominent role in railway construction than Latin Americanists generally recognize," argues Paul J. Dosal. In a detailed study, Alfonso W. Quiroz challenges the traditional assumption "that *private domestic finance* played a negligible role in pre-1950 Peru." Dosal, *Doing Business with the Dictators* (Wilmington: Scholarly Resources, 1993), 28; Quiroz, *Domestic and Foreign Finance in Modern Peru* (Pittsburgh: University of Pittsburgh Press, 1993), x; Jaime Domínguez, *La Dictadura de Heureaux* (Santo Domingo: Editora Universitaria, 1986), 69.

20. Local capital was largely devoted to state loans and investments in sugar plantations of the merchant capitalists themselves. Little local capital remained for financing other sugar plantations and railroads. William Bass, owner of a large sugar estate, told Heureaux that obtaining capital in the United States was a requirement for Dominican planters. "It is necessary that the northern backers become so largely interested and actively occupied with the estates," Bass wrote, "that they cannot recede and in order that the enterprises do not become dependant [sic] upon advances of the local merchants, whose capital being small soon runs out and then the enterprise has neither northern or southern resources." W.L. Bass [unsigned] to Ulises Heureaux, 30 Sept. 1897, leg. 18, CE.

21. Contracts may not of course accurately reflect the actual amounts lent. All values are expressed in U.S. gold dollars. Alfonso Huet, "Juan B. Vicini y la Acumulación Originaria, 1870–1900" (Master's essay, Universidad Autónoma de Santo Domingo, 1980), 64.

22. The country's other leading merchant capitalist, Cosme Battle, for example, lent the government $207,000 in 1893, $346,242 in 1895, and participated in a $100,000 loan with Vicini and another lender in 1895. "Case of the United States," 46–47.

23. The dictator borrowed money from European houses including Vinamata & Huttlinger, Frame Alston & Co., as well as J. Sala & Co., the latter a Dominican firm with offices in New York. Heureaux to I. Mendel, 14 April 1898, tomo 34, UH.

24. At various times Heureaux articulated this preference. "What the government wants and imperatively needs is to liberate itself from its current domestic debts, which incur an excessively high rate of interest and absorb resources that could be used to guarantee much larger loans than those to which they are now dedicated." Heureaux to I. Mendel, 7 Aug. 1897, tomo 61, UH.

25. Juan B. Vicini actually signed the SDIC's first contract with the Dominican government. The contract pledged the company to pay 199,000 mexican pesos — about $100,000 gold — to Vicini and slightly larger sums to Cosme Battle and to Pedro A. Lluberes, the latter one of Heureaux's cabinet ministers. *Colección de Leyes*, 1893, 24–25.

26. The exact operation of these contracts with Battle remains obscure. Heureaux to Ch. W. Wells, 4 Dec. 1896, tomo 56, UH.

27. According to Francisco Henríquez y Carvajal, who played a pivotal role in negotiations with the SDIC and the State Department after Heureaux's assassination, "it is more or less confirmed that Heureaux's administration was spending over $200,000 gold each month." The government's monthly allowance from the SDIC was only $90,000. Francisco Henríquez y Carvajal, *Cayacoa y Cotubanama* (Santo Domingo: ONAP, 1985), 104.

28. Memorandum, 17 Oct. 1894, tomo 42, UH.

29. In one letter seeking new funds Heureaux drew attention to his courteous demeanor: "I hope you will note the marked deference with which I address you, and my interest in increasing the business I conduct with you." Heureaux to J. Sala & Ca, 19 Dec. 1895, tomo 37, UH.

30. "I will continue to guarantee ever more resolutely the interests that I am obliged to safeguard, including yours and those of the others which have grown under the protection of my regime," the dictator assured one leading merchant. Heureaux to Cosme Battle, 12 Sept. 1895, tomo 48, UH.

31. Detailed studies of the merchant lender group are few. Huet's "Juan B. Vicini" provides valuable information about the loans and sugar investments of the country's leading merchant lender.

32. Memorandum dated 17 Oct. 1894, prepared for Comisionado Confidencial in his meeting with Smith M. Weed and Charles W. Wells in New York, tomo 42, UH.

33. The local lenders played a pivotal role until the very end of Heureaux's regime. In 1896, Heureaux reported that Vicini had refused to accept checks from the government and that "I was forced to accept to my great disadvantage" an arrangement to get payment. In July Heureaux wired Wells in Paris: "It is impossible: I can't make any sort of arrangement with Vicini. He insists that his notes be paid by you." In 1897 Heureaux reported "Vicini and Cosme are demanding payment . . . they refuse to accept my notes." Indeed, the day before Heureaux was assassinated he negotiated a new loan from merchants in the Cibao city of Moca. Heureaux to C.W. Wells, 27 June 1896, tomo 52; quoted in Heureaux to Pedro A. Lluberes, 14 July 1896, tomo 53; Heureaux to I. Mendel, 14 Oct. 1897, tomo 62, UH; Adriano Miguel Tejada, *El Ajusticiamiento de Lilís* (Santo Domingo: Editora Corripio, 1995), 17.

34. It is true that the director of the Regie was an American employee of the SDIC. But this was basically a clerical position, and the director of the Regie had little influence over the Dominican government.

35. "Minor Keith was not a Wall Street tycoon who exploited the tropics from a Manhattan office." The characterization does, however, fit the directors of the SDIC. Paul J. Dosal, *Doing Business with the Dictators* (Wilmington, DE: Scholarly Resources, 1993), 55–56.

36. The system naturally worked to the disadvantage of small merchants unable to lend money and obtain free entry of goods. "How can other merchants get ahead when Don Cosme can do whatever he feels like doing?" Zóilo Garcia to Ulises Heureaux, 30 Jan. 1893, CE.

37. Of course, small merchants as well as large did all they could to avoid paying duties. One merchant explained the system to Heureaux in frank detail: "As a merchant, I always did what the other merchants did and still do. I presented phony bills of lading to the custom inspectors, concealed from them all that I could, and tried to pass one article off as another, and so on, being just as devious as the other merchants were." Zóilo Garcia to Ulises Heureaux, 22 Feb. 1897, CE.

38. After Heureaux's assassination, the SDIC provided a candid portrait of these operations. "The President needed for his purposes, say $100,000. He would borrow it from some local merchants of wealth, promising to pay back $200,000 or even more, with interest . . . as the merchants were importers and exporters, he would authorize them to apply the Customs Duties they incurred to the payment of this multiplied debt," adding that "the *Regie* protested, but was powerless." "Case of the United States before the Commission of Arbitration," United States [vs.] the Dominican Republic, [n.p.], 12 Feb. 1904, 18.

39. In 1897 Heureaux apologized to the SDIC for taking the unusual step of appointing a new inspector in Samaná "without getting the company's approval beforehand," but promised that government "will abstain . . . for the time being from naming any new customs officials." Heureaux to Ch. W. Wells, 15 April 1897, tomo 58, UH.

40. Heureaux to Charles W. Wells [Paris], 2 June 1896, tomo 52, UH. Earlier Heureaux had assured the SDIC "in all honesty I must tell you that the customs inspectors do their duties well." Heureaux to Charles W. Wells, 25 May 1894, tomo 40, UH.

41. "I imagine that with the reforms that I intend to introduce in the customs service, the income of the government will increase considerably," Heureaux pledged in July 1896. In January 1898 Heureaux told Wells, "You know my firm resolve to reorganize the custom houses with new personnel and new discipline so that the receipts will be higher than ever before." Heureaux to I. Mendel, 14 Feb. 1897, tomo 57; Heureaux to Ch. Wells, 14 July 1896, tomo 53; Heureaux to Charles W. Wells, 14 Jan. 1898, tomo 64, UH.

42. In 1897, Heureaux acknowledged that it was necessary to "better organize and manage the Caja de Recaudación, making this institution a serious control over our customs service." Later the dictator commented that "I think the money we spend on the personnel of the Caja de Recaudación is wasted. Each month they consume $4,500 in gold, paid by the government, and in the end they do nothing but live like princes." Heureaux to I. Mendel, 16 April 1897 and 13 Sept. 1897, tomos 58 and 61, UH.

43. The pattern occurred in other peripheral states, where the interests of foreign lenders and local borrowers interpenetrated so thoroughly that they could be put asunder only by force. David S. Landes has described the relationship of French banker Edouard Dervieu to Ismael, the viceroy of Egypt in the 1860s, in similar terms. "There was little Dervieu could do about this particular client. Dervieu's prestige and profits depended on the favor of the Viceroy. . . . At the same time, there was no way in the world of preventing Ismael from borrowing from Oppenheim, Pastré, or any other banker." Landes, *Bankers and Pashas*, 159–160.

44. The approach of the deadline for interest payments on the loans provoked panic at predictable, six-month intervals. In November 1894 Heureaux commented to Wells that "payment of the coupon in January, saves our credit: and you know very well that, with well grounded credit, all negotiations will find an easy [way]." A year later the dictator advised Wells, "In December I will put at your disposal in Europe . . . the amount needed to cover the deficit in favor of the Caja de Recaudación, which is destined to pay the interest coupon of January 1896. . . . I don't think I'll be able to remit to you in December the rest of the 250 thousand pesos . . . that would put me in a very difficult situa-

tion." Heureaux to Charles W. Wells, 25 Nov. 1894, tomo 36, original in English; Heureaux to Charles W. Wells, 9 Nov. 1895, tomo 36, UH.

45. On another occasion he lectured Wells that "I have advanced you 279,000 francs . . . to pay the coupon of July. I do not claim their immediate payment, but I have drawn on you to cover my engagements with the Bank." On another he commented that "to settle my most pressing obligations and save my credit . . . I have been forced to promise everything I own and be very careful to honor the drafts that have been submitted to me for payment." Later Heureaux took personal responsibility for payments that should have been made by the Regie. "Until now the interest payments have been made religiously. Through March I was seeing to these payments personally, because I have the obligation to do so. In the future, however, it will be the exclusive function of the Caja de Recaudación, which is responsible therefor." Since a representative of the Belgian bondholders had become co-director of the Regie, the dictator was anxious to transfer responsibility for paying interest back to that institution. If interest payments were not made, warned Heureaux, "the creditors will have no right to complain about the government, since the Caja de Recaudación . . . is now able to service the external debt and so fulfill its function as representative of the bondholders. It will be their fault, not the government's, if their own employees, through malfeasance or incompetence, damage their interests." Heureaux to Charles W. Wells, 7 Oct. 1896, tomo 54, original in English; Heureaux to I. Mendel, 14 April 1898, tomo 34; Heureaux to I. Mendel, 14 April 1898, tomo 66, UH.

46. In fact, Heureaux commanded a substantial fortune as a private citizen. In 1895 he acknowledged that he personally had a one-third interest in the purchase of the Banco Nacional and owned $510,000 pesos of Reclamation Consols. Heureaux to I. Mendel, 11 Nov. 1895, tomo 36; Heureaux to C. W. Wells, 26 Oct. 1896, tomo 55, UH. See also *Resumen General del Activo y Pasivo de la Sucesión Heureaux* (Santo Domingo: Garcia Hermanos, 1900).

47. According to the secretary of the Corporation of Foreign Bondholders, the SDIC's business was "a very paying one." [James P. Cooper to S.A. Braithwaite, 27 Feb. 1901, St. Domingo Press Copy, vol. V, Guildhall ms. 15,802.

48. Heureaux to Charles W. Wells, 7 Aug. 1897, tomo 61, UH.

49. The incident is described in detail in David Charles MacMichael, "The United States and the Dominican Republic, 1871–1940" (unpublished Ph.D. diss., University of Oregon, 1964), 100–117, and Edgar Charles Duin, "Dominican-American Diplomatic Relations, 1895–1907" (unpublished Ph.D. diss., Georgetown University, 1955), 13–17.

50. Explanatory Memo, attached to A. W. y Gil to Secretary of State, 5 Feb. 1895, volumes 3–4, DL.

51. "Upon presentation of the matter to Secretary of State Gresham and President Cleveland, the United States intervened in Paris, so effectually, that the French Government proposed an amendment." "Case of the United States," 12. According to one scholar, "American representations to Paris were concerned only with the welfare of the Improvement Company. Nothing was said of the Monroe Doctrine, or even simple justice." MacMichael, "United States and Dominican Republic," 109, 112.
52. Heureaux to Charles W. Wells, 14 Jan. 1895, tomo 43; Heureaux to Charles W. Wells, 20 Feb. 1895, tomo 44, UH.
53. Heureaux to Charles W. Wells, 14 March 1895, tomo 45, UH.
54. Like Ulises Heureaux, some historians have minimized the effectiveness of the SDIC's contacts in Washington as revealed by the bank incident. Richard Collin concludes that "the United States had in fact done very little." Since both diplomatic and military resources had been mobilized on behalf of the company, however, it is difficult to imagine what more the government might have done. Richard Collin, *Theodore Roosevelt's Caribbean* (Baton Rouge: Louisiana State University Press, 1990), 367.
55. Heureaux to Smith M. Weed, 21 March 1895, and to Charles W. Wells, 26 March 1895, tomo 45, UH.
56. H. F. Pollock, a member of parliament who acted as solicitor for the Dominican government in London, related the incident to another m.p. in 1897: "Mr. Smith M. Weed . . . in his capacity as President of the Improvement Co. went to Washington, announced what the French Republic had done, and thereupon the American Minister in Paris was instructed to call on [foreign minister] Hanotaux and inform him that if France took any such high-handed proceedings as sending her War Ships to San Domingo to enforce her supposed claim, then in such case America would send her War Ships also in order to protect the rights of the San Domingo Improvement Co." The Foreign Office did not accept all Pollock's assertions at face value, but showed real concern about official backing of the SDIC. H. F. Pollock to G. N. Curzon, 6 July 1897, Dominica (Diplomatic, Consular & Treaty), V. Consul at San Domingo, 1897, FO 23/93.
57. In 1897, the dictator asked Isidor Mendel to try to "convince Wells or induce him somehow to accept my coinage plan." Heureaux to I. Mendel, 14 Oct. 1897, tomo 62, UH.
58. "It isn't possible for me to authorize the Bank emission . . . even if it might temporarily provide relief, it would overcommit our resources." Despite his misgivings, Heureaux later released the notes, causing a run on the Banco Nacional and forcing the dictator to arrange an emergency loan from local merchants. Heureaux to I. Mendel, 13 Jan. 1896, tomo 49; Heureaux to Charles W. Wells, 25 Feb. 1896; tomo 50, UH.

59. Heureaux to Charles W. Wells, 13 July 1897, tomo 60, UH.
60. "Though I had hoped that by this new conversion I would have been enabled to liquidate these debts and to free me of all obligations, I am sorry to say that by the new conditions and charges made in our conversion scheme this will be an impossibility. I therefore have been seriously studying in what way I could make a clean slate and discharge my Government of any liability outside of those deriving from formal contracts. The means of doing so are following: I want to make an issue of $1.500.000 in paper money . . . in order to pay of[f] the several loans that my Government has still outstanding with the principal merchants of this country." Heureaux to Charles W. Wells, 7 Aug. 1897, tomo 61, original in English, UH.
61. To Wells the dictator explained, "it will seem strange to you that I now feel that the emission should be limited to $1,000,000 . . . but one doesn't argue with necessity. The circumstances demand a reduction and we must accept that fact." Heureaux to Charles W. Wells, 15 Dec. 1897, tomo 63, UH.
62. No final sums can be given for the emissions. These numbers are taken from the report of acting British vice-consul H. Gosling's report, "Trade of Santo Domingo for the year 1898–99," No. 2313, Annual Series, Diplomatic and Consular Reports, Foreign Office, July, 1899, FO 23/96. Julio C. Estrella's history of Dominican banks and finances gives no figure for the period but notes that the coinage of 1897 varied between 66 and 80 percent copper. Estrella, *La Moneda, La Banca y las Finanzas en la República Dominicana* (Santiago: Universidad Católica Madre y Maestra, 1971), 1: 58–60, 734.
63. Heureaux to Charles W. Wells, 15 Dec. 1897, tomo 63, UH.
64. Heureaux to Aristides Patino, 15 July 1897; see also Heureaux to Manuel M. Castillo, 9 July 1897, tomo 60, UH.
65. GO, 4 March 1899.
66. Heureaux to Y. Mendel, 14 Oct. 1897, tomo 62, and to Charles [W.] Wells, 7 Oct. 1896, tomo 54, UH.
67. "The organization of the exhibit and the objects displayed deserve our praise," wrote a Dominican official in Europe, "as they did from his majesty the king of the Belgians, who reviewed our display and examined our products with lively interest." Heureaux praised the Dominican consul in Brussels for arranging the exhibit "in the most attractive and favorable manner for the prestige of our country and the beneficial display or our products." Emanuel de Almeda to Ulises Heureaux, 15 May 1897, CE; Heureaux to J. Penso, 12 July 1897, tomo 60, UH.
68. Undated newspaper clipping attached to A. Cohen to Ulysses Heureaux, 10 June 1897, CE.
69. Heureaux predicted "good harvests that will relieve the economic distress that the country has experienced in recent months." Heureaux to J. Tornabells, 30 Aug. 1897, tomo 61, UH.

70. That is, exports more than tripled, while imports increased about 40 percent. Given the manipulation of customs receipts described above, neither import nor export statistics are wholly reliable. Since merchants presumably undervalued both imports and exports, figures were probably even larger. Statistics compiled by Helen Ortiz, "The Era of Lilís: Political Stability and Economic Change in the Dominican Republic" (unpublished Ph.D. diss, Georgetown Univ., 1975), 337.

71. The situation in the late 1890s paralleled that earlier in the decade, as described in chapter 4, in which inflation of silver currency favored exporters, who opposed the imposition of the gold standard. In 1898, however, the government did take the step of requiring payment of export taxes in gold. GO, 4 March 1899.

72. H. Gosling, "Trade of Santo Domingo for 1898–99," FO 23/96.

73. Unsigned letters to Heureaux dated 4 April 1899 and 9 April 1899, 1892–99, CE.

74. Quoted in Raymundo González, *Bonó, un intelectual de los pobres* (Santo Domingo: Editora Buho, 1994), 12.

75. Heureaux also threatened to take action against farmers and plantation owners who took advantage of the inflated currency. "If during October the financial situation doesn't improve, and the exporters continue to take advantage as they have so far, the Government will be forced to defend itself, especially from the large planters, who have benefitted most." Heureaux to Manuel Ma. Castillo, 4 Aug. [sic: actually Oct.] 1898 and to Teofilo Cordero y Bidó, 26 Sept. 1898, tomo 69, UH.

76. One well-known figure in Baní complained that "six months have passed without paying the public employees of this district." [Manuel Puello] to Ulises Heureaux, 9 Aug. 1898, CE.

77. From La Vega, Manuel Decamp reported that employees and those receiving "asignaciones" had accepted a 25 percent reduction in their income without complaint "because we are convinced of the imperious necessity constraining the Government." When the actual budget arrived, however, they were shocked to find that some salaries had been cut 66 percent, "that doesn't even permit us to take care of our most urgent needs." [illegible], governor of Distrito Pacificador, to Ulises Heureaux, 5 Feb. 1897; Manuel Decamp to Ulises Heureaux, 20 Jan. 1897; see also Manuel Pichardo to Ulises Heureaux, 25 Jan. 1897; all in CE.

78. Heureaux to C.I.[sic] Wells, 7 Oct. 1896, tomo 54, and to Zoilo Garcia, 23 Sept. 1898, tomo 69, UH.

79. See chapter 1, pp. 26–27. John Bassett Moore, "Counter-Case of the United States before the Commission of Arbitration," United States [vs.] Dominican Republic, [n.p.], 12 April 1904, 97, 106–7.

80. Heureaux did not object to the appointment of the Belgian "Controlador," but did find it unfair that his salary, along with those of the officials of the Regie, would be paid from his country's treasury. Heureaux even arranged for the newcomer to live near him so that "we will be neighbors and I will have a chance to cultivate his friendship." Heureaux to I. Mendel, 7 Aug. and 13 Sept. 1897, tomo 61, UH.

81. "Without first freeing up these *apartados* from the obligations that now weigh upon them, it is legally impossible to apply them to the guarantee and payment of the new loan, since as long as they are not redeemed, which the government seeks to do at once, they belong by right to the creditors to whom they were given as a surety." Heureaux to Charles W. Wells, 7 Aug. 1897, tomo 61, UH.

82. "I promised Vicini and the other holders of the internal debt to redeem the *apartados* that are now dedicated to paying their loans in order to deliver them to the Belgian control." Vicini demanded "in exchange the 10% surcharge as a guarantee for the sums he is owed." Heureaux to Charles W. Wells, 15 March and 13 May 1898, tomos 65 and 66, UH.

83. Heureaux to I. Mendel, 14 March 1898, tomo 65, UH.

84. "I must suggest that you don't overlook the possibility of having the bondholders' committees force Wells to accept the new conversion plan, or even, if it be necessary, having them retire the powers granted to him in order to deal directly with the Dominican government." Heureaux to I. Mendel, 13 March 1897, tomo 57, UH.

85. "It seems that just as you deny that Wells enjoys considerable influence in Europe," wrote Heureaux, "you likewise underestimate his rights, which so far have allowed him to oppose the plan that you are trying to put together. . . . Besides being the legal representative of the bondholders, the [SDIC] officials themselves hold a considerable quantity of bonds. . . . Prior to the creation of any combination that might affect the interests of the majority, they should have stripped the company of its legal character. . . . so that the government could have had a legal entity with which to negotiate new operations without accepting the dangerous responsibility of arbitrarily suppressing the rights of the Improvement." Heureaux to Ch. W. Wells, 15 April 1897, and to I. Mendel, 16 April 1897, tomo 58, and 12 July 1897, tomo 60, UH.

86. Heureaux to Miguel Pichardo, 19 April 1898, tomo 66, UH.

87. The dictator permitted covert support of the Cuban rebels, and even provided money to José Martí and Máximo Gómez at the outset of the struggle "He may have done much harm in Santo Domingo," Máximo Gómez wrote of Heureaux in 1900, "but he did much good for Cuba." *Papeles Domincanos de Máximo Gómez*, ed. Emilio Rodríguez Demorizi (Santo Domingo: Editora Montalvo, 1954), 180; see also 97 and 253n, as well as *Martí en Santo Domingo* (Barcelona: Gráfica Pareja, 1978), 120–24, by the same editor.

88. It was in Spain's best interest, Heureaux wrote, "to reduce the scattering of immigrants, encouraging them to settle among Latinos, where they will conserve their filial devotion to Spain." Heureaux to Prudencio Rabell, 5 June 1895, tomo 46, UH.

89. The leader hoped to buy 15 to 20 cannon and two small warships. Heureaux to José Ladislao de Escoriaza, 10 Aug. 1898, tomo 68, UH.

90. The plan is described by Duin, "Dominican-American Diplomatic Relations," 19–20.

91. Heureaux to José Ladislao de Escoriaza, 24 April 1896, tomo 51, UH.

92. Heureaux to Alejandro Wos y Gil, 30 March 1898, tomo 65, UH. The shifts in American attitude are summarized in Joseph Smith, *The Spanish American War* (New York: Longman, 1994), 37–40.

93. Heureaux to José Ladislao de Escoriaza, 14 May 1898, tomo 66, UH.

94. Historians have doubted that the United States took these offers seriously. David Charles MacMichael finds that events during the Spanish-Cuban-American War provide "more evidence that the American desire for the possession of Samaná is a myth." MacMichael, "United States and Dominican Republic," 128. Heureaux's failed negotiations are discussed in Tansill, "Diplomatic Relations," 198–201.

95. A. S. Crowninshield to Secretary of the Navy, 28 Feb. 1898, in William Rufus Day papers, Library of Congress Manuscript Division, Washington, D.C.

96. Heureaux's earlier efforts to reach a new reciprocity accord with the United States are described in Henry M. Smythe to Richard W. Olney, 4 Jan. 1897, vol. 3, USM.

97. Edward Younger, *John A. Kasson* (Iowa City: State Historical Society of Iowa, 1955), 364–69.

98. In late March Kasson told Smith M. Weed about snags in negotiations for lease of the bay. "Nothing is finally settled," he wrote, and he was reluctant "to offer now as good terms as were offered before. The use proposed would be a positive benefit to that people, with its incidental expenditures, and its moral protection against foreign outrages. But Heureaux, and any successor of his, we fear would be finding pretexts for claiming more money, or for making trouble of other kinds for the lessee. It is better for us to look elsewhere; or wait for some distinct proposition from Heureaux. Meantime I hold up our reciprocity arrangement with them." John A. Kasson to Smith M. Weed, 31 March 1898, Records of the Reciprocity Commissioner (RG59), Letters sent by the reciprocity commissioner 22 Oct. 1897–3 July 1899, box 1, entry 1023, U.S. National Archives. See also translation of cablegram from Heureaux to Charles W. Wells advising "I shall be very glad to meet confidentially the Special Agent of the United States . . . to make the combined treaty," undated, folder 478, Archibald Grimké papers, Moorland-Springarn Research Center, Howard University,

Washington, D.C. Even to the Dominican consul in New York, Heureaux vigorously denied that his government had received propositions from the United States and that he had any intention of leasing a coaling station. Heureaux to Alejandro W. y Gil, 21 April 1898, tomo 66, UH.

99. Archibald H. Grimké to William Rufus Day, 7 April 1898, Despatches from U.S. Consuls in Santo Domingo, U.S. National Archives.

100. Heureaux to John S. Durham, 5 July 1898, tomo 67, UH.

101. Grimké to Heureaux, 14 July 1898, folder 479; Heureaux to Grimké, 4 Aug. and 11 Sept. 1898, folder 477, Archibald H. Grimké papers, Moorland-Springarn Research Center, Howard University, Washington, D.C.

102. Heureaux hoped to achieve the goals of "reducing the interest charged on the external debt, and removing the North American company as representative of that debt." Heureaux's offer to the French government included the lease of Samaná Bay as a coaling station. Ulises Heureaux to Camilo Jalouzet, 14 Sept. 1898, série B, carton 49, dossier 3, Republique Dominicaine, Relations avec la France, 1896–1914.

103. Heureaux to José L. de Escoriaza, 10 Nov. 1898 and 13 Oct. 1898, tomos 70 and 69, UH.

104. Heureaux to José Ladislao de Escoriaza, 15 Sept. 1898, tomo 69, UH.

105. The incident is described by César A. Herrera, *Las Finanzas de la República Dominicana* (Santo Domingo: Impresora Dominicana, 1955), 1: 229–232.

106. Heureaux's last days are described in Adriano Miguel Tejada, *El Ajusticiamiento de Lilís* (Santo Domingo: Editora Corripio, 1995), 13–22.

107. The arrival of the SDIC signaled "the financial predominance of the United States in the Dominican Republic . . . the presence of the Improvement Company completed the domination of, and dependence on, the United States," according to Mu-Kien Adriana Sang Ben, *Ulises Heureaux* (Santo Domingo: Editora Corripio, 1987), 158.

108. Louis A. Pérez, Jr., "Dependency," in Michael J. Hogan and Thomas G. Patterson, eds., *Explaining the History of American Foreign Relations* (New York: Cambridge University Press, 1992), 109.

109. The Foreign Office carefully considered what its position toward the international committee should be. See, for example, H. F. Pollock to G. N. Curzon, 5 Feb. 1897, and Foreign Office annotations thereon, in FO 23/93.

110. Albert Fishlow, "Lessons from the past: capital markets during the 19th century and the interwar period," *International Organization* 39: 3 (Summer 1985), 400.

111. The 85 percent tariff reduction given to Puerto Rican sugar in 1900 became free entry in 1901, while Cuba received a preferential tariff in 1902. Paul Mutto, "Desarrollo de la Economía de Exportación Dominicana, 1900–1930," *Eme Eme* 3: 15 (1974), 75.

6. Old Wine in New Skins

1. R.P. Rodgers to Commander in Chief, 7 October 1899, AF.
2. Smith M. Weed, *NYT*, 6 May 1902, 8.
3. Boletín del Archivo General de la Nación 16: 76 (Enero-Marzo 1953), 164.
4. During whole era of Heureaux "the Improvement hardly gave signs of life. Once Heureaux was dead, it reappeared with contract in hand, diligently seeking to extract the government from its financial difficulties." Henríquez y Carvajal, *Cayacoa*, 147.
5. After Heureaux's death, "the entire country dreamed of the complete regeneration of the public administration." *El Nuevo Régimen* (Santo Domingo), 5 Dec. 1900.
6. "Case of the United States before the Commission of Arbitration," United States [vs.] the Dominican Republic, [n.p.], 12 Feb. 1904, 38; David Charles MacMichael, "The United States and the Dominican Republic, 1871–1940: A Cycle in Caribbean Diplomacy" (unpublished Ph.D. diss, University of Oregon, 1964), 148.
7. Dominican historian César A. Herrera calls Vásquez and Jimenes "symbols of two parties devoid of ideals." Herrera, *Las Finanzas de la República Dominicana* (Santo Domingo: Impresora Dominicana, 1955), 1: 233.
8. "The Cibao district is not likely to remain quiet long unless immediate and effective measures are taken to recall the paper currency with which the country is flooded and to rectify the other abuses from which the country is suffering to such an extent as to be unsupportable to the poorer classes," reported the British vice-consul in Santo Domingo a few days after Heureaux's death. H. H. Gosling to Marquis of Salisbury, 4 Aug. 1899, FO 140/7.
9. Early in 1903, the U.S. minister reported to Washington on political unrest arising from "the refusal on the part of the Government to continue the monthly pay of a number of men who are termed chiefs in their districts; these men do not fill any public office . . . they are expected in the case of an insurrection . . . to fight on the side of the President." W. F. Powell to John Hay, 14 Jan. 1903, vol. 7, USM. TK
10. H. H. Gosling to Marquis of Salisbury, 4 Sept. 1899, FO 140/7.
11. "The attention of the public, both Dominicans and foreigners, is fixed upon it, because of the vital financial role the company plays, as well as for the issues of rights and morality that are involved." Henríquez y Carvajal, *Cayacoa*, 181. The SDIC charged that "the press was freely used to urge the withdrawal of the Companies and even their expulsion from the country." "Case of the United States," 23.
12. R. P. Rodgers to Commander in Chief, 7 Oct 1899, AF.
13. "Case of the United States," 21–22.

14. John Bassett Moore, "International Arbitration: The United States and Santo Domingo; Case of the San Domingo Improvement Company, 1903–1905," in *Collected Papers*, 3: 174.

15. F. Henríquez y Carvajal to Encargado de Negocios in New York, 20 Jan. 1900, 1898–1901, MRE.

16. Henríquez y Carvajal to John Hay, 20 Feb. 1901, DL; Herrera, *Finanzas*, 2: 237; William H. Wynne, *State Insolvency and Foreign Bondholders* (New Haven: Yale University Press, 1951), 2: 225–26.

17. F. Velázquez H. in *El Nuevo Régimen*, 17 April 1900; "Case of the United States," 25.

18. The Corporation of Foreign Bondholders warned one investor that the new contract was "dependent on the consent of the general body of Bondholders, and as there is considerable opposition in Belgium, where most of the bonds are held, it is not certain that it will be carried out." C. J. Henry [Wuck?] to First General Manager, 3 Sept. 1900, CFB.

19. W. F. Powell to John Hay, 10 Sept. 1900, vol. X, USM; Corporation of Foreign Bondholders, *Twentieth-Eighth Annual Report of the Council of the Corporation of Foreign Bondholders, for the year 1900–1901* (London: Council House, 1901), 339.

20. H. H. Gosling to A. Cohen, 31 Jan. 1901, FO 140/7.

21. H. H. Gosling to A. Cohen, 31 Jan. 1901, FO 140/7; "Case of the United States," 27; quoted in "Argument of the Dominican Republic [before the Commission of Arbitration, United States vs. the Dominican Republic, n.d., n.p.], 3.

22. *NYT*, 12 Jan. 1901, 1.

23. F. L. Vásquez to John Hay, 16 Jan. 1901, DL; Francisco Henríquez y Carvajal to John Hay, 20 Feb. 1901, 5, 15, 16, DL.

24. See, for example, calls in the Dominican congress for negotiations with the SDIC "on the basis of a previous liquidation of accounts" and an editorial demanding that the company "settle its accounts and justify its claims." *El Nuevo Régimen*, 25 and 11 April 1900, AGN.

25. W. F. Powell to John Hay, 12 Oct. 1901, vol. 5, USM.

26. "Recently the Dominican Government has put forward as a pretext for not coming to a settlement with the Improvement Company," reported the CFB, "the plea that the Company has failed to render a proper statement of accounts. . . . We have positive assurances from the Improvement Company that they are ready to render this statement to the Government." Acknowledging "no doubt the accounts are extremely complicated," and that "it is difficult for us to judge as to the rights and wrongs of the dispute . . . as to the accounts," the CFB complained that the issue was "being used as an excuse to obscure the main issue" — paying the bondholders. James P. Cooper to Under Secretary

of State for Foreign Affairs, 20 Dec. 1901 and to H. H. Gosling, 26 Dec. 1901 and 13 March 1902, CFB.

27. Charles Lipson has noted that the United States and other industrial powers sought to establish the legal security of foreign property abroad but "tried to limit the direct imposition of political and military controls, which were expensive and difficult to manage." Submitting contractual disputes to international arbitration often proved the best way for the developed countries to force less-developed regions to conform their laws to the needs of the global capitalist order. Indeed, arbitration would soon become the State Department's preferred solution in the Dominican case. Charles Lipson, *Standing Guard* (Berkeley: University of California Press, 1985), 15.

28. *NYT*, 19 Feb. 1901, 5.

29. The SDIC agreed to accept annual payments of only $200,000, while the European contract provided for a minimum annual payment of $300,000, with special guarantees from the customs revenue of the two most important southern ports, Santo Domingo and San Pedro de Macoris. Wynne, *State Insolvency*, 228.

30. After the contract's repudiation, Henríquez y Carvajal resigned from the cabinet, and the Jimenes government faced a new revolutionary outbreak. W. F. Powell to John Hay, 12 Oct. 1901, vol. 5, USM.

31. This biographical summary draws on the *Dictionary of American Biography*, Supplement Four (New York: Scribner's, 1974) 597–600; *Memorial Book 1948* (New York: Association of the Bar of the City of New York, no date), 65–66; and Richard Megargee, "Realism in American Foreign Policy: The Diplomacy of John Bassett Moore" (unpublished Ph.D. diss., Northwestern Univ., 1963), the only full-length study of Moore's influence on foreign policy. In his preface (viii) Megargee notes that "neither the extensive papers of Moore [in the Library of Congress] or his contemporaries provided clear information about the lawyer's role in relation to specific events in United States diplomacy." Like other scholars, Megargee was unaware of a large but uncatalogued collection of Moore's papers at the Columbia University School of Law.

32. Moore had joined the State Department as a clerk in Alvey Adee's Diplomatic Bureau. A year later, in 1886, Moore became third assistant secretary, a post he held until 1891, when he accepted a newly created professorship in law and diplomacy at Columbia University. Moore retained contacts in the State Department and pursued his interest in international relations, especially the settlement of interstate conflicts, as discussed below. Moore's memo on Panama and the meeting with Roosevelt are discussed in David H. Burton, *Theodore Roosevelt: Confident Imperialist* (Philadelphia: University of Pennsylvania Press, 1968), 125–26.

33. Theodore Roosevelt to Jacob Hollander, quoted in memo dated 30 March 1905, JBM.

34. Moore qualifies as a "servant of power" or "action intellectual" as identified recently by Thomas McCormick. Rather than "selling [government] decisions to the private sector," however, Moore put his global vision simultaneously at the service of a private company and the U.S. government. McCormick and Walter LaFeber, *Behind the Throne: Servants of Power to Imperial Presidents, 1898–1968* (Madison: University of Wisconsin Press, 1993), xi.

35. Moore's correspondence with the Improvement Company before 1903 does not survive, but later letters make reference to his representation of the company from that date. See Memorandum of Agreement, November 1904, JBM.

36. "I think it right to advise you that the question of taking legal action against your Company will be considered by the Council at its next meeting," the secretary of the council warned the London representative of the SDIC in 1900. Secretary of the CFB to A. Thorp, 28 Sept. 1900, CFB.

37. "Since 1897 the exterior floating debt has largely passed into the hands of British subjects"; "large amounts of the bonds had . . . passed into the hands of companies and private firms who had made advances against them to the Improvement Company." James P. Cooper to Under Secretary of State for Foreign Affairs, 20 Dec. 1901, and to Jacob H. Hollander, 20 June 1905, CFB.

38. Estimate of British holdings in James P. Cooper to Under Secretary of State for Foreign Affairs, 21 April 1902, St. Domingo Press Copy, vol. VI, CFB; estimate of total debt given by Henríquez y Carvajal, *Cayacoa*, 128.

39. C. W. Fremantle, no addressee, 24 April 1902, FO 23/99; James P. Cooper to Tony Chauvin, Association Nationale des Porteurs Français de Valeures Etrangeres, 4 April 1901, CFB.

40. The council's position toward the SDIC corresponded to official British acceptance of U.S. hegemony in the Caribbean, a private parallel to the "great rapprochement" taking place in the diplomatic plane. See Bradford Perkins, *The Great Rapprochement* (London: Gollancz, 1969), 7–11, 186–194.

41. Note initialed A.L., 1 Jan. 1902, attached to 20 Dec. 1901 letter from Council of Foreign Bondholders, FO 25/1.

42. Powell insisted that the SDIC had once offered to render its accounts to Henríquez y Carvajal. The Dominican admitted that the SDIC had offered "the accounts to me privately, or better still, confidentially," but had declined to accept because he "judged that the offer had nothing to do with my mission at the time." W. F. Powell to Juan F. Sánchez, 3 Dec. 1902, enclosure with W. F. Powell to John Hay, 6 Dec. 1902; Henríquez y Carvajal to Encargado de Negocios, 5 March 1902, enclosure with W. F. Powell to John Hay, 11 March 1902, vols. 7 & 5, USM.

43. W. F. Powell to F. Henríquez y Carvajal, 20 March 1902, enclosed with Powell to John Hay, 20 March 1902, vol. 5, USM.
44. Henríquez y Carvajal to Encargado de Negocios, 17 March 1902, enclosed with W. F. Powell to John Hay, 20 March 1902, vol. 5, USM.
45. W. F. Powell to F. Henríquez y Carvajal, 7 March 1902, enclosed with W. F. Powell to John Hay, 11 March 1902, emphasis in original; W. F. Powell to John Hay, 26 April 1902; vol. 5, USM.
46. W. F. Powell to John Hay, 16 June 1902, vol. 6, USM.
47. Juan F. Sánchez to Encargado de Negocios, 1 Dec. 1902, enclosure with W. F. Powell to John Hay, 6 Dec. 1902, vol. 7, USM.
48. On U.S. pressure on the Dominican Republic to submit to arbitration, see MacMichael, "The United States and the Dominican Republic," 150–56.
49. W. F. Powell to Juan F. Sánchez, 23 Jan. 1903, enclosure with W. F. Powell to John Hay, 26 Jan. 1903; W. F. Powell to John Hay, 20 Jan. 1903; vol. 7, USM.
50. See Powell to Alfau, 3 Dec. 1903, and to Machado, 12 Dec. 1903, *FRUS 1904.*

7. A Reign of Law Among Nations

1. John Bassett Moore, "Argument of the United States before the Commission of Arbitration," United States [vs.] the Dominican Republic, [n.d., n.p.], 31.
2. John Bassett Moore, "Santo Domingo and the United States," in *Collected Papers of John Bassett Moore* (New Haven: Yale University Press, 1944), 3: 185.
3. According to Frederick William Holls, who represented the United States at the first peace conference at the Hague, publication of the *Digest* was "a significant event in the history of arbitration" that showed "the applicability of judicial methods to a large variety of international disagreements" and which "furnishes a valuable body of precedents for the guidance of future tribunals." Ironically, Holls had served as attorney for the SDIC at the time of its founding; see chapter 1. Frederick W. Holls, *The Peace Conference at the Hague* (New York: Macmillan, 1900), 236. See also *The Collected Papers of John Bassett Moore* (New Haven: Yale University Press, 1944).
4. Moore, "Application of the Principle of International Arbitration on the American Continents," 59, in *Collected Papers*, vol. III.
5. A review of arbitration cases involving the United States and Latin American countries from 1870 to 1914 that appear in A. M. Stuyt's compendium confirms the tendency. Nearly all the cases concern loss or seizure of ships, private and mutual claims (including violation of contract), and personal injuries. In nearly every case, the Latin American nation paid a cash settlement to the United States. A.M. Stuyt, *Survey of International Arbitration, 1794–1989* (Boston: Martinus Nijhoff, 1990). See also Richard Langhorne, "Arbitration: the first

phase, 1870–1914," 52–55, in Michael Dockrill and Brian McKercher, *Diplomacy and world power* (Cambridge: Cambridge University Press, 1996).

6. Another measure of the degree to which arbitration favored metropolitan over peripheral nations was the ineffectiveness of "Calvo clauses." These contract features sought to annul the right of foreigners to appeal to their home governments for intervention in the case of a dispute. In practice, Calvo clauses were routinely interpreted not to be "a bar to proceedings before an international tribunal." Calvo clauses did little more than reaffirm the traditional usage holding that foreigners must exhaust local remedies before appealing to outside intervention, always assuming that local courts were not "obviously insufficient" because they failed to meet "minimum standards" under general international law. J.L. Simpson and Hazel Fox, *International Arbitration* (London: Stevens & Sons, 1959), 121, 117.

7. Moore, "International Law: Its Present and Future," in *Collected Papers* 3: 272.

8. Moore, "International Law," in *Collected Papers* 2, 29. "The general rule followed by the United States" according to a classic 1915 study, was that "a contract claim cannot give rise to the diplomatic intervention of the government unless, after an exhaustion of local remedies, there has been a denial of justice, or some flagrant violation of international law." Edwin M. Borchard, *The Diplomatic Protection of Citizens Abroad* (New York: Kraus Reprint, 1970), 285.

9. The "building of a legal framework for development" in less-developed countries continues to concern enlightened representatives of global capitalism. A recent World Bank report on judicial reform in Latin America urges the region to "foster an enabling legal and judicial environment that is conducive to trade, financing, and investment." Warning that "the alternative to law is chaos," the report notes that "rule of law is a precondition for private sector development . . . since it creates certainty and predictability, clarifies and protects property rights, and enforces contractual obligations." The World Bank, *Judicial Reform in Latin America and the Caribbean* (Washington, D.C.: World Bank, 1995), vii, 13, 2.

10. No extant documents explain why the State Department allowed Moore to play this dual role. By 1903, however, the SDIC's dealings had moved beyond exploiting a small Caribbean country and had begun to disturb U.S. relations with the "creditor powers" of Europe. Since both Assistant Secretary of State Francis B. Loomis, who handled Dominican affairs in Washington, and Secretary of State John Hay, knew Moore well, they may have looked on the expert in international relations as a type of *intendant* of a private firm whose operations had significant foreign policy implications. Moore to Charles W. Wells, 7 September 1904, JBM.

11. Moore to F. B. Loomis, 21 April 1904, JBM.

12. "Argument of the United States," 22, 63.

13. "Argument of the United States," 64, 21, 22.

14. "Argument of the United States," 28.

15. "In general, it may be said that intervention is not warranted in the case of honest inability of a state to pay its debts, but only when, the means being at hand, the debtor state willfully refuses to pay." Borchard, *Diplomatic Protection*, 312; "Argument of the Dominican Republic," 9–10.

16. "Argument of the United States," 22, 23, 26, 28.

17. For reports on the struggle for power, see W. F. Powell to John Hay, 31 Jan., 13 Feb., and 27 Feb. 1904, vol. 10, USM.

18. "Argument of the United States," 65.

19. "Argument of the United States," 139, 112, 113.

20. "Argument of the United States," 22, 55, 56.

21. "Argument of the United States," 68, 103.

22. It was probably no coincidence that in March 1904, U.S. Minister W. F. Powell suggested a plan of reform that resembled Moore's blueprint in some ways. Powell recommended that the United States "take charge of the Custom Revenue," "disband" the army, and create a "Rural Guard." Powell felt these steps would create such prosperity "that there would be a universal demand coming from the people themselves" to join the United States. "If annexation is forced upon the people," Powell warned, "we would have a sullen foe that would constantly give us trouble . . . until the Republic was completely subjugated." Powell to John Hay, 13 March 1904, vol. 11, USM. For a summary, see David Healy, *Drive to Hegemony* (Madison: University of Wisconsin, 1988), 115–17.

23. "Argument of the United States," 54, 55.

24. The assurance and apparent objectivity that allowed the metropolitans to impose their representation of the Dominican state corresponds to what Timothy Mitchell, describing the European conception of Egypt, identifies as "its remarkable claim to certainty or truth: the apparent certainty with which everything seems ordered and organised, calculated and rendered unambiguous." Similarly, in his discussion of the protection of foreign capital in the developing world, Charles Lipson notes that "the symbolic role of international law is particularly noteworthy, since it can sometimes turn questionable claims into approved obligations. . . . legal symbols, by abstracting from and disguising material relations, can serve to authenticate them ethically across nations and social classes." Timothy Mitchell, *Colonising Egypt* (Berkeley: University of California Press, 1991), 13; Lipson, *Standing Guard*, 55.

25. "Argument of the Dominican Republic [before the Commission of Arbitration, United States vs. the Dominican Republic, n.d., n.p.], 3.

26. George Gray served as Senator from Delaware, where Moore's family had been prominent for generations. Gray, described as "an old family friend" in the 1880s, helped Moore begin work at the State Department when he was in his

twenties. Richard Megargee, "The Diplomacy of John Bassett Moore: Realism in American Foreign Policy" (unpublished Ph.D. diss., Northwestern University, 1963), 20. On Carlisle's likely acquaintance with Smith M. Weed, see Richard Collin, *Theodore Roosevelt's Caribbean* (Baton Rouge: Louisiana State University Press, 1990), 402–3.

27. W. F. Powell to John Hay, 3 Dec. 1903, vol. 9, USM; Rufino Martínez, *Diccionario Biográfico-Histórico Dominicano* (Santo Domingo: Editora UASD, 1971), 187–188.

28. The text of the arbitral award appears in *FRUS* 1904, 274–79. On the tribunal's failure to consider European protocols, see Collin, *Roosevelt's Caribbean*, 404; for a description of the European claims and the award, see Wynne, *State Insolvency*, 234–39.

29. Juan Francisco Sánchez to Manuel de J. Galván, 2 August 1904, JBM; Carlos Morales to Emilio Joubert, 22 Nov. 1904, tomo 11, CM.

30. For Drago's famous note, see *FRUS* 1903, 1–5; Carlos Morales Languasco to Emilio C. Joubert, 30 Sept. 1904, tomo 19, CM.

31. Enclosure no. 5 with T.C. Dawson to John Hay, 6 Oct. 1904, vol. 12, USM. John Bassett Moore refuted the Dominican objections point by point in a memo to Secretary of State Hay. Moore to Hay, 7 Jan. 1905, JBM.

32. Luis M. Drago, "State Loans in their Relation to International Policy," *American Journal of International Law* (New York) 50: 2 (July and Oct. 1907), 710–11.

33. In the words of Lester D. Langley, "Drago proposed a Pan-American corollary to the Monroe Doctrine; TR responded with the Roosevelt corollary." Langley, *America and the Americas* (Athens: University of Georgia Press, 1989), 108.

34. In the final negotiations for creation of the American customs receivership in January 1905, one of the few points the Dominicans insisted on was that John T. Abbott not be appointed collector. Thomas C. Dawson to Secretary of State, 2 Jan. 1905 and 13 Feb. 1905, in *FRUS* 1905, 298, 329.

35. John Bassett Moore to the Secretary of State, handwritten draft, 18 July 1904, JBM.

36. J. B. Loomis to John Bassett Moore, 28 July 1904, JBM. Moore's machinations help explain the otherwise strategically unsound decision to appoint Abbott. Dexter Perkins refers to "the American financial agent, curiously enough an official of the Improvement Company." Dexter Perkins, *The Monroe Doctrine, 1867–1907* (Baltimore: Johns Hopkins University Press, 1937), 427.

37. In September 1904, Thomas C. Dawson forwarded to Secretary of State Hay copies of two letters from Abbott, noting that he had discussed several issues with Abbott "in his private capacity as representative of the improvement company." *FRUS* 1904, 281.

38. F. B. Loomis to John Bassett Moore, 10 Feb. 1905, JBM.

39. John Bassett Moore to Charles W. Wells, 4 Oct. 1904, JBM.
40. Undated telegram in John Bassett Moore papers, pinned to 3 October 1904 telegram from Dawson to Secretary of State. A paraphrase of the telegram appears in *FRUS* 1904, 283.
41. John Bassett Moore to F. Van Dyne, 14 Oct. 1904, JBM.
42. A.G. Vansittart to Marquis of Landsdowne, 9 Nov. 1904, FO 23/106.
43. Charles W. Wells to John Bassett Moore, 5 Oct. 1904, JBM.
44. Thomas C. Dawson to John Hay, 3 Oct. 1904, vol. 12, USM. For European reaction, see Dana G. Munro, *Intervention and Dollar Diplomacy in the Caribbean, 1900–1921* (Princeton: Princeton University Press, 1964), 97.
45. For European pressure on the United States, see Robert James Neymeyer, "The Establishment and Operation of the Dominican Customs Receivership, 1905–1916" (unpublished Ph.D. diss., University of Iowa, 1990), 77–78.
46. "Argument of the United States," 38. In mid-September, the State Department asked Moore to analyze several European claims against the Dominican Republic and comment on how the SDIC award would affect their settlement. Since Moore had presented the government's case to the arbitral board himself, he maintained that all European claims had been fully considered and seized the opportunity to uphold both the legality and viability of the SDIC award. John Bassett Moore to Secretary of State, 1 Oct. 1904, JBM.
47. Richard Collin observes that "Hay particularly took the high road . . . indicating that the arbitral tribunal had considered all claims before making its independent finding." Collin, *Roosevelt's Caribbean*, 405. But Hay was simply paraphrasing Moore's letter to the Secretary of State, 1 Oct. 1904, JBM.
48. The State Department asked Moore to evaluate Italian claims against the Dominican government, and in his 2 February 1905, reply to the Secretary of State Moore insisted that the arbitrators "took into account the Italian protocols and endeavored so to frame their award as not to interfere with the rights of other creditors or with the power of the Dominican Government to give them effect." Moore to John Hay, 2 Feb. 1905, JBM.
49. Thomas C. Dawson to John Hay, 3 Oct. 1904, vol. 12, USM.
50. Morales to Federico Velásquez, 22 Aug. 1904, and to Guarin González, 16 Dec. 1904, tomos 10 and 11, CM.
51. With typical moderation, Moore showed himself unwilling to criticize the U.S. minister: "Of course I have no wish to defend Dawson against anything that he has done out of the way, but I do not feel at all sure that I know what he has done." Charles W. Wells to John Bassett Moore, 6 Oct. 1904; Moore to Charles W. Wells, 7 Oct. 1904, JBM.
52. "By thus holding the Dominicans to arrangements which favored United States creditors over their European fellows, the State Department helped to create the dissatisfactions to which so many European governments finally found it

necessary to respond." Healy, *Drive to Hegemony*, 120. Richard Collin notes that "Hay's instructions and Dawson's negotiations with the troubled Dominicans almost always cited the higher authority of the sacred arbitration commission as the source of Dominican discontent, averring that the Americans could not change an independent legal decision even if they wanted to, an argument that offended everyone and convinced no one." This position, which inflamed European creditors and their governments, was not simply a strategic decision rationally made at Foggy Bottom, but the fruit of persistent pressure by the SDIC in the person of John Bassett Moore. Collin, *Roosevelt's Caribbean*, 404.

53. Turning the ports of Monte Cristy, Sánchez, and Samaná over to the American agent was a way for Morales to keep the customs revenue from falling into the hands of his political rivals, who dominated the northern region. T. C. Dawson to John Hay, 21 Nov. 1904, vol. 12, USM.

54. John Hay to John Bassett Moore, 1 Nov. 1904, JBM.

55. Paul Morton to Secretary of State, 29 Oct. 1904, JBM.

56. John Bassett Moore to F. B. Loomis, 4 Nov. 1904, JBM. Moore reminded Loomis that Abbott had discussed the question of a warship with Roosevelt, who agreed that a ship's "moral support" would be helpful. Moore insisted that Abbott was "a discreet man" who did not have in mind "anything antagonistic to the wishes of the Dominican Government." JBM to F. B. Loomis, 21 Nov. 1904, JBM.

57. Undated memo, JBM.

8. *A World Safe for Capitalism*

1. Carlos Morales Languasco to Emilio C. Joubert, 27 March 1905, CML.

2. Luis M. Drago, "State Loans and their Relation to International Policy," *American Journal of International Law* 1: 2 (July and Oct., 1907), 705.

3. H. M. Durand to Marquis of Lansdowne, 20 March 1905, FO 23/106, PRO.

4. Albert S. Dillingham to Secretary of the Navy, 5 June 1904, vol. 267, AF.

5. Quoted in Emily Rosenberg, *Financial Missionaries to the World* (Cambridge: Harvard University Press, 1999), 63.

6. Washington had good reasons to avoid deeper intervention in Santo Domingo. "Direct and frequent interventions promised immediate and direct gains. Yet such a course was both risky and costly. . . . British policy in Latin America . . . was founded on the idea that it was cheaper to bear the immediate costs of occasional bond defaults than to risk sabotaging local governments by frequent interventions." Britain "was defining the risks the state would bear for foreign investors, and it was defining them narrowly." Charles Lipson, *Standing Guard* (Berkeley: University of California Press, 1985), 44–45, 49.

7. Roosevelt to Joseph Bucklin Bishop, 23 Feb. 1904, and to Theodore Roosevelt, junior, 10 Feb. 1904; *Letters of Theodore Roosevelt*, ed. Elting E. Morison (Cambridge: Harvard University Press, 1951), [4]: 734, 723.

8. American minister W. F. Powell explained that he would recognize Morales because "the present Government is more favorably disposed towards us than that of Mr. Jimenez." Powell to John Hay, 14 Jan. 1904, vol. 9, USM. "I believe that Jimenez is making every endeavor to excite public opinion against the United States and against Morales' people, claiming that Morales is playing into the hands of the United States," commander Albert Dillingham reported. Dillingham to Secretary of the Navy, 17 Jan. 1904, vol. 265, AF; *NYT*, 29 Jan. 1905, 3: 4.

9. For discussion of the role of the navy in Dominican political events, see Richard H. Collin, "The 1904 *Detroit* Compact: U.S. Naval Diplomacy and Dominican Revolutions," *Historian* 52 (May 1990), 432–52; and Robert James Neymeyer, "The Establishment and Operation of the Dominican Customs Receivership, 1905–1916" (unpublished Ph.D. diss., University of Iowa, 1990), especially 18–92.

10. Commander Albert S. Dillingham's recommendation that "a permanent passive naval force here will help greatly to maintain the status quo" was noted with approval by the Secretary of State and acted upon by the Navy. John Hay to Secretary of the Navy, 23 April 1904, vol. 266, AF.

11. Sigsbee, as commander of the ill-fated *Maine*, had played a similar role in Cuba in 1898. See, for example, David F. Trask, *The War with Spain in 1898* (New York: Macmillan, 1981), xii, 25–26.

12. Dillingham to Secretary of the Navy, 16 May 1904, vol. 267, AF.

13. Dillingham to Secretary of the Navy 23 May and 5 June 1904, vol. 267, AF.

14. Dillingham to Secretary of the Navy, 11 Feb. 1904; Sigsbee to Secretary of the Navy, 29 Jan. 1905, vols. 265 & 268, AF.

15. Before late in 1904, Roosevelt and Hay seemed relatively unconcerned about great-power forays into the Dominican Republic. "Hay had scoffed at the danger of foreign intervention," reports David Charles MacMichael, and in late March scarcely showed "any concern for foreign threats." MacMichael, "The United States and the Dominican Republic, 1871–1940: A Cycle in Caribbean Diplomacy" (unpublished Ph.D. diss., University of Oregon, 1964), 167.

16. Carlos Morales to Theodore Roosevelt, 8 Jan. 1904; Juan Francisco Sánchez to Francis B. Loomis, 8 Feb. 1904; both in vol. 5, DL. The lease of Samaná is described in David Healy, *Drive to Hegemony* (Madison: University of Wisconsin Press, 1988), 113.

17. Roosevelt to Joseph Bucklin Bishop, 23 Feb. 1904, *Letters* 4, 734.

18. Roosevelt to George Dewey, 20 Feb. 1904, *Letters* 4, 734; Healy, *Hegemony*, 117; Loomis, "Memorandum for the Secretary of State on the Dominican Republic," 19 March 1904, JBM.

19. Hay to Loomis, 28 March 1904, vol. 5, DL.

20. Juan Francisco Sánchez to John Hay, 28 March 1904, vol. 5, DL.

21. Luis Drago, the Argentinian statesman who championed Latin American sovereignty, drew attention to a contradiction in the forced collection of public debts by European powers, where "the costly naval expeditions and blockades [were] so entirely out of proportion with their immediate object and apparent aim." Luis M. Drago, "State Loans and their Relation to International Policy," *American Journal of International Law* 1: 2 (July and Oct., 1907), 712.

22. Sigsbee to Secretary of the Navy, 29 Jan. 1905, vol. 268, AF.

23. Sigsbee to Thomas Dawson, 23 Jan. 1905, vol. 268, AF.

24. Juan Francisco Sánchez to United States Consul, Santo Domingo, 30 June 1905, tomo 58, MRE.

25. A. W. Lithgow to F. B. Loomis, 19 Feb. 1904, vol. 265, AF.

26. E. Tejera to U.S. Minister Resident, Santo Domingo, 1 Jan. 1906, tomo 58, MRE.

27. The policy continued even after Morales was overthrown by Ramón Cáceres in 1906. The new leader, with the support of the U.S. Navy, "one by one crushed his opponents" and launched "a modest but popular program of public works." Lester D. Langley, *Banana Wars: United States Intervention in the Caribbean, 1898–1934* (Lexington: University Press of Kentucky, 1985), 33; Healy, *Hegemony*, 124.

28. Carlos Vilas has observed that the weakness of states in the Caribbean region, "generally reduced to an inefficient mechanism for collecting revenue — has favored the expansion of the United States in the Caribbean economically, politically, and militarily, substituting for the peripheral state its own state." Carlos Vilas, "El Estado Dominicano," *Estudios Sociales Latinoamericanos* 24 (Sept.-Dec. 1979), 125–26.

29. In an interesting article that treats an earlier period of Dominican history, Detlev Julio K. Peukert notes that Dominican regimes throughout the nineteenth century tried "to end the insane political instability by importing the instruments of state infrastructure." "Anhelo de dependencia: Las ofertas de anexión de la República Dominicana a los Estados Unidos en el siglo XIX," *Jahrbuch für Geschichte von Staat, Wirstschaft und Gesellschaft Lateinamerikas,* 23 (1986), 315.

30. "The United States Government . . . ought to allow Italy to collect the quota due her directly from the custom houses of the Republic assigned for this purpose, or, if your Government has occupied some of the custom houses, as it appears to have done, it should assume the obligation of paying on behalf of San Domingo the amounts to which we are entitled." Royal Italian Embassy to John Hay, 24 December 1904, JBM.

31. After the meeting of 17 December 1904, mentioned above, Jusserand met with Hay again on December 24 or 25 and told him that "the limit had been reached in Santo Domingo." He noted that Hay was noncommittal about international control "because of the more and more marked desire of the American government to forbid any action by foreigners in the Americas." Cypher telegram from Jusserand to Ministère des Affaires Etrangères, 26 December 1904, série B, carton 38, dossier 3.

32. The background of the sugar tax dispute is given in W. F. Powell to John Hay, 27 April 1904, vol. 11, USM.

33. Frank Schaffer to Thomas Dawson, 13 Sept. 1904, enclosure with Thomas Dawson to John Hay, 16 Sept. 1904, vol. 12, USM.

34. W. F. Powell to John Hay, 27 April 1904, vol. 11, USM.

35. Thomas Dawson to Frank Schaffer, 15 Sept. 1904, vol. 12, USM.

36. In December 1904 the department instructed Dawson to use his good offices "to prevent the collection of the sugar tax." Dawson to John Hay, 26 April 1905, vol. 14, USM.

37. *Presidential Addresses and State Papers of Theodore Roosevelt, Part Three* (New York: Kraus Reprint Co., 1970), 175–177.

38. See *FRUS* 1905, 298–301.

39. John Bassett Moore to Charles W. Wells, 20 Jan. 1905 [misdated 1904], JBM.

40. Several clauses of the original protocol were unacceptable to the State Department, but it set forth the basic structure of the customs receivership that, with minor modifications, went into effect under the "modus vivendi" declared by Roosevelt on 28 March 1905. See *FRUS* 1905, 301–367, for details of negotiations and text of draft and final protocol.

41. Carlos Morales to José Bordas, 24 Jan., to Francisco Vásquez, 15 March, and to Augustin Reves, 25 Jan. 1905, CM.

42. Charles W. Wells to John Bassett Moore, 26 Jan. and 9 Feb. 1905, JBM.

43. The protocol signed on January 21 was to take effect on February 11, not leaving time for the Senate to debate and ratify the measure. W. Stull Holt describes the conflict fully in *Treaties Defeated by the Senate* (Gloucester, MA: Peter Smith, 1964), 202, 212–29. For the opposition of leading senators, see *New York Sun*, 26 Jan. 1905, 5, and *NYT*, 24 Jan. 1905, 6.

44. Moore's recent contract with the SDIC is discussed at the end of chapter 7.

45. *NYT*, 21 March 1905, 6; *New York Sun*, 31 March 1905, 4.

46. Roosevelt had sketched the terms of the corollary that bears his name as early as 20 May 1904, in a letter read by Secretary of War Elihu Root at a dinner celebrating Cuban independence. For the history of the corollary, see Dexter Perkins, *The Monroe Doctrine* (Baltimore: Johns Hopkins University Press, 1937) 419–433, and Collin, *Roosevelt's Caribbean*, 385, 409–25; for adumbra-

tions see J. Fred Rippy, "Antecedents of the Roosevelt Corollary of the Monroe Doctrine," *Pacific Historical Review* 9 (1940), 267–79.

47. International law at the time permitted the use of force for debt collection. "Enforcement was unilateral. If a state chose to espouse the private claims of its nationals, it could use diplomacy, arbitration, or force." Lipson, *Standing Guard*, 54.

48. Roosevelt noted that when payments are made to American creditors under an arbitral award "some foreign Government complains that the award conflicts with its rights, as a creditor, to some portion of these revenues." "Message," 241–43, 245.

49. Moore describes his meetings with the President in an 8-page handwritten memorandum, JBM.

50. The memorandum that Moore gave to Roosevelt, with his handwritten revisions and the President's insertion as mentioned above, survives in the special collection at the Columbia University School of Law. A comparison of that document with Roosevelt's final message to Congress reveals that Roosevelt incorporated whole cloth into the final version of his message some 350 words written by Moore. Draft bearing annotation "Revised text, sent to Loomis, Jan. 31, 1905, of memo presented to the President, Jan. 28, 1905," JBM.

51. "Message from the President of the United States, transmitting a protocol of an agreement between the United States and the Dominican Republic, providing for the collection and disbursement by the United States of the customs revenues of the Dominican Republic, signed on February 4, 1905," in *Presidential Addresses*, 241–260.

52. "Message," 256.

53. S. Nelson Drew, *NSC — 68: Forging the Strategy of Containment* (Washington: National Defense Univ., 1994), 66, 54.

54. "Message," 248.

55. New York *Sun*, 17 February 1905, 1; Jusserand to Delcassé, 20 February 1905, records of the Ministère des Affaires Etrangères, série B, carton 38, dossier 3.

56. Dana C. Munro, quoted in Lipson, *Standing Guard*, 63.

57. Emily Rosenberg, *Financial Missionaries to the World* (Cambridge: Harvard University Press, 1999), 43, 2.

58. "Message," 256. The American press echoed this theme. "[Intervention] is a course commended to us by prudence and by the desire to remove possible causes of difference with friendly foreign nations." *NYT*, 17 Feb. 1905, 8.

59. On British naval reductions in Latin America, see Kneer, *Great Britain and the Caribbean*, 100. For German attempts to create an anti-British league and the British reaction, see Raymond A. Esthus, *Theodore Roosevelt and the International Rivalries* (Waltham, MA: Ginn-Blaisdell, 1970), 43–48. Roosevelt's role in the Russo-Japanese peace talks and in the French-German conflict over

Morocco is discussed in Lewis L. Gould, *The Presidency of Theodore Roosevelt* (Lawrence: University of Kansas Press, 1991), 179–89 and 189–95.

60. The *Outlook* (London), quoted in *New York World*, 12 Feb. 1905, 2E. Dexter Perkins reviews the European reaction in *Monroe Doctrine*, 446–51. A note by an official at the Quay d'Orsay, composed before Roosevelt's February 15 message, conveys the mixed feelings of the French foreign ministry: "If this event marks a step forward for American hegemony in the Antilles and can be considered regrettable from the point of view of European politics generally, it certainly brings immediate and concrete benefits for French interests in the Dominican Republic." Note [signature illegible] dated 27 Jan. 1905, records of Ministère des Affaires Etrangères, série B, carton 38, dossier 3.

9. From the Gilded Age to Dollar Diplomacy

1. Unpublished letter to New York newspaper by former Dominican President Carlos Morales Languasco, June 7, 1907, translated by John T. Abbott, in JBM.
2. Jacob H. Hollander to Jacob H. Schiff, April 25, 1907, box 4, JHH.
3. Thomas Dawson to Jacob Hollander, July 23, 1906, box 4, JHH.
4. Even before the protocol was submitted to Congress in mid-February, Moore was supplying the State Department with examples of international agreements that had been approved by a simple majority rather than a two-thirds vote of the Senate. Moore also furnished precedents for using force to take over the revenue of another sovereign state and apparently lobbied individual senators to support the Dominican plan. In early March, Moore reviewed a State Department memorandum describing precedents for international protocols "by which revenues are appropriated." Moore added brief descriptions of arrangements in China, Colombia, Costa Rica, Ecuador, Mexico, Peru, as well as the creation of the fiscal agent in the Dominican Republic. Memo included with letter from John Bassett Moore to Andrew H. Allen, 3 March 1905, JBM. In a note to F. B. Loomis, Moore attached "some memoranda of cases in which force was resorted to for the purpose of obtaining redress, pecuniary or otherwise." John Bassett Moore to F. B. Loomis, 3 March 1905. For evidence of Moore's lobbying efforts, see letters of 28 Jan. 1905, JBM.
5. See Dawson's chronology, *FRUS* 1906, 597.
6. Charles Sigsbee to Desiderio Arias, 7 and 8 Feb. 1905, vol. 268, AF.
7. Roosevelt's action is described in page-one stories in the *New York Tribune*, the *New York Times*, the *New York Sun*, and the *Washington Post*, all of 29 March 1905. The SDIC's reaction was expressed by Charles W. Wells to John Bassett Moore, 29 March 1905, JBM.
8. Charles W. Wells to John Bassett Moore, 29 March 1905, JBM.

9. Moore's financial history appears in *FRUS* 1905, 344–49. Roosevelt's brief statement of March 28 said that "Mr. Hollander will thoroughly investigate these claims, including the claim of the American Improvement Company, and will report in detail all the information he is able to gather." *FRUS* 1905, 360–61.

10. *Chicago Tribune*, 5 April 1905, 8.

11. Hugh O'Beirne to Marquis of Lansdowne, 26 May 1905, FO 23/106.

12. John Bassett Moore to E. M. Hood, 25 April 1905, JBM.

13. In the memorandum Moore wrote that "it seems proper that his Majesty's Government should make this statement, if only for the purpose of expressing its confidence that nothing will be done to put in doubt the execution of legal obligations of the Dominican Government . . . in the full discharge of which the subjects of his Majesty have an important interest." Memorandum enclosed with cover letter from Moore to John T. Abbott, 24 April 1905, JBM.

14. Hugh J. O'Beirne to F. B. Loomis, 26 May 1905, *FRUS* 1905, 374–375; O'Beirne to John Bassett Moore, 23 May 1905, JBM; Herbert H. D. Peirce, Acting Secretary of State, to Hugh J. O'Beirne, 27 June 1905, *FRUS* 1905, 377–378.

15. John Bassett Moore to Hugh J. O'Beirne, 28 May 1905, JBM.

16. On rejection of award by Dominican congress, see W. W. Langhorne to Secretary of State, 13 July 1905, vol. 14, USM; John Bassett Moore to Secretary of State, 20 June 1905, JBM.

17. W. L. Penfield to John Bassett Moore, June 22, 1905, JBM.

18. John Bassett Moore to W. L. Penfield, 23 June 1905, JBM.

19. W. L. Penfield to John Bassett Moore, 24 June 1905, JBM.

20. Herbert H.D. Peirce to John Bassett Moore, 26 June 1905, JBM.

21. Undated memorandum describing 12 June 1905 meeting with Jacob Hollander, JBM.

22. Wynne, *State Insolvency*, 248.

23. Roosevelt to Jacob H. Hollander, July 3, 1905, in Elting E. Morison, *Letters of Theodore Roosevelt*, IV (Cambridge: Harvard University Press, 1951), 1259.

24. John T. Abbott to John Bassett Moore, 20 Sept. 1905, JBM.

25. Jacob H. Hollander to John Bassett Moore, 22 Sept. 1905, JBM.

26. John T. Abbott to John Bassett Moore, 27 Sept. 1905, JBM.

27. Smith M. Weed to John Bassett Moore, 9 Oct. 1905, JBM.

28. Jacob Hollander, "Debt of Santo Domingo," 59th Congress, 1st Session [1905], Exc. Doc. No. 1, 43.

29. Hollander, "Debt of Santo Domingo," 43–44.

30. "Confidential Memoranda submitted to the President in connection with 'A Report on the Debt of Santo Domingo,'" undated, box 2, JHH.

31. See, for example, William Salomon to Jacob Hollander, 20 July 1906 and Jacob H. Hollander to Robert Bacon, 4 Aug. 1906, box 3, JHH.
32. Jacob H. Hollander to Charles H. Allen, 28 June 1906, box 3, JHH.
33. Charles H. Allen to Jacob H. Hollander, 9 July 1906, box 3, JHH.
34. "Confidential Memoranda," 10 August 1905, box 2, JHH.
35. Jacob H. Schiff to Robert Bacon, First Assistant Secretary of State, 13 August 1906, copy in box 3, JHH.
36. John T. Abbott to John Bassett Moore, 1 Aug. 1906, JBM.
37. "THERE IS NO NECESSITY for this whatever," Abbott continued, ". . . there is plenty of money to pay the whole *Award*." John T. Abbott to John Bassett Moore, 16 Oct. 1906, JBM.
38. James P. Cooper, secretary of the CFB, paraphrased Hollander's comments in a letter to Charles W. Wells, 20 March 1907, JBM.
39. Hollander's refunding plan and the SDIC objections to it are described in detail by Wynne, *State Insolvency*, 248–261; the plan is also discussed in César A. Herrera, *Las Finanzas de la República Dominicana* (Santo Domingo: Impresora Dominicana, 1955), 1: 279–286 and 2: 9–22.
40. In 1907, Moore commented to the British chargé d'affaires in Washington "how unfortunate would have been the predicament of the English and American interests if they had carried their opposition to the point of being held responsible by the Government of the United States for the failure of its efforts to solve the Dominican problem." John Bassett Moore to Esmé Howard, 9 Feb. 1907, JBM.
41. John Bassett Moore to Charles H. Allen, 5 Jan. 1907, JBM.
42. Decoded telegram, John Bassett Moore to Charles H. Allen, 5 Jan. 1907, JBM; for pressures on SDIC, see Wynne, *State Insolvency*, 254–57.
43. Kuhn, Loeb & Co. to John Bassett Moore, 7 Oct. 1907; John Bassett Moore to Kuhn, Loeb & Co., 10 Oct. 1907, JBM.
44. On attempts to reconstruct the Dominican state by the U.S. customs receivership and military government, see Robert James Neymeyer, "The Establishment and Operation of the Dominican Customs Receivership, 1905–1916 (unpublished Ph.D diss., University of Iowa, 1990), especially 103–63, and Bruce Calder, *The Impact of Intervention* (Austin: University of Texas Press, 1984), 32–114.
45. *Plattsburgh Sentinel*, 14 Feb. 1908, 1.
46. The incident is recounted in Collin, *Roosevelt's Caribbean*, 459.
47. *Dictionary of American Biography*, Supplement Four (New York: Scribner's, 1974), 599. On Moore's work for Standard Oil, see JBM.

Conclusion

1. On the Dominican Republic as the model for the new Dollar Diplomacy, see Emily Rosenberg, *Financial Missionaries to the World: The Politics and Culture*

of Dollar Diplomacy, 1900–1930 (Cambridge: Harvard University Press,1999), 31–60.

2. See Martin Sklar, *The Corporate Reconstruction of American Capitalism* (New York: Cambridge University Press, 1988), especially 20–40.

3. Robert James Neymeyer, "The Establishment and Operation of the Dominican Republic Customs Receivership, 1905–1916" (unpublished Ph.D. dissertation, University of Iowa, 1990), 139, 140.

4. A recent study of the near-annexation of the Dominican Republic by the United States after the Civil War justifies its reliance on government sources and its "emphasis on North American participants" based on the inescapable fact of "Dominican helplessness as compared to the strength of the United States." William Javier Nelson, *Almost a Territory: America's Attempt to Annex the Dominican Republic* (Newark, DE.: University of Delaware Press, 1990), 9.

5. Louis A. Pérez, Jr., *Cuba and the United States: Ties of Singular Intimacy* (Athens: University of Georgia Press, 1990), 107.

6. "The commitment of the United States to the explicit purpose of promoting virtuous self-government meant that its imperialistic role was never intended to be complete or lasting," according to Dexter Perkins. Richard Collin concludes that Roosevelt's Caribbean strategy was "fundamentally altruistic and benign." Perkins, Collin, and John Lewis Gaddis recognize the agency of peripheral actors and the limits on U.S. power in order to vindicate both the motives and achievements of American expansionists. Perkins, *Constraint of Empire* (Westport, CT: Greenwood Press, 1981), xiv; Collin, "Symbiosis versus Hegemony: New Directions in the Foreign Relations Historiography of Theodore Roosevelt and William Howard Taft," *Diplomatic History* 19: 3 (Summer 1995), 492; see also John Lewis Gaddis, "New Conceptual Approaches to the Study of American Foreign Relations: Interdisciplinary Perspectives," *Diplomatic History* 14:3 (Summer 1990), 411–12.

7. John Gallagher and Ronald Robinson, "The Imperialism of Free Trade," *Economic History Review* 6: 1 (1953), 3; Emily S. and Norman L. Rosenberg, "From Colonialism to Professionalism: The Public-Private Dynamic in United States Foreign Financial Advising, 1898–1929," *Journal of American History* 74: 1 (June 1987), 61.

8. On Root's decisive role in reorganizing the department, see Richard Hume Werking, *The Master Architects* (Lexington: University of Kentucky Press, 1977), 88–120.

9. Sklar, *Corporate Reconstruction*, 27.

10. Sklar, *Corporate Reconstruction*, 338

11. "Expansion unleashed such disruptive forces upon the indigenous structures that they tended to wear out and even collapse," Gallagher and Robinson write. "Indigenous local governments," Hobsbawm notes, disintegrated "due to the undermining of local structures by economic penetration." LaFeber attributes

extraordinary causal power to United States expansion, finding that the American "quest for opportunities . . . destroyed order" in many parts of the world. As the United States rose to world power, major revolts broke out from Russia and China to Mexico, Cuba, the Philippines, and El Salvador. LaFeber concludes that "American policy played some role in all of these outbreaks, and in most it was a determinative force." Gallagher and Robinson, "Imperialism of Free Trade," 13; Eric Hobsbawm, *The Age of Empire* (New York: Pantheon, 1987), 69; LaFeber, *Cambridge History of American Foreign Relations* vol. II (New York: Cambridge University Press, 1995), 234.

12. On attempts to reconstruct the Dominican state by the United States customs receivership and military government, see Neymeyer, "Dominican Customs Receivership," especially 103–63, and Bruce Calder, *The Impact of Intervention* (Austin: University of Texas Press, 1984), 32–114.

Bibliography

Archival Sources

UNITED STATES NATIONAL ARCHIVES, WASHINGTON, D.C.

State Department (record group 59):
  Despatches from United States Ministers to the Dominican Republic
  Diplomatic Instructions of the Department of State, Haiti and Santo Domingo
  Notes from the Legation of the Dominican Republic in the United States to
      the Department of State
Department of the Navy (record group 45):
  Area File of the Naval Records Collection, Area 8

OTHER ARCHIVES

Benjamin Feinberg Library, Plattsburgh State University, Plattsburgh, NY
  Smith M. Weed papers
Guildhall Library, London, England
  Records of the Council of the Corporation of Foreign Bondholders
Moorland-Springarn Research Center, Howard University, Washington, DC
  Archibald H. Grimké papers
Rare Book and Manuscript Library, Columbia University, New York, NY
  Frederick William Holls papers
Special Collections, Columbia University School of Law, New York, NY
  John Bassett Moore papers
  Jacob H. Hollander papers

Library of Congress, Manuscript Division, Washington, D.C.:
    Grover Cleveland papers
    Walter Q. Gresham papers
Public Record Office, Kew, England, Foreign Office:
    General Correspondence before 1906, Dominican Republic (FO 23)
    Embassy and Consular Archives, Dominican Republic (FO 140)
Ministère des Affaires Etrangères, Paris, France:
    Amerique du Sud, Republique Dominicaine, Dossier General
Archivo General de la Nación, Santo Domingo, Dominican Republic:
    Presidencia de la República, Copiadores de Ulises Heureaux
    Correspondencia epistolar de Ulises Heureaux
    Presidencia de la República, Copiadores de Carlos Morales
    Ministerio de Hacienda y Comercio
    Ministerio de lo Interior y Policía
    Ministerio de Relaciones Exteriores
    El Republicano
    Oiga
    El Eco de la Opinión
    Gaceta Oficial
    Las Noticias

Periodicals

Bradstreet's
New York Times
New York Tribune

Secondary Sources

Abrahams, Philip. The Foreign Expansion of American Finance and its Relationship to the Foreign Economic Policies of the United States, 1907–1921. New York: Arno Press, 1976.

Acevedo, Octavio A. "Dominican Republic or Republic of Santo Domingo." Washington, D.C.: [n.p.], 1902.

Aguilar, Luis E. "Cuba, c. 1860–c. 1930." *Cuba: A Short History*, ed. Leslie Bethell. New York, 1993.

Alix, Juan Antonio. *Décimas Políticas*. Santo Domingo: Editora de Santo Domingo, 1977.

Alvarez Léal, Francisco. *La Republique Dominicaine*. Paris: Lucien Beillet, 1888.

"Argument of the Dominican Republic [before the Commission of Arbitration, United States vs. the Dominican Republic, n.d., n.p.].

"Argument of the United States before the Commission of Arbitration," United States [vs.] the Dominican Republic, [n.d., n.p.].

Báez Evertsz, Franc. *Azúcar y Dependencia en la República Dominicana*. Santo Domingo: UASD, 1978.

Baud, Michiel. *Historia de un Sueño*. Santo Domingo, Fundación Cultural Dominicana, 1993.

Baud, Michiel. "Ideología y Campesinado: El Pensamiento de José Ramón López." *Estudios Sociales* 64 (April–May 1986).

Baud, Michiel. "The Origins of Capitalist Agriculture in the Dominican Republic." *Latin American Research Review* 22: 2 (1987).

Baud, Michiel. "Sugar and Unfree Labour: Reflections on Labour Control in the Dominican Republic, 1870–1935." *Journal of Peasant Studies* 19: 2 (Jan. 1992).

Bauer, Arnold J. "Rural Workers in Spanish America: Problems of Peonage and Oppression." *Hispanic American Historical Review* 59: 1 (1979).

Becker, William H. *The Dynamics of Business-Government Relations*. Chicago: University of Chicago Press, 1982.

Beisner, Robert L. *From the Old Diplomacy to the New, 1865–1900*. Arlington Heights, IL: Harlan Davidson, 1986.

Benson, Lee. *Merchants, Farmers and Railroads*. Cambridge, MA: Harvard University Press, 1955.

Bergeron, David M. *English Civic Pageantry 1558–1642*. London: Edward Arnold, 1971.

Borchard, Edwin M. *The Diplomatic Protection of Citizens Abroad*. New York: Kraus Reprint, 1970.

Bosch, Juan. *Capitalismo Tardío en la República Dominicana*. Santo Domingo: Alfa y Omega, 1990.

Bourne, Kenneth. *Britain and the Balance of Power in North America, 1815–1908*. London: Longmans, 1967.

Brea, Ramonina. *La Formación del Estado Capitalista en Haiti y Santo Domingo*. Santo Domingo: Editora Taller, 1982.

Bryan, Patrick E. "La cuestión obrera en la industria azucarera de la República Dominicana a finales del siglo [XIX] y principios del XX." *Eme Eme* 7: 41 (mayo–abril 1979).

Bryan, Patrick E. "La Producción Campesina en la República Dominicana a Principio del Siglo XX." *Eme Eme* 7: 42 (Mayo–Junio 1979).

Bureau of the American Republics. *Handbook of Santo Domingo*. Washington: Government Printing Office, 1894.

Burns, E. Bradford. *The Poverty of Progress*. Berkeley: University of California Press, 1980.

Burton, David H. *Theodore Roosevelt: Confident Imperialist*. Philadelphia: University of Pennsylvania Press, 1968.

Cairncross, A. K. *Home and Foreign Investment, 1870–1913*. Cambridge: Cambridge University Press, 1953.

Calder, Bruce. *The Impact of Intervention*. Austin: University of Texas Press, 1984.

Cambranes, J.C. *Coffee and Peasants*. Stockholm: Institute of Latin American Studies, 1985.

Campillo Pérez, Julio G. *Historia Electoral Dominicana, 1848–1986*. Santo Domingo: Editora Corripio, 1986.

"Case of the Dominican Republic [before the Commission of Arbitration," United States vs. the Dominican Republic, n.d., n.p.].

"Case of the United States before the Commission of Arbitration," United States [vs.] the Dominican Republic, 12 Feb. 1904, [n.p.].

Cassá, Roberto. *Historia Social y Económica de la República Dominicana*, vol 2. Santo Domingo: Alfa y Omega, 1992.

Castro, Victor M. de. *Cosas de Lilís*. Santo Domingo: Editora Taller, 1986.

Cecco, Marcello de. *Money and Empire*. London: Blackwell, 1974.

Censo de Población y Otros Datos Estadísticos. Santo Domingo: J.R. Vda. Garcia, 1909. *Censo y Catastro de la Comun de Santo Domingo, Año 1919*. Santo Domingo: El Progreso, 1919.

Cestero, Tulio M. *La Sangre*. Santo Domingo: [n.p., n.d.]

Clayton, Lawrence A. "The Nicaragua Canal in the Nineteenth Century: Prelude to American Empire in the Caribbean." *Journal of Latin American Studies* 19: 2 (Nov. 1987).

Colección de Leyes, Decretos y Resoluciones Emanados de los Poderes Legislativo y Ejecutivos de la República Dominicana, Tomo 13. Santo Domingo: Imprenta del Listin Diario, 1929.

Collin, Richard H. "The 1904 *Detroit* Compact: U.S. Naval Diplomacy and Dominican Revolutions." *Historian* 52 (May 1990).

Collin, Richard H. "The Caribbean Theater Transformed: Britain, France, Germany, and the U.S., 1900–1906." *The American Neptune* 52 (Spring 1992).

Collin, Richard H. "Symbiosis versus Hegemony: New Directions in the Foreign Relations Historiography of Theodore Roosevelt and William Howard Taft." *Diplomatic History* 19: 3 (Summer 1995).

Collin, Richard H. *Theodore Roosevelt's Caribbean*. Baton Rouge: Louisiana State University Press, 1990.

Cooling, Benjamin Franklin. *Gray Steel and Blue Water Navy*. Hampton, CT: Archon Books, 1979.

Cooper, Frederick. *From Slaves to Squatters*. New Haven: Yale University Press, 1980.

Corporation of Foreign Bondholders, *Twentieth-Eighth Annual Report of the Council of the Corporation of Foreign Bondholders, for the year 1900–1901* (London: Council House, 1901).

Corrigan, Philip and Derek Sayer. *The Great Arch: English State Formation as Cultural Revolution*. New York: Blackwell, 1985.

Crapol, Edward P. "Coming to Terms with Empire: The Historiography of Late-Nineteenth-Century American Foreign Relations." *Diplomatic History* 16 (Fall 1992).

del Castillo, José. "Azucar & Braceros: Historia de un Problema." *Eme Eme* 10: 58 (Enero-Febrero 1982).

Demorizi, Emilio Rodríguez, ed. *Cancionero de Lilís*. Santo Domingo: Editora del Caribe, 1962.

Demorizi, Emilio Rodríguez, ed. *Martí en Santo Domingo*. Barcelona: Gráficas M. Pareja, 1978.

Demorizi, Emilio Rodríguez, ed. *Papeles de Pedro F. Bonó*. Barcelona: Gráficas M. Pareja, 1980.

Demorizi, Emilio Rodríguez, ed. *Papeles Dominicanos de Máximo Gómez*. Santo Domingo: Editora Montalvo, 1954.

Díaz, Virgil. *Lilís*. Santo Domingo, [n.p., n.d.].

Dictionary of American Biography, Supplement Four. New York: Scribner's, 1974.

Domínguez, Jaime de Jesús. *La Dictadura de Heureaux*. Santo Domingo: Editora Universitaria, 1986.

Domínguez, Jaime de Jesús Domínguez. *La Sociedad Dominicana a Principios del Siglo XX*. Santo Domingo: Editora Taller, 1994.

Dosal, Paul. *Doing Business with the Dictators*. Wilmington: Scholarly Resources, 1993.

Drago, Luís. "State Loans in their Relation to International Policy." *American Journal of International Law* 50: 2 (July and October, 1907).

Drew, S. Nelson. *NSC — 68: Forging the Strategy of Containment*. Washington: National Defense University, 1994.

Duin, Edgar Charles. "Dominican-American Diplomatic Relations, 1895–1907." Unpublished Ph.D. diss., Georgetown University, 1955.

Dunn, Frederick Sherwood. *The Protection of Nationals*. Baltimore: Johns Hopkins University Press, 1932.

Esthus, Raymond A. *Theodore Roosevelt and the International Rivalries*. Waltham, MA: Ginn-Blaisdell, 1970.

Estrella, Julio C. *La Moneda, La Banca y las Finanzas en la República Dominicana*. Santiago: Universidad Católica Madre y Maestra, 1971.

Felix, David. "Alternative Outcomes of the Latin American Debt Crisis." *Latin American Research Review* 22: 2 (1987).

Fishlow, Albert. "Lessons from the past: capital markets during the 19th century and the interwar period." *International Organization* 39: 3 (Summer 1985).

Foner, Eric. *Nothing but Freedom*. Baton Rouge: Louisiana State University Press, 1983.

Foner, Eric. *Reconstruction*. New York: Harper & Row, 1988.

Forbes, Ian L.D. "German Informal Imperialism in South America before 1914." *Economic History Review* 31: 3 (Aug. 1978).

Franks, Julie. "The *Gavilleros* of the East: Social Banditry as Political Practice in the Dominican Sugar Region, 1900–1924." *Journal of Historical Sociology* 8: 2 (June 1995).

Friedlander, Heinrich. *Historia Económica de Cuba*. Havana: Editorial de Ciencias Sociales, 1978.

Gaddis, John Lewis. "New Conceptual Approaches to the Study of American Foreign Relations: Interdisciplinary Perspectives." *Diplomatic History* 14: 3 (Summer 1990).

Gallagher, John and Ronald Robinson. "The Imperialism of Free Trade." *Economic History Review* 6: 1 (1953).

Geertz, Clifford. *Negara*. Princeton: Princeton University Press, 1980.

Gómez, Luis. *Relaciones de Producción Dominantes en la Sociedad Dominicana, 1875–1975*. Santo Domingo: Alfa y Omega, 1984.

González, Raymundo. *Bonó, Un Intelectual de los Pobres*. Santo Domingo: Centro de Estudios Sociales, 1994.

González, Raymundo. "Ideología de progreso y campesinado en el siglo XIX." *Ecos* 2 (1993).

Gootenberg, Paul. "Beleaguered Liberals: The Failed First Generation of Free Traders in Peru," in Love and Jacobsen, *Guiding the Invisible Hand*.

Gould, Lewis L. *The Presidency of Theodore Roosevelt*. Lawrence: University of Kansas Press, 1991.

Grafenstein, Johanna von. *Haití 2*. Mexico City: Instituto de Investigaciones, 1989.

Gudmundson, Lowell and Héctor Lindo-Fuentes. *Central America, 1821–1871: Liberalism before Liberal Reform*. Tuscaloosa: University of Alabama, 1995.

Gunn, L. Ray. *The Decline of Authority*. Ithaca: Cornell University Press, 1988.

Hahn, Steven. "Hunting, Fishing, and Foraging: Common Rights and Class Relations in the Postbellum South." *Radical History Review* 26 (1982).

Hale, Charles A. "Political and Social ideas," in *Latin America: Economy and Society, 1870–1930*, ed. Leslie Bethell. New York: Cambridge University Press, 1989.

Healy, David. *Drive to Hegemony*. Madison: University of Wisconsin Press, 1988.

Henríquez y Carvajal, Francisco. *Cayacoa y Cotubanama*. Santo Domingo: ONAP, 1985.

Herrera, César A. *Las Finanzas de la República Dominicana*. Santo Domingo: Impresora Dominicana, 1955.

Hobsbawm, Eric. *The Age of Empire*. New York: Pantheon, 1987.

Hobson, J.A. *Imperialism*. London: J. Nisbet, 1902.

Hoetink, Harry. "El Cibao 1844–1900: Su Aportación a la Formación Social de la República," in *Santo Domingo y El Caribe*. Santo Domingo: Fundación Cultural Dominicana, 1994.

Hogan, Michael J. "Corporatism: A Positive Appraisal." *Diplomatic History* 10: 4 (Fall 1986).

Holden, Robert and Eric Zolov, eds. *Latin America and the United States: A Documentary History*. New York: Oxford University Press, 2000.

Hollander, Jacob H. "Report on the Debt of Santo Domingo." 59th Congress, 1st Session, Executive Document No. 1.4, Washington, D.C.

Holls, Frederick W. *The Peace Conference at the Hague*. New York: Macmillan, 1900.

Holt, Thomas C. *The Problem of Freedom*. Baltimore: Johns Hopkins University Press, 1992.

Holt, W. Stull. *Treaties Defeated by the Senate*. Gloucester, MA: Peter Smith, 1964.

Hostos, Eugenio Maria de. "Civilización o Muerte," in *Páginas Dominicanas*, ed. E. Rodriguez Demorizi. Santo Domingo: Editora Taller, 1979.

Huet, Alfonso. "Juan B. Vicini y la Acumulación Originaria, 1870–1900." Master's essay, Universidad Autonoma de Santo Domingo, 1980.

Huskey, James L. "The Cosmopolitan Connection: Americans and Chinese in Shanghai during the Interwar Years. *Diplomatic History* 11 (Summer 1987).

In Memoriam: Frederick William Holls. Privately printed, 1904.

The Inter-Oceanic Canal of Nicaragua. New York: Nicaragua Canal Construction Company, 1891.

Iriye, Akira. "Culture and Power: International Relations as Intercultural Relations." *Diplomatic History* 3 (Spring 1979).

Jonas, Manfred. *The United States and Germany*. Ithaca: Cornell University Press, 1984.

Kay, Cristóbal. *Latin American Theories of Development and Underdevelopment*. New York: Routledge, 1989.

Keller, Morton. *Affairs of State*. Cambridge: Harvard University Press, 1977.

Klarén, Peter F. and Thomas J. Bossert. *Promise of Development*. Boulder, CO: Westview, 1986.

Kneer, Warren H. *Great Britain and the Caribbean, 1901–1913*. East Lansing: Michigan State University Press, 1975.

LaFeber, Walter. *Cambridge History of American Foreign Relations*, vol. II. New York: Cambridge University Press, 1995.

LaFeber, Walter. *The New Empire*. Ithaca: Cornell University Press, 1963.

Landes, David. *Bankers and Pashas*. New York: Harper & Row, 1958.

Langhorne, Richard. "Arbitration: the first phase, 1870–1914," in Michael Dockrill and Brian McKercher. *Diplomacy and World Power*. Cambridge: Cambridge University Press, 1996.

Langley, Lester D. *America and the Americas*. Athens: University of Georgia Press, 1989.

Langley, Lester D. *Banana Wars: United States Intervention in the Caribbean, 1898–1934*. Lexington: University Press of Kentucky, 1985.

Langley, Lester D. *Struggle for the American Mediterranean*. Athens: University of Georgia Press, 1976.

Laughlin, J. Laurence. "Gold and Silver in Santo Domingo." *Journal of Political Economy* 2 (Dec. 1893–Sept. 1894).

Laughlin, J. Laurence. "Monetary Reform in Santo Domingo." *Atlantic Monthly* 74: 441 (July 1894).

Léal, Franciso Alvarez. *La Republique Dominicaine*. Paris: Lucien Beillet, 1888.

Lilley, Charles R. and Michael H. Hunt. "On Social History, the State, and Foreign Relations: Commentary on 'The Cosmopolitan Connection.'" *Diplomatic History* 11 (Summer 1987).

Lipson, Charles. *Standing Guard*. Berkeley: University of California Press, 1985.

Love, Joseph L. and Nils Jacobsen. *Guiding the Invisible Hand*. New York: Praeger, 1988.

McCormick, Richard L. *The Party Period and Public Policy*. New York: Oxford University Press, 1986.

McCormick, Thomas. "Something Old, Something New: John Lewis Gaddis's 'New Conceptual Approaches.'" *Diplomatic History* 14 (Summer 1990).

McCormick, Thomas and Walter LaFeber. *Behind the Throne: Servants of Power to Imperial Presidents, 1898–1968*. Madison: University of Wisconsin Press, 1993.

McFeely, William S. *Frederick Douglass*. New York: W. W. Norton, 1991.

McGuire, James K., ed. *The Democratic Party of the State of New York*. New York: United States History Co. 1905.

McKitrick, Eric. "The Study of Corruption." *Political Science Quarterly* 72 (Dec. 1957).

McLean, David. "Finance and 'Informal Empire' Before the First World War." *Economic History Review* 29: 2 (May 1976).

MacMichael, David Charles. "The United States and the Dominican Republic, 1871–1940." Unpublished Ph.D. diss., University of Oregon, 1964.

Mallon, Florencia. *The Defense of Community in Peru's Central Highlands*. Princeton: Princeton University Press, 1983.

Marichal, Carlos. *A Century of Debt Crises in Latin America*. Princeton: Princeton University Press, 1989.

Martí, José. *Inside the Monster*, ed. Philip Foner. New York: Monthly Review, 1975.

Martínez, Rufino. *Diccionario Biográfico-Histórico Dominicano*. Santo Domingo: Editora UASD, 1971.

Megargee, Richard. "Realism in American Foreign Policy: The Diplomacy of John Bassett Moore." Unpublished Ph.D. diss., Northwestern University, 1963.

Miner, Dwight. *Fight for the Panama Route*. New York: Columbia University Press, 1940.

Mitchell, Timothy. *Colonising Egypt*. Berkeley: University of California Press, 1991.

Moore, John Bassett. *Collected Papers of John Bassett Moore*. New Haven: Yale University Press, 1944.

Moreno, Guillermo. "De la Propiedad Comunera a la Propiedad Privada Moderna, 1844–1924." *Eme Eme* 9: 51, (Nov.–Dic., 1980).

Morison, Elting E., ed. *Letters of Theodore Roosevelt*. Cambridge: Harvard University Press, 1951.

Moya Pons, Frank. "Datos Sobre la Economía Dominicana durante la Primera República." *Eme Eme* 4: 24 (Mayo–Junio 1976).

Moya Pons, Frank. *Manual de Historia Dominicana*. Santo Domingo: Editora Corripio, 1984.

Moya Pons, Frank. "Nuevas Consideraciones sobre la Historia de la Población Dominicana." *Eme Eme* 3: 15 (Nov.–Dic. 1974).

Munro, Dana G. *Intervention and Dollar Diplomacy in the Caribbean, 1900–1921*. Princeton: Princeton University Press, 1964.

Murphy, Martin F. *Dominican Sugar Plantations*. New York: Praeger, 1991.

Mutto, Paul. "Desarrollo de la Economía de Exportación Dominicana, 1900–1930." *Eme Eme* 3: 15 (1974).

Mutto, Paul. "The Illusory Promise: The Dominican Republic and the Process of Economic Development, 1900–1930." Unpublished Ph.D. diss., University of Washington, 1976.

Nelson, William Javier. *Almost a Territory: America's Attempt to Annex the Dominican Republic*. Newark: University of Delaware Press, 1990.

Nevins, Allan. *Grover Cleveland: A Study in Courage*. New York: Dodd, Mead, 1932.

Neymeyer, Robert James. "The Establishment and Operation of the Dominican Customs Receivership, 1905–1916." Unpublished Ph.D. diss., University of Iowa, 1990.

Ninkovich, Frank. "Theodore Roosevelt: Civilization as Ideology." *Diplomatic History* 10: 3 (Summer 1986).

Ortiz, Helen. "The Era of Lilís: Political Stability and Economic Change in the Dominican Republic." Unpublished Ph.D. diss, 1975, Georgetown University.

Pérez, Louis A., Jr. *Cuba and the United States: Ties of Singular Intimacy*. Athens: University of Georgia Press, 1990.

Pérez, Louis A., Jr. *Cuba: Between Reform and Revolution*. New York: Oxford University Press, 1988.

Pérez, Louis A., Jr. "Dependency." in Michael J. Hogan and Thomas G. Patterson, eds. *Explaining the History of American Foreign Relations*. New York: Cambridge University Press, 1992.

Perkins, Bradford. *The Great Rapprochement*. London: Gollancz, 1969.

Perkins, Dexter. *The Monroe Doctrine, 1867–1907*. Baltimore: Johns Hopkins Press, 1937.

Peukert, Detlev Julio K. "Anhelo de dependencia: Las ofertas de anexión de la República Dominicana a los Estados Unidos en el siglo XIX." *Jahrbuch für Ge-schichte von Staat, Wirstschaft und Gesellschaft Lateinamerikas,* 23 (1986).

Peynado, Francisco José. "Por la inmigración," in *Papeles y Escritos de Francisco José Peynado,* ed. Juan Daniel Balcácer. Santo Domingo: Fundación Peynado Alvarez, 1994.

Pletcher, David M. *The Diplomacy of Trade and Investment: American Economic Expansion in the Hemisphere, 1865–1900.* Columbia: University of Missouri Press, 1998.

Pletcher, David M. "Rhetoric and Results: A Pragmatic View of American Economic Expansionism, 1865–98." *Diplomatic History* 5 (Spring 1981).

Plummer, Brenda Gayle. *Haiti and the Great Powers.* Baton Rouge: Louisiana State University Press, 1988.

Presidential Addresses and State Papers of Theodore Roosevelt, Part Three. New York: Kraus Reprint Co. 1970.

Quiroz, Alfonso W. *Domestic and Foreign Finance in Modern Peru.* Pittsburgh: University of Pittsburgh Press, 1993.

Resumen General del Activo y Pasivo de la Sucesión Heureaux. Santo Domingo: Garcia Hermanos, 1900.

Rippy, J. Fred "Antecedents of the Roosevelt Corollary of the Monroe Doctrine." *Pacific Historical Review* 9 (1940).

Rippy, J. Fred. "The British Bondholders and the Roosevelt Corollary of the Monroe Doctrine." *Political Science Quarterly* 49: 2 (June, 1934).

Rippy, J. Fred. *British Investments in Latin America, 1822–1949.* New York: Arno Press, 1977.

Roseberry, William. *Coffee and Capitalism in the Venezuelan Andes.* Austin: University of Texas Press, 1983.

Roseberry, William. "Hegemony and the Language of Contention," in Gilbert M. Joseph and Daniel Nugent, eds., *Everyday Forms of State Formation.* Durham: Duke University Press, 1994.

Rosenberg, Emily S. *Financial Missionaries to the World: The Politics and Culture of Dollar Diplomacy.* Cambridge: Harvard University Press, 1999.

Rosenberg, Emily S. and Normal L. Rosenberg. "From Colonialism to Professionalism: The Public-Private Dynamic in United States Foreign Financial Advising, 1898- 1929." *Journal of American History* 74 (June 1987).

Sahlins, Marshall. "Cosmologies of Capitalism: The Trans-Pacific Sector of 'The World System,'" in Nicholas B. Dirks, et al., eds., *Culture/Power/History.* Princeton: Princeton University Press, 1994.

Said, Edward. *Orientalism.* New York: Random House, 1979.

San Miguel, Pedro. "The Dominican Peasantry and the Market Economy: The Peasants of the Cibao, 1880–1960." Unpublished Ph.D. diss., Columbia University, 1987.

Sang Ben, Mu-Kien Adriana. *Ulises Heureaux*. Santo Domingo: Editora Corripio, 1987.

Scott, James C. *Comparative Political Corruption*. Englewood Cliffs, N.J.: Prentice-Hall, 1972.

Scott, James C. *The Moral Economy of the Peasant*. New Haven: Yale University Press, 1976.

Scott, Rebecca J. *Slave Emancipation in Cuba*. Princeton: Princeton University Press, 1985.

Simpson, J. L. and Hazel Fox. *International Arbitration*. London: Stevens & Sons, 1959.

Sklar, Martin. *The Corporate Reconstruction of American Capitalism*. New York: Cambridge University Press, 1988.

Sklar, Martin. "Dollar Diplomacy According to Dollar Diplomats: American Development and World development" in *The United States as a Developing Country*. New York: Cambridge University Press, 1992.

Skowronek, Stephen. *Building a New American State*. New York: Cambridge University Press, 1982.

Smith, Joseph. *Illusions of Conflict*. Pittsburgh: University of Pittsburgh Press, 1979.

Smith, Joseph. *The Spanish American War*. New York: Longman, 1994.

Smith, Tony. *The Pattern of Imperialism*. New York: Cambridge University Press, 1981.

Socolofsky, Homer E. and Allan B. Spetter. *The Presidency of Benjamin Harrison*. Lawrence: University Press of Kansas, 1987.

Spanish American Commercial Union, Proceedings at the Banquet. New York: El Avisador Hispano-Americano Publishing Co. 1889.

Stead, William T. *The Americanisation of the World, or the Trend of the Twentieth Century*. London: Review of Reviews, 1902.

Stuyt, A. M. *Survey of International Arbitration, 1794–1989*. Boston: Martinus Nijhoff, 1990.

Tansill, Charles Callan. *The United States and Santo Domingo, 1798–1873*. Gloucester, MA: Peter Smith, 1967.

Tansill, William Raymond. "Diplomatic Relations Between the United States and the Dominican Republic, 1874–1899." Unpublished Ph.D. diss., Georgetown University, 1951.

Tate, Merze. *Hawaii: Reciprocity or Annexation* East Lansing: Michigan State University Press, 1968.

Taussig, F. W. *The Tariff History of the United States*. New York: Capricorn, 1964.

Tejada, Adriano Miguel. *El Ajusticiamiento de Lilís*. Santo Domingo: Editora Corripio, 1995.

Terrill, Tom E. *The Tariff, Politics, and American Foreign Policy*. Westport, CT: Greenwood, 1973.

Trask, David F. *The War with Spain in 1898*. New York: Macmillan, 1981.

Trouillot, Michel-Rolph. "Discourses of rule and the acknowledgment of the peasantry in Dominica, W.I., 1838–1928." *American Ethnologist* 16: 4 (Nov. 1989).

Tyler, Alice Felt. *The Foreign Policy of James G. Blaine* Hamden, CT: Archon Books, 1965.

Vanderwood, Paul J. *Disorder and Progress: Bandits, Police, and Mexican Development*. Wilmington, DE: Scholarly Resources, 1992.

Vilas, Carlos. "El Estado Dominicano." *Estudios Sociales Latinoamericanos* 24 (Sept–Dic. 1979).

Waller, Altina. "The Political Economy of the New York State Prison System." Unpublished paper, Special Collections, Feinberg Library, SUNY/Plattsburgh.

Wallerstein, Immanuel. *The Politics of the World-Economy*. New York: Cambridge University Press, 1984.

Welch, Richard E., Jr. *The Presidencies of Grover Cleveland*. Lawrence: University Press of Kansas, 1988.

Wells, Sumner. *Naboth's Vineyard*. New York: Payson & Clarke, 1928.

Werking, Richard Hume. *The Master Architects*. Lexington: University of Kentucky Press, 1977.

Wilkins, Myra. *The Emergence of Multinational Enterprise: American Business Abroad from the Colonial Era to 1914*. Cambridge: Harvard University Press, 1970.

Williams, William Appleman. *The Tragedy of American Diplomacy*. New York: Dell, 1962.

World Bank. *Judicial Reform in Latin America and the Caribbean*. Washington, D.C.: World Bank, 1995.

Wynne, William H. *State Insolvency and Foreign Bondholders*. New Haven: Yale University Press, 1951.

Younger, Edward. *John A. Kasson*. Iowa City: State Historical Society of Iowa, 1955.

Zakaria, Fareed. *From Wealth to Power: The Unusual Origins of America's World Role*. Princeton: Princeton University Press, 1998.

Index

Columbia Studies in Contemporary American History Series

Alan Brinkley, General Editor

Lawrence S. Wittner, *Rebels Against War: The American Peace Movement, 1941–1960*   1969

Davis R. B. Ross, *Preparing for Ulysses: Politics and Veterans During World War II*   1969

John Lewis Gaddis, *The United States and the Origins of the Cold War, 1941–1947*   1972

George C. Herring, Jr., *Aid to Russia, 1941–1946: Strategy, Diplomacy, the Origins of the Cold War*   1973

Alonzo L. Hamby, *Beyond the New Deal: Harry S. Truman and American Liberalism*   1973

Richard M. Fried, *Men Against McCarthy*   1976

Steven F. Lawson, *Black Ballots: Voting Rights in the South, 1944–1969*   1976

Carl M. Brauer, *John F. Kennedy and the Second Reconstruction*   1977

Maeva Marcus, *Truman and the Steel Seizure Case: The Limits of Presidential Power*   1977

Morton Sosna, *In Search of the Silent South: Southern Liberals and the Race Issue*   1977

Robert M. Collins, *The Business Response to Keynes, 1929–1964*   1981

Robert M. Hathaway, *Ambiguous Partnership: Britain and America, 1944–1947*   1981

Leonard Dinnerstein, *America and the Survivors of the Holocaust*   1982

Lawrence S. Wittner, *American Intervention in Greece, 1943–1949*   1982

Nancy Bernkopf Tucker, *Patterns in the Dust: Chinese-American Relations and the Recognition Controversy, 1949–1950*   1983

Catherine A. Barnes, *Journey from Jim Crow: The Desegregation of Southern Transit*   1983

Steven F. Lawson, *In Pursuit of Power: Southern Blacks and Electoral Politics, 1965–1982*   1985

David R. Colburn, *Racial Change and Community Crisis: St. Augustine, Florida, 1877–1980*   1985

Henry William Brands, *Cold Warriors: Eisenhower's Generation and the Making of American Foreign Policy*   1988

Marc S. Gallicchio, *The Cold War Begins in Asia: American East Asian Policy and the Fall of the Japanese Empire.*   1988

Melanie Billings-Yun, *Decision Against War: Eisenhower and Dien Bien Phu*   1988

Walter L. Hixson, *George F. Kennan: Cold War Iconoclast*   1989

Robert D. Schulzinger, *Henry Kissinger: Doctor of Diplomacy*   1989

Henry William Brands, *The Specter of Neutralism: The United States and the Emergence of the Third World, 1947–1960*   1989

Mitchell K. Hall, *Because of Their Faith: CALCAV and Religious Opposition to the Vietnam War*   1990

David L. Anderson, *Trapped By Success: The Eisenhower Administration and Vietnam, 1953–1961*   1991

Steven M. Gillon, *The Democrats' Dilemma: Walter F. Mondale and the Liberal Legacy*   1992

Wyatt C. Wells, *Economist in an Uncertain World: Arthur F. Burns and the Federal Reserve, 1970–1978*   1994

Stuart Svonkin, *Jews Against Prejudice: American Jews and the Fight for Civil Liberties*   1997

Doug Rossinow, *The Politics of Authenticity: Liberalism, Christianity, and the New Left in America*   1998

Campbell Craig, *Destroying the Village: Eisenhower and Thermonuclear War*   1998

Brett Gary, *The Nervous Liberals: Propaganda Anxieties from World War I to the Cold War*   1999

Andrea Friedman, *Prurient Interests: Gender, Democracy, and Obscenity in New York City: 1909–1945*   2000

Eric Rauchway, *The Refuge of Affections: Family and American Reform Politics, 1900–1920*   2000

Robert C. Cottrell, *Roger Nash Baldwin and the American Civil Liberties Union*   2000

Wyatt Wells, *Antitrust and the Formation of the Postwar World*   2002